REA

AC
DIS
D0342607

6-17-75

Booker T. Washington and His Critics

PROBLEMS IN AMERICAN CIVILIZATION

Under the editorial direction of

the late Edwin C. Rozwenc
Amherst College

Booker T. Washington and His Critics

Black Leadership in Crisis

Second Edition

Edited and with an introduction by

Hugh Hawkins
Amherst College

D. C. HEATH AND COMPANY
Lexington, Massachusetts   Toronto   London

Published simultaneously in Canada.

Printed in the United States of America.

International Standard Book Number: 0-669-87049-8

Library of Congress Catalog Card Number: 74-4727

CONTENTS

INTRODUCTION vii

CONFLICT OF OPINION xv

I BOOKER T. WASHINGTON AND HIS PROGRAM

O. K. Armstrong
BOOKER T. WASHINGTON—APOSTLE OF GOOD WILL 3

Booker T. Washington
THE EDUCATIONAL OUTLOOK IN THE SOUTH 10

Booker T. Washington
THE ATLANTA EXPOSITION ADDRESS 17

Emmett J. Scott and Lyman Beecher Stowe
BOOKER T. WASHINGTON: BUILDER OF A CIVILIZATION 32

II W. E. B. DU BOIS AND THE REEMERGENCE OF PROTEST

W. E. Burghardt Du Bois
MY EARLY RELATIONS WITH BOOKER T. WASHINGTON 47

W. E. Burghardt Du Bois
OF MR. BOOKER T. WASHINGTON AND OTHERS 55

Francis L. Broderick
THE FIGHT AGAINST BOOKER T. WASHINGTON 67

Ray Stannard Baker
AN OSTRACIZED RACE IN FERMENT 81

Kelly Miller
WASHINGTON'S POLICY 87

III HENRY M. TURNER AND THE BACK-TO-AFRICA MOVEMENT

Henry M. Turner
TWO EDITORIALS 97

Edwin S. Redkey
BLACK EXODUS 101

Booker T. Washington
THE FUTURE OF THE AMERICAN NEGRO 108

IV THE CHALLENGE FROM THE NAACP

THE NATIONAL NEGRO COMMITTEE ON MR. WASHINGTON, 1910 121

Basil Matthews
AN EXCHANGE BETWEEN BOOKER T. WASHINGTON AND OSWALD GARRISON VILLARD 124

August Meier
BOOKER T. WASHINGTON AND THE "TALENTED TENTH" 127

V CHANGING PERSPECTIVES ON BOOKER T. WASHINGTON

Horace Mann Bond
THE INFLUENCE OF PERSONALITIES ON THE PUBLIC EDUCATION OF NEGROES IN ALABAMA 141

C. Vann Woodward
THE ATLANTA COMPROMISE 156

Samuel R. Spencer, Jr.
THE ACHIEVEMENT OF BOOKER T. WASHINGTON 167

Harold Cruse
BEHIND THE BLACK POWER SLOGAN 174

Louis R. Harlan
THE SECRET LIFE OF BOOKER T. WASHINGTON 183

SUGGESTIONS FOR ADDITIONAL READING 204

INTRODUCTION

Although it destroyed chattel slavery, the American Civil War did not end "the race question." It left in physical proximity two races whose contrasting heritages were fastened in the minds of men by a difference in pigmentation. The resulting relationships were beset by problems that brought misery to individual human beings and challenged the sincerity of the highest ideals professed by Americans.

The war had given the former slave a semblance of freedom, but it had certainly not given him equality. Nor did two amendments to the Constitution and a dozen years of "reconstruction" significantly change the situation. Most blacks remained inferior to most whites in economic status, political power, and the exercise of civil rights, to say nothing of self-esteem or social prestige. The history of black Americans since 1865 has been in large part the story of changing strategies in the struggle against the inferior status in which they found themselves.

The nationwide attention which Civil War and Reconstruction focused on Americans of African ancestry reappeared only in the aftermath of World War II with such dramatic developments as the school desegregation decision, the emergence of direct-action nonviolent protest, and the black ghetto uprisings. During the years between these peaks of national concern, no movement affecting black life was more important than the program Booker Taliaferro Washington, principal of Tuskegee Normal and Industrial Institute, presented for the betterment of his race. A former slave, Washington received some of the most effusive praise ever given a living American; he received also some of the most extreme denunciations. The sharp contrasts in the judgments of his contemporaries recur in later estimations by historians.

By 1877, when the last federal troops were withdrawn from the South, the North seemed satisfied to leave the race problem to white Southerners who "understood the Negro." Immediate repression did not occur. During the 1880s, black men continued to vote in the South (though their votes were usually controlled by white men), and the physical segregation of the races which a later generation took for granted was not a codified system and was at times ignored. The origins of worsening race relations in the 1890s were complex. Particularly important were the division of the whites by the Populist movement of the early nineties, the resultant threat of political power for blacks, the fears aroused in the conservatives (traditionally paternalistic in race relations), and the frustration of the Populists.

Yet even before the rise of populism, in 1890, Mississippi had adopted several devices—notably the "understanding clause"—to disfranchise blacks. All other Southern states had followed suit by 1910. The annual rate of lynchings reached 235 in 1892 and did not drop below 100 until 1902. A long period of agricultural depression was intensified by the general depression that began in 1893; black farmers—and many of their white neighbors—were held in virtual debt peonage by the crop-lien system. Jim Crow laws for railroads began appearing ever more rapidly, and after 1900 such laws spread to nearly every facet of Southern life.

In the midst of these worsening conditions, Booker T. Washington was invited to speak before a biracial audience gathered for the opening of the 1895 Atlanta Cotton States and International Exposition. He sensed the great potential for good or ill in the situation, since he would be the first black ever to address such a large group of Southern whites. He decided to be "perfectly frank and honest"; he decided also "not to say anything that would give undue offense to the South." He thus set himself a prodigious task.

Essentially, the program that he outlined at Atlanta pointed to the abundance that characterized America and urged both races to find their salvation there. It told white and black to turn to their own economic betterment, a goal more important than their differences. To whites Washington said, only by lessening your antagonism to the Negro can you properly use him in getting rich. To blacks he said, political and social equality are less important as present goals than economic respectability. His call for "a willing obedience among all classes to the mandates of law" rested directly on his economic premise. To whites he said, it is profitable to give the Negro equal protection of the laws. To blacks he said, gain an economic foot hold and equal protection of the laws is more likely to be yours. The program of industrial education which Washington had been promoting since 1881 at Tuskegee was similarly in accord with his underlying economic appeal.

His auditors overwhelmed him with applause. The editor of the Atlanta *Constitution* at once hailed the address as "a platform upon which blacks and whites can stand with full justice to each other," and other editors joined in a chorus of approval. Typifying the general assent of Northerners was President Grover Cleveland, who wrote thanking Washington for what he had done. From the moment of this address until his death in 1915, Washington remained one of the most powerful men in America. As adviser to presidents, philanthropists, and editors, and as a sought-after writer and speaker, he influenced the life and thought of the entire nation. His program for solving "the Negro question" was supported by millions of Americans, white and black. The years 1895 to 1915 have, in fact, been called "The Era of Booker T. Washington." Honors were heaped upon him, and the publication in 1901 of his autobiography, *Up from Slavery,* raised him to the pantheon of American heroes. It was the day of Horatio Alger, but Alger had never written a story to equal the rise of the ex-slave whom Queen Victoria invited for tea.

Certain black Americans raised their voices in opposition to this "Atlanta Compromise" with its admonition to work and wait. They could not topple Washington from power, but one of them did win recognition as leader of the opposition. The life of W. E. Burghardt Du Bois differed radically from that of Washington. He was born in Great Barrington, Massachusetts, shortly after the Civil War. His family had long been free, and he grew up in an environment containing little overt race prejudice. In fact, when he first entered the South to attend Fisk University, the degradation of black life shocked him profoundly. He decided to dedicate his life to his people, to serve them through knowledge and through protest. He studied in Germany and in 1895 won a Ph.D. at Harvard. Soon he was a professor at Atlanta University, producing scientific monographs on the condition of the Negro.

Though not at first an opponent of Washington's program, Du Bois began publicly criticizing it in 1903. He later led the vigorous protest of the Niagara Movement and in 1910 became editor of *Crisis,* journal of the newly organized National Association for the Advancement of Colored People. No just estimate of Booker T. Washington can be made without a thorough examination of the criticisms by Du Bois and his colleagues. They pointed to the worsening conditions of the Negro at the very time when Washington was calling for patience and accommodation. Three injurious trends, Du Bois charged, had been aided by Washington's activities: the loss of political rights, the erection of caste barriers, and the deflection of funds from academic education for leaders to industrial education for the masses. He charged too that Washington and the "Tuskegee Machine" maintained a dictatorial control over black affairs that stifled other efforts for racial betterment. Though Washington grew more outspoken about discrimination before his death, he never joined the NAACP. In an obituary article, Du Bois repeated his criticisms of 1903.

Du Bois best symbolizes the anti-Washington movement and accordingly appears in this collection immediately after Washington's basic position is presented. Next in appearance (though it began somewhat earlier) is the program for blacks of Henry M. Turner, a bishop of the African Methodist Episcopal church. Born free in the slave South, Turner was considerably older than Washington. Shortly after the Atlanta address, Turner declared that Washington would "have to live a long time to undo the harm he has done our race," since his remarks about social equality would be used by whites "to prove that the Negro race is satisfied with being degraded."

Instead of accommodationist measures, the bishop called for emigration to Africa by large numbers of black Americans, and he urged blacks to think of themselves as a separate nation. More pessimistic than either Washington or Du Bois about America's ability to fulfill its promises of liberty and equality for all, he denounced racial injustice in pungent language. Partly because of his leadership in the black church, Turner was influential among his own race, though completely unknown to most white Americans. Especially poor farmers, who made up the majority of the black population, responded to his African dream. Thousands gave money to projects which promised to help them emigrate to Africa. Some of these undertakings were swindles, others hopelessly mismanaged. Of the few hundred blacks who did reach Liberia from the United States in

Turner's day, many died from tropical diseases and others returned to America sorely disappointed. More significant than the physical emigration, however, was the protest represented by the back-to-Africa movement. Through it, blacks could at least symbolically challenge the oppression of American life. They could refuse to limit their choice to being either second-class Americans waiting for promotion, or men without a country. Here in provocative form was the idea of black nationhood.

Although both Washington and Du Bois showed concern for Africa and criticized white imperialism (Du Bois in a remarkable series of writings and activities that lie beyond the scope of this volume), they both rejected proposals for black emigration to Africa. But black nationalism is a complex of beliefs and feelings which can express itself in many forms. In some ways, both Washington and Du Bois asserted black nationalist ideals, as the reader can discover in this collection, though the focus is primarily on Washington. His calls for solidarity and self-help tapped the vein of race pride in his fellow blacks. Accepting separation of the races, at least for a period, Washington wanted blacks to seize the "advantages of the disadvantages" in efforts which gave racial unity an economic cast, such as the National Negro Business League, founded in 1900. Cultural black nationalism was suggested in Washington's calls for the study of black history and recognition of black heroes. It should not be particularly surprising, then, that a black nationalist leader like Marcus Garvey, whose back-to-Africa movement of the 1920s reminds one of Turner's, could in fact claim to have been inspired by Washington, and that in the late 1960s Washington could be called by some a forerunner of "Black Power."

No present-day scholar is likely to deny that among Washington's ultimate goals was the achievement of all the rights of American citizenship for members of his race. But no two scholars agree completely on the wisdom of the means he chose. Which course was most appropriate—compromise with current prejudices and concentration on economic self-improvement, insistent demands for full civil and political equality, or dramatization of separate black identity through advocacy of emigration to Africa? If Washington's overall approach is rejected, can any part of his program be declared valid? To what extent could he have adopted an alternative course in 1895 or later? What about Washington's relationship to the black masses? Did he legitimately speak for them? Did his message reach them? Assuming that black heroes were needed at a time of deep racial demoralization, was Washington a good candidate for the role? Was the abolitionist Frederick Douglass a superior model? Although the contrasts among Washington, Du Bois, and Turner are pronounced, it is worth inquiring what views these leaders shared. What meaning did each find in blackness? In American life? What can be learned about white Americans from the fact that they responded enthusiastically to Washington's approach? Not just a man and a program, but a nation and an era that elevated Washington to fame and power are up for judgment.

The articles presented in this volume represent a variety of approaches to these and other questions. Some stress the personality of the man, others the legend he inspired. The conflicts of class, race, and region in the society of his time are emphasized in others. Some are pro-Washington, some anti-Washington. None is indifferent to him.

The opening article presents Washington to readers of a popular magazine, suggesting a man of heroic proportions. Washington speaks for himself in the next two selections. The first, an address given in 1884, is an early description of his program, especially its educational side. The second, from his autobiography, tells of his hopes and fears at the time of the Atlanta address. He includes the full text of that address, which is properly considered the focal document of this collection. Then two of Washington's supporters, in a collaborative study written shortly after his death, defend his program and indicate the stands he took for the civil rights of blacks.

The next five documents trace the emergence of opposition to Washington and his program among better-educated blacks. Here Du Bois is the central figure. In a passage from his autobiography, he recalls the relationship between himself and Washington at the turn of the century and the background of his decision to oppose Washington publicly. There follows the widely known essay of 1903 in which Du Bois carefully launched his criticism. A biographer of Du Bois, Francis L. Broderick, then traces the early similarity of views between the two men, seeks causes for their break, and follows Du Bois as far as the organizing of the Niagara Movement. The next two items, by Ray Stannard Baker, a white journalist, and Kelly Miller, a black professor, were written while the Washington-

Du Bois controversy was growing in intensity. Though offering quite different interpretations, these two writers seek to find merit in both the Tuskegeean and his challenger.

The possibilities of building an alternative to Washington's program through an intense black nationalism are examined in the next section, where Bishop Turner speaks his mind. The scholar Edwin S. Redkey examines reasons for the failure of the back-to-Africa movement and points out some dilemmas peculiar to nationalism among black Americans. In a selection that recognizes the back-to-Africa proposals, Washington rejects them, but advocates other expressions of black pride and solidarity.

A later period of Washington's life gets the spotlight in Section Four. The first two selections comprise a statement issued from NAACP headquarters to counteract reports on American race relations given by Washington in England and part of a letter in which Washington defends his course to one of the white organizers of the NAACP. Although not centered on the NAACP, August Meier's study of the Talented Tenth shows that many blacks active in that group took ambivalent positions on Booker T. Washington and his program.

The concluding section reveals both changing attitudes of scholars toward Washington and more recently developed information about him. Horace Mann Bond, basing his interpretation on class relationships, includes a provocative passage on the importance of myths and heroes. C. Vann Woodward draws on his knowledge of the Southern society in which Washington built up his program and reaches an essentially negative judgment of the man's work. Both a deep faith in the integrationist solution to racial conflicts and a positive appraisal of Washington mark the selection from the biography of Washington by Samuel R. Spencer, Jr. Next, the challenging question of how Washington can be related to the Black Power advocates is addressed by Harold Cruse. The last article, by Louis R. Harlan, Washington's most recent biographer, takes us behind the public facade and lets us refine our thinking about the man's goals and means. Equally important, it reminds us that we should try, not merely to reconstruct a part of the American past and to face a persisting social problem, but to understand a fellow human being.

At the height of the civil rights movement in the 1960s, a leader of a small black community in North Carolina appeared late one morning at breakfast, having read far into the night in Charles Silberman's *Crisis in Black and White.* "Well!" she exclaimed to the assembled white and black student workers in the cause, "I can see now that Booker T. Washington was nothing but an Uncle Tom!" It was probably good to have the anti-Washington view more widely known in a community where male children were often honored with the name "Booker T." by their parents. But the judgment was essentially mistaken. Booker Washington is too complicated a figure to deserve a "nothing but" label. The pages that follow seek to explore some of the complexities involved and to give grounds for the reader's own careful judgment.

Conflict of Opinion

The president of Tuskegee Institute makes a speech in Atlanta in 1895:

> Our greatest danger is that in the great leap from slavery to freedom we [Negroes] may overlook the fact that the masses of us are to live by the productions of our hands, and fail to keep in mind that we shall prosper in proportion as we learn to dignify and glorify common labor and put brains and skill into the common occupations of life. . . . You [Southern white people] can be sure in the future, as in the past, that you and your families will be surrounded by the most patient, faithful, law-abiding, and unresentful people that the world has seen. . . . In all things that are purely social we can be as separate as the fingers, yet one as the hand in all things essential to mutual progress.
>
> BOOKER T. WASHINGTON

In 1903, a black scholar decries this approach:

> As a result of this tender of the palm branch, what has been the return? In these years there have occurred:
>
> 1. the disenfranchisement of the Negro
> 2. the legal creation of a distinct status of civil inferiority for the Negro
> 3. the steady withdrawal of aid from institutions for the higher training of the Negro
>
> These movements are not, to be sure, direct results of Mr. Washington's teachings; but his propaganda has, without a shadow of doubt, helped their speedier accomplishment.
>
> W. E. B. DU BOIS

The same year, a black bishop objects to the proposals of both Washington and his critics among black intellectuals:

> Anything less than separation and the black man relying upon himself is absolutely nonsense. Negro nationality is the only remedy, and time will show it.
>
> HENRY M. TURNER

But a noted black lawyer says in 1915:

> While most of us were agonizing over the Negro's relation to the State and his political fortunes, Booker Washington saw that there was a great economic empire that needed to be conquered. He saw an emancipated race chained to the soil by the Mortgage Crop System, and other devices, and he said, "You must own your own farms"—and

forthwith there was a second emancipation. He saw the industrial trades and skilled labor pass from our race into other hands. He said, "The hands as well as the head must be educated."

WILLIAM HENRY LEWIS

Yet a historian insists that even in historical context Washington's program was misdirected:

The shortcomings of the Atlanta Compromise, whether in education, labor, or business, were the shortcomings of a philosophy that dealt with the present in terms of the past. Not that a certain realism was lacking in the Washington approach. It is indeed hard to see how he could have preached or his people practiced a radically different philosophy in his time and place. The fact remains that Washington's training school, and the many schools he inspired, taught crafts and attitudes more congenial to the premachine age than to the twentieth century; that his labor doctrine was a compound of individualism, paternalism, and anti-unionism in an age of collective labor action; and that his business philosophy was an anachronism.

C. VANN WOODWARD

A biographer of Washington makes a more favorable estimate:

His predecessors had taken their lead from Thomas Jefferson. Washington took his from Benjamin Franklin, and by doing so, introduced a strain into the Negro's Americanism which strengthened his claim to full citizenship.

SAMUEL R. SPENCER, JR.

But another scholar suggests that the heritage from Washington is not so much "Americanism" as black nationalism:

Black Power is nothing but the economic and political philosophy of Booker T. Washington given a 1960s militant shot in the arm and brought up to date.

HAROLD CRUSE

A recent biographer of the man offers a new way of looking at him:

What strikes a later generation about Washington is not so much his accommodation to segregation and other aspects of white supremacy, which has long been recognized, but his complexity, his richness of strategic resource, his wizardry.

LOUIS R. HARLAN

I BOOKER T. WASHINGTON AND HIS PROGRAM

O. K. Armstrong

BOOKER T. WASHINGTON—APOSTLE OF GOOD WILL

This succinct and colorful sketch of Booker T. Washington is based largely on his autobiography, Up from Slavery, *and on a visit to the Tuskegee Institute campus some thirty years after Washington's death. The appearance of this article in a popular magazine in 1947 followed Washington's election to the Hall of Fame a year earlier. The effort to give Washington heroic stature was doubtless related to the effects of World War II. The restatements of democratic ideology during the war and the horrors of Nazi racism had evoked strong objections to the unequal treatment of black Americans, especially segregation.*

On the campus of Tuskegee Institute in Alabama stands a monument to Booker T. Washington, the great Negro educator who founded the school. Beneath his statute is this tribute: "He lifted the veil of ignorance from his people and pointed the way to progress through education and industry."

He it was who first raised the American Negroes from their knees and taught them that by their own efforts they could strike off their chains of economic slavery and win the respect and cooperation of their white neighbors. And no man knew better than Booker T. Washington how hard that was to do.

Booker was born April 5, 1856, in a one-room cabin on a plantation in Virginia. The boy's food was a piece of bread here, a scrap of meat there. His clothes were a shirt and pants. No Negro he had ever heard of could read or write.

When he was nine, the Confederacy sank in defeat. But the lot of the Negro was little better than before. For emancipation carried with it responsibility, which in turn called for training. The shattered South was unable to cope with the schooling of its former slaves.

So Booker's mother and her children migrated, most of the way on foot, to West Virginia. There Booker worked in coal mines, sawed wood, and plowed fields. At night he attended an elementary school for colored children. When his teacher asked his name, Booker, aim-

From O. K. Armstrong, "Booker T. Washington—Apostle of Good Will," *Reader's Digest*, February 1947, pp. 25–30.

ing as high as he could, said it was Washington. And indeed he became the father of his people.

Hearing two miners talk about a Negro school at Hampton, Virginia, he set out at the age of seventeen, with a few dollars in his pocket, to cover the 500 miles to the institution. A teacher told him to sweep the room. Characteristically, he swept it three times and dusted it four. He was forthwith accepted.

To pay his board he worked as a janitor and waiter; to fit himself for a trade he studied bricklaying. Soon after graduation he was given a place on the faculty.

Down at Tuskegee, Alabama, a white merchant, George Campbell, and his friend Lewis Adams, a skilled Negro workman, conceived the idea of a training school for the black race. Through a friend in the state legislature, Campbell secured an appropriation of $2000. When he wrote to Hampton Institute for a principal, Booker T. Washington was recommended. Arriving at Tuskegee, the eager young principal asked, "Where's the school?"

"There isn't any—yet," he was told. Undismayed, he declared he would build one. In the meantime he obtained permission to use a small Negro church. Then he went about making friends and inviting young Negroes to come to Tuskegee.

What Washington saw in the Alabama countryside would have discouraged a man of less vision and determination. Most Negroes worked for a pittance. Their houses were shacks, their clothing coarse homespun, their food a diet of salt pork and beans. Disease was prevalent.

Professor Washington decided that cultural education without vocational training would be a waste of time. He named the school "Tuskegee Normal and Industrial Institute," and announced that every student would have to work with his or her hands.

Opening day was July 4, 1881. Thirty persons came in, mostly from nearby cotton fields. The roof leaked so badly that on rainy days the pupils held umbrellas over their heads. Later, with $500 Washington borrowed from friends at Hampton, they bought an old plantation near town and laid the foundation for Porter Hall, their first building.

Booker Washington was forced to meet deep-seated prejudices. "Educate a Negro and he won't work!" was an oft-repeated maxim among Southern white people. Among Negro freedmen was the persistent belief that the one purpose of education was to prepare a person to live in leisure without hard work. A delegation of Negroes protested against manual labor as a part of the institute's program. Washington told them, "There is as much dignity in tilling a field as in writing a poem. And it is as important for your girls to know how to set a table and keep a house as it is to read Latin."

On one occasion, a spirited young teacher hired from a Northern school, unused to the ways of the Deep South, angered a Tuskegee merchant. A mob quickly marched to the campus, demanding the "insolent" teacher. Washington faced them calmly.

"We Negroes are handicapped by ignorance, therefore we may break the law. But you, our white friends, know the law, and therefore respect and obey it. We want to learn from you. Now you wouldn't want to bring shame on Tuskegee by a lawless act, would you?" The mob dispersed.

Resolutely the Tuskegee schoolman took his crusade to the piney woods and the plantations, speaking at church meetings and visiting hundreds of homes to explain patiently how trained hands were needed with trained minds. "Our children must learn to do by doing," he would say. "We should not always look to the white race for leadership. Let us develop our own leaders."

Washington's sincerity won friends. Negroes began bringing gifts or volunteering their labor for the struggling school. White citizens of Tuskegee made donations. During the first five years, courses were established in bricklaying, carpentry, blacksmithing, and farming for the boys and cooking, sewing, and housekeeping for the girls. It was Washington's pride that no youth was ever turned away for lack of money. Every student spent some hours in study, and other hours in physical labor. They made the furniture for the buildings—beds from pine trees, mattresses from cotton cloth stuffed with pine needles, tables, chairs. Strict discipline was the rule, for Washington believed that education should develop character. Students were taught courtesy in manners and speech and respect for the rights of others. "We cannot fail," the principal warned his teachers, "for then people would say that Negroes are not capable of self-education."

With courage, tact, and patience, Washington used the institute to draw into closer understanding and cooperation the people of both races. Once as he was passing the Varner mansion, Mrs. Varner, not knowing him by sight, called out to him to chop some wood. Professor Washington pulled off his coat, seized the axe, cut a pile of wood, and carried it into the kitchen. A servant girl recognized him and told her mistress, "That was Professor Washington."

Early next morning Mrs. Varner entered his office and said, "I have come to apologize. I did not know it was you I put to work."

"It's entirely all right, madam," Washington responded. "I like to work, and I'm delighted to do favors for my friends."

From that day, Mrs. Varner was the institute's friend. She got wealthy acquaintances to give thousands of dollars for the school.

In the fall of 1895 the Cotton States Exposition was held in Atlanta. One pavilion was set aside for the products of Negro farmers. Professor Washington was invited to speak. Georgia's Governor Bullock introduced the colored leader to the several thousand people of both races in the exposition hall—probably the first time that an important white official had presented a Negro to a Southern audience.

Not a person stirred as the tall, neatly dressed Negro eloquently explained his plan of education, pleading for understanding and cooperation. Turning to the distinguished white men on the platform, he said: "As we have proved our loyalty to you in nursing your children and watching by the sickbeds of your mothers and fathers, so in the future in our humble way we will stand by you with devotion; interlacing our industrial, commercial, civil, and religious life with yours in a way that shall make the interests of both races one."

As the speech ended Governor Bullock grasped the Negro's hand, while men and women stood cheering. The speech was printed in countless publications. President Cleveland sent a warm letter of congratulation. The occasion made Booker T. Washington a national figure, the recognized spokesman of his race in America.

Later, in Chicago, he addressed an audience of 16,000 people, in which sat President McKinley as the guest of honor. In countless communities of the South his were the first meetings ever to bring white and colored people together. He encouraged frank discussion of mutual problems. He told many a white audience, "You must understand the troubles of the man farthest down before you can help him." He also had the courage to tell them, "The time to test a true gentleman is to observe him when he is in contact with individuals of a race less fortunate than his own."

With friendly persistence, he urged wealthy men and women "to invest in the future of the Negro race." One of the first he visited was Collis P. Huntington, noted railway magnate, who impatiently cut him off with, "Here is two dollars for your school." But the gentle black man persisted, and presently Huntington gave him a check for $50,000, and later enough additional money to build Huntington Hall.

Shrewdly the principal would ask benefactors to underwrite various projects rather than give sums of money. Andrew Carnegie presented a library building. Later he gave $600,000 in one sum. Washington's faith in himself and his cause never wavered. If a new building was needed he would say, "Start the construction; I'll get the money."

By comradeship in toil, and with simple eloquence, he inspired his students. Teachers were required to send slothful workers to his office. Washington would remind them sternly; then, his face softening, he would say, "Come show me the trouble." Together they would go to the field or bench, and the professor would painstakingly demonstrate how the work should be done.

In 1896 Washington talked the Alabama legislature into creating the Tuskegee Agricultural Experiment Station, "maintained for training colored students in scientific agriculture." He heard of the soil experiments of George Washington Carver, a former slave. "You are just the man to head our station," he said. "Find out what can be raised from this southern clay." During nearly half a century, Professor Carver's experiments brought forth hundreds of new products, enriching American agriculture for people of all races.

Booker Washington carried the institute out to the farms. He and Professor Carver would load a wagon with implements and drive around giving demonstrations. Morris K. Jesup, New York philanthropist, donated a two-horse vehicle equipped to display all sorts of farming tools, and the Jesup wagon became famous as the "movable school."

The principal invited Seaman A. Knapp, of the Department of Agriculture, to Tuskegee, and showed him the demonstration wagon. From that visit grew agricultural extension work for Negroes. In charge of the Jesup wagon was an intelligent, vigorous young Negro, Thomas M. Campbell. In 1906 he became the first colored field worker under the Department of Agriculture. Today, from his office at Tuskegee, Tom Campbell directs agricultural extension among farmers of his race in six Southern states. In two generations he and his associates have helped triple the productiveness of Southern Negro farms.

Far beyond the school he founded, Booker T. Washington advanced the progress of Negro education in America. He began by inducing Henry H. Rogers, Standard Oil executive, to help improve the schools of Macon County, of which Tuskegee is county seat. Rogers agreed to donate $600 per month for the first year. The results were so satisfactory that Rogers extended the aid to several counties. Then the principal brought Julius Rosenwald to Alabama, drove him about the countryside, and told him, "Every dollar invested in rural schools in the South will return many dollars in progress for the Negro race."

Mr. Rosenwald consented to finance a number of new buildings. Washington insisted that colored people of each community raise money to provide the land for their school, and that county officials extend the school term. Thus he enlisted the active support of both white and Negro citizens.

The Rosenwald Fund was formed. It has made possible more than 5,000 Negro rural schools in all the Southern states. It has helped provide for the education of nearly three-quarters of a million colored children since its beginning.

Honors came to Booker T. Washington from near and far. President Theodore Roosevelt found in the vigorous Negro a kindred spirit and the two exponents of the strenuous life became fast friends. Washington's advice was constantly sought by business, educational, and religious leaders. President Charles W. Eliot of Harvard, presenting to him the first degree [i.e., honorary degree—Ed.] awarded by the university to a Negro, called him "teacher, wise helper of his race, good servant of God and country."

Washington's constant traveling and speaking, added to his duties on the ever-expanding campus, literally wore out his great heart. His wife and associates begged him to take long rests, but he answered, "No—there is so much to do, and time is so short." In November 1915 he fell ill in New York, and arrived at his beloved school only a few hours before he died.

Today Tuskegee has a staff of 310, with a student enrollment of about 2,000. There are 133 buildings and 3,550 acres of campus and farms. Seventeen similar industrial schools for Negroes have been founded by alumni of Tuskegee.

New honors signify the greatness of Booker T. Washington. The National Education Association included him in a list of ten who have contributed most to the development of education in America. A memorial fund has been established to build an institute at his birthplace, and the Treasury has issued special 50-cent coins to aid the project.

In May 1946, Booker Washington's likeness was placed in the American Hall of Fame at New York University. It reveals a brow furrowed by years of toil and responsibility, a mouth rich in humor yet determined. The lips seem still to be saying to us all, black and white, as they often said during his lifetime: "In all things that are purely social we can be as separate as the fingers, yet one as the hand in all things essential to mutual progress."

About a dozen elderly former associates of Professor Washington still serve Tuskegee. All fondly remember the principal's friendliness, his wondrous faith, and his exacting discipline. With tear-dimmed eyes Dr. Emmett J. Scott, who was for nineteen years his secretary, repeated to me Washington's words which all Tuskegee students have heard: "No matter how poor you are, how black you are, or how obscure your present position, each one should remember there is a chance for him, and the more difficulties he has to overcome, the greater can be his success."

Those deep words remind us to be conscious primarily, not of our race, but of our humanity. In the long climb upward of that common humanity, few have done more to help so many on their way than that man of good will, Booker T. Washington.

Booker T. Washington

THE EDUCATIONAL OUTLOOK IN THE SOUTH

Washington's first major address to a national audience was delivered in 1884. It expressed themes that underlay his activities for the rest of his life. Quite apart from his "message," Washington's straightforward style and down-to-earth imagery help one understand his growing popularity as a speaker. His reference to "civil rights" reveals his reaction to a decision of the Supreme Court the year before. The Court had declared unconstitutional those provisions of the Civil Rights Act of 1875 outlawing racial discrimination in public places, such as theaters, trains, and hotels.

Fourteen years ago it is said that Northern teachers in the South for the purpose of teaching colored schools were frightened away by the whites from the town of Tuskegee, Alabama. Four years ago the democratic members of the Alabama legislature from Tuskegee voluntarily offered and had passed by the General Assembly a bill, appropriating $2,000 annually to pay the salaries of teachers in a colored normal school to be located at Tuskegee. At the end of the first session of the school the legislature almost unanimously passed a second bill appropriating an additional $1,000 annually, for the same purpose. About one montn ago one of the white citizens of Tuskegee who had at first looked on the school in a cold, distant kind of a way said to me, "I have just been telling the white people that the Negroes are more interested in education than we, and are making more sacrifices to educate themselves." At the end of our first year's work, some of the whites said, "We are glad that the Normal School is here because it draws people and makes labor plentiful." At the close of the second year, several said that the Normal School was beneficial because it increased trade, and at the close of the last session more than one has said that the Normal School is a good institution, it is making the colored people in this state better citizens. From the opening of the school to the present, the white citizens of Tuskegee have been among its warmest friends.

From Booker T. Washington, "The Educational Outlook in the South," *Journal of the Proceedings and Addresses of the National Educational Association, Session of the Year 1884, at Madison, Wis.* (Boston, 1885), pp. 125–130.

FIGURE 1. Booker T. Washington (1856–1915). *(The Granger Collection)*

They have not only given of their money but they are ever ready to suggest and devise plans to build up the institution. When the school was making an effort to start a brickyard, but was without means, one of the merchants donated an outfit of tools. Every white minister in the town has visited the school and given encouraging remarks. When the school was raising money to build our present hall, it occurred to one of the teachers that it would be a good idea to call on the white ladies for contributions in the way of cakes, etc., toward a fair. The result was that almost every lady called on gave something and the fair was made up almost entirely of articles given by these friends. A former slaveholder working on a Negro normal-school building under a Negro master carpenter is a picture that the last few years have made possible.

Any movement for the elevation of the Southern Negro in order to be successful, must have to a certain extent the cooperation of the Southern whites. They control government and own the property—whatever benefits the black man benefits the white man. The proper education of all the whites will benefit the Negro as much as the education of the Negro will benefit the whites. The governor of Alabama would probably count it no disgrace to ride in the same railroad coach with a colored man, but the ignorant white man who curries the governor's horse would turn up his nose in disgust. The president of a white college in Tuskegee makes a special effort to furnish our young men work that they may be able to remain in school, while the miserable unlettered "brother in white" would say, "You can't learn a nigger anything." Brains, property, and character for the Negro will settle the question of civil right. The best course to pursue in regard to the civil rights bill in the South is to let it alone; let it alone and it will settle itself. Good school teachers and plenty of money to pay them will be more potent in settling the race question than many civil rights bills and investigating committees. A young colored physician went into the city of Montgomery, Alabama, a few months ago to practice his profession—he was the first to professionally enter the ex-Confederate capital. When his white brother physicians found out by a six days' examination that he had brains enough to pass a better examination, as one of them said, than many of the whites had passed, they gave him a hearty welcome and offered their services to aid him in consultation or in any other way possible—and they are standing manfully up to their promise. Let there be in a community a Negro who by virtue of his superior knowledge of the chemistry of the soil, his acquaintance with the most improved tools and best breeds of stock, can raise fifty bushels of corn to the acre while his white neighbor only raises thirty, and the white man will come to the black man to learn. Further, they will sit down on the same train, in the same coach, and on the same seat to talk about it. Harmony will come in proportion as the black man gets something that the white man wants, whether it be of brains or of material. Some of the county whites looked at first with disfavor on the establishing of a normal school in Tuskegee. It turned out that there was no brickyard in the county; merchants and farmers wanted to build, but bricks must be brought from a distance or they must wait for one house to burn down before building another. The normal school with student labor started a brickyard. Several kilns of bricks were burned; the whites came miles around for bricks. From examining bricks they were led to examine the workings of the school. From the discussion of the brickyard came the discussion of Negro education—and thus many of the "old masters" have been led to see and become interested in Negro education. In Tuskegee a Negro mechanic manufactures the best tinware, the best harness, the best boots and shoes, and it is common to see his store crowded with white customers from all over the county. His word or note goes as far as that of the whitest man.

I repeat for emphasis that any work looking towards the permanent improvement of the Negro South, must have for one of its aims the fitting of him to live friendly and peaceably with his white neighbors both socially and politically. In spite of all talk of exodus, the Negro's home is permanently in the South: for coming to the bread-and-meat side of the question, the white man needs the Negro, and the Negro needs the white man. His home being permanently in the South, it is our duty to help him prepare himself to live there an independent, educated citizen.

In order that there may be the broadest development of the colored man and that he may have an unbounded field in which to labor, the two races must be brought to have faith in each other. The teachings of the Negro in various ways for the last twenty years have been rather too much to array him against his white brother than to put the two races in cooperation with each other. Thus, Massachusetts supports the Republican party, because the Republican party supports Massachusetts with a protective tariff, but the Negro supports the Republican party simply because Massachusetts does. When the colored man is educated up to the point of reasoning that Massachusetts and Alabama are a long ways apart and the conditions of life are very different, and if free trade enables my white neighbor across the street to buy his plows at a cheaper rate it will enable me to do the same thing, then will he be consulted in governmental questions. More than once have I noticed that when the whites were in favor of prohibition the blacks led even by sober upright ministers voted against it simply because the whites were in favor of it and for that reason the blacks said that they knew it was a "Democratic trick." If the whites vote to levy a tax to build a schoolhouse it is a signal for the blacks to oppose the measure, simply because the whites favor it. I venture the assertion that the sooner the colored man South learns that one political party is not composed of all angels and the other of all devils, and that all his enemies do not live in his own town or neighborhood, and all his friends in some distant section of the country, the sooner will his educational advantages be enhanced manyfold. But matters are gradually changing in this respect. The black man is beginning to find out that there are those even among the Southern whites who desire his elevation. The Negro's new faith in the white man is being reciprocated in proportion as the Negro is rightly educated. The white brother is beginning to learn by degrees that all Negroes are not liars and chicken thieves. A former owner of 75 or 100 slaves and now a large planter and merchant said to me a few days ago, "I can see every day the change that is coming about. I have on one of my plantations a colored man who can read and write and he is the most valuable man on the farm. In the first place I can trust him to keep the time of the others or with any thing else. If a new style of plow or cotton planter is taken on the place he can understand its construction in half the time that any of the others can."

My faith is that reforms in the South are to come from within. Southern people have a good deal of human nature. They like to receive the praise of doing good deeds, and they don't like to obey orders that come from Washington telling them that they must lay aside at once customs that they have followed for centuries, and henceforth there must be but one railroad coach, one hotel, and one schoolhouse for ex-master and ex-slave. In proof of my first assertion, the railroads in Alabama required colored passengers to pay the same fare as the whites, and then compelled the colored to ride in the smoking car. A committee of leading colored people laid the injustice of the matter before the railroad commissioners of Alabama, who at once ordered that within thirty days every railroad in the state should provide equal, but separate, accommodations for both races. Every prominent newspaper in the state pronounced it a just decision. Alabama gives $9,000 annually towards the support of colored normal schools. The last legislature increased the annual appropriation for free schools by $100,000, making the total annual appropriation over $500,000, and nearly half of this amount goes to colored schools, and I have the first time to hear of any distinction being made between the races by any state officer in the distribution of this fund. Why, my friends, more pippins are growing in the South than crabapples, more roses than thorns.

Now, in regard to what I have said about the relations of the two races, there should be no unmanly cowering, or stooping to satisfy unreasonable whims of Southern white men, but it is charity and wisdom to keep in mind the 200 year's schooling in prejudice against the Negro, which exslaveholders are called upon to conquer. A certain class of whites South object to the general education of the colored man, on the ground that when he is educated he ceases to do manual labor, and there is no evading the fact that much aid is withheld from Negro education in the South, by the states, on these grounds. Just here the great mission of *Industrial Education,* coupled with the mental comes in. "It kills two birds with one stone," viz.: secures the cooperation of the whites, and does the best possible thing for the black man. An old colored man in a cottonfield in the middle of July lifted his eyes toward heaven and said, "De cotton is so grassy, de work is so hard, and de sun am so hot, I believe dis darkey am called to preach." This old man, no doubt, stated the true reason why not a few enter school. Educate the black man, mentally and industrially, and there will be no doubt of his prosperity; for a race who have lived at all, and paid for the last twenty years, 25 and 30 percent interest on the dollar advanced for food, with almost no education, can certainly take care of themselves when educated mentally and industrially.

The Tuskegee Normal School, located in the black belt of Alabama, with an ignorant, degraded Negro population of 25,000 within a radius of twenty miles, has a good chance to see the direct needs of the people; and to get a correct idea of their condition one must leave the towns and go far out into the country, miles from any railroad, where the majority of the people live. They need teachers with not only trained heads and hearts, but with trained hands. Schoolhouses are needed in every township and county. The present wrecks of log cabins and bush harbors, where many of the schools are now taught, must be replaced by comfortable, decent houses. In many schoolhouses rails are used for seats, and often the fire is on the outside of the house, while teacher and scholars are on the inside. Add to this a teacher who can scarcely write his name, and who is as weak mentally as morally, and you then have but a faint idea of the educational condition of many parts of the South. It is the work of Tuskegee to send into these places teachers who will not stand off and tell the people what to do, or what ought to be done, but to send those who can take hold and show the people *how* to do. The blacksmiths, carpenters, brickmasons, and tinners, who learned their trades in slavery, are dying out, and slavery having taught the colored boy that labor is a disgrace few of their places are being filled. The Negro now has a monopoly of the trades in the South, but he can't hold it unless the young men are taught trades while in school. The large number of educated loafers to be seen around the streets of our large cities furnishes another reason in favor of industrial education. Then the proud fop with his beaver hat, kid gloves, and walking cane, who has done no little to injure the cause of education South, by industrial training, would be brought down to something practical and useful. The Tuskegee Normal School, with a farm of 500 acres, carpenter's shop, printing office, blacksmith shop, and brickyard for boys and a sewing department, laundry, flower gardening, and practical housekeeping for girls, is trying to do its part toward furnishing industrial training. We ask help for nothing that we can do for ourselves; nothing is bought that the students can produce. The boys raise the vegetables, have done the painting, made the brick, the chairs, the tables, the desks; have built a stable, a carpenter's shop, and a blacksmith's shop. The girls do the entire housekeeping, including the mending, ironing, and washing of the boys' clothes; besides they make many garments to sell.

The majority of the students are poor and able to pay but little cash for board; consequently, the school keeps three points before it. First, to give the student the best mental training; secondly, to furnish him with labor that will be valuable to the school, and that will enable the student to learn something from the labor per se; thirdly, to teach the dignity of labor. A *chance* to help himself is what we want to give to every student; this is the chance that was given me ten years ago when I entered the Hampton Institute with but fifty cents in my pocket, and it is my only ambition in life to do my part in giving it to every other poor but worthy young man and woman.

As to morals, the Negro is slowly but surely improving. In this he has had no standard by which to shape his character. The masses in too many cases have been judged by their so-called leaders, who are as a rule ignorant, immoral preachers or selfish politicians. The number of these preachers is legion. One church near Tuskegee has a total membership of 200, and 19 of these are preachers.

Poverty and ignorance have affected the black man just as they affect the white man. They have made him untruthful, intemperate, selfish, caused him to steal, to be cheated, and made the outcast of society, and he has aspired to positions which he was not mentally and morally capable of filling. But the day is breaking, and education will bring the complete light. The scales of prejudice are beginning to drop from the eyes of the dominant classes South, and through their clearer and more intelligent vision they are beginning to see and recognize the mighty truth that wealth, happiness, and permanent prosperity will only come in proportion as the hand, head, and heart of both races are educated and Christianized.

Booker T. Washington

THE ATLANTA EXPOSITION ADDRESS

Included in the following excerpt from Washington's autobiography is the full text of his most famous address, given in 1895 at the opening of a world's fair in Atlanta. It is, in fact, one of the most important speeches ever made by an American. Washington recalls the situation that led to his giving the address and the reaction that followed. Atlanta was the center of the "New South" movement, which stressed industrial advancement of the region, reduction of antagonism between North and South, and an end to Northern "interference" in Southern race relations. In the closing passage of this selection, Washington clarifies his position on political rights, especially the right to vote.

I have often been asked how I began the practice of public speaking. In answer I would say that I never planned to give any large part of my life to speaking in public. I have always had more of an ambition to *do* things than merely to talk *about* doing them. It seems that

From Booker T. Washington, *Up from Slavery: An Autobiography* (New York: Doubleday, Page & Co., 1901), pp. 199–201, 206–230, 234–237.

I went North with General Armstrong to speak at the series of public meetings to which I have referred, the president of the National Educational Association, the Hon. Thomas W. Bicknell, was present at one of those meetings and heard me speak. A few days afterward he sent me an invitation to deliver an address at the next meeting of the Educational Association. This meeting was to be held in Madison, Wisconsin. I accepted the invitation. This was, in a sense, the beginning of my public-speaking career.

On the evening that I spoke before the association there must have been not far from 4,000 persons present. Without my knowing it, there were a large number of people present from Alabama, and some from the town of Tuskegee. These white people afterward frankly told me that they went to this meeting expecting to hear the South roundly abused, but were pleasantly surprised to find that there was no word of abuse in my address. On the contrary, the South was given credit for all the praiseworthy things that it had done. A white lady who was teacher in a college in Tuskegee wrote back to the local paper that she was gratified, as well as surprised, to note the credit which I gave the white people of Tuskegee for their help in getting the school started. This address at Madison was the first that I had delivered that in any large measure dealt with the general problem of the races. Those who heard it seemed to be pleased with what I said and with the general position that I took.

When I first came to Tuskegee, I determined that I would make it my home, that I would take as much pride in the right actions of the people of the town as any white man could do, and that I would, at the same time, deplore the wrongdoing of the people as much as any white man. I determined never to say anything in a public address in the North that I would not be willing to say in the South. I early learned that it is a hard matter to convert an individual by abusing him, and that this is more often accomplished by giving credit for all the praiseworthy actions performed than by calling attention alone to all the evil done.

While pursuing this policy I have not failed, at the proper time and in the proper manner, to call attention, in no uncertain terms, to the wrongs which any part of the South has been guilty of. I have found that there is a large element in the South that is quick to respond to straightforward, honest criticism of any wrong policy. As a rule, the place to criticize the South, when criticism is necessary, is in the South—not in Boston. A Boston man who came to Alabama to criticize Boston would not effect so much good, I think, as one who had his word of criticism to say in Boston. . . .

I now come to that one of the incidents in my life which seems to have excited the greatest amount of interest, and which perhaps went further than anything else in giving me a reputation that in a sense might be called national. I refer to the address which I delivered at the opening of the Atlanta Cotton States and International Exposition, at Atlanta, Georgia, September 18, 1895.

So much has been said and written about this incident, and so many questions have been asked me concerning the address, that perhaps I may be excused for taking up the matter with some detail. The five-minute address in Atlanta, which I came from Boston to deliver, was possibly the prime cause for an opportunity being given me to make the second address there. In the spring of 1895 I received a telegram from prominent citizens in Atlanta asking me to accompany a committee from that city to Washington for the purpose of appearing before a committee of Congress in the interest of securing government help for the exposition. The committee was composed of about twenty-five of the most prominent and most influential white men of Georgia. All the members of this committee were white men except Bishop Grant, Bishop Gaines, and myself. The mayor and several other city and state officials spoke before the committee. They were followed by the two colored bishops. My name was the last on the list of speakers. I had never before appeared before such a committee, nor had I ever delivered any address in the capital of the nation. I had many misgivings as to what I ought to say, and as to the impression that my address would make. While I cannot recall in detail what I said, I remember that I tried to impress upon the committee, with all the earnestness and plainness of any language that I could command, that if Congress wanted to do something which would assist in ridding the South of the race question and making friends between the two races, it should, in every proper way, encourage the material and intellectual growth of both races. I said that the Atlanta Exposition would present an opportunity for both races to show what advance they had made since freedom, and would at the same time afford encouragement to them to make still greater progress.

I tried to emphasize the fact that while the Negro should not be deprived by unfair means of the franchise, political agitation alone would not save him, and that back of the ballot he must have property, industry, skill, economy, intelligence, and character, and that no race without these elements could permanently succeed. I said that in granting the appropriation Congress could do something that would prove to be of real and lasting value to both races, and that it was the first great opportunity of the kind that had been presented since the close of the Civil War.

I spoke for fifteen or twenty minutes, and was surprised at the close of my address to receive the hearty congratulations of the Georgia committee and of the members of Congress who were present. The committee was unanimous in making a favorable report, and in a few days the bill passed Congress. With the passing of this bill the success of the Atlanta Exposition was assured.

Soon after this trip to Washington the directors of the exposition decided that it would be a fitting recognition of the colored race to erect a large and attractive building which should be devoted wholly to showing the progress of the Negro since freedom. It was further decided to have the building designed and erected wholly by Negro mechanics. This plan was carried out. In design, beauty, and general finish the Negro Building was equal to the others on the grounds.

After it was decided to have a separate Negro exhibit, the question arose as to who should take charge of it. The officials of the exposition were anxious that I should assume this responsibility, but I declined to do so, on the plea that the work at Tuskegee at that time demanded my time and strength. Largely at my suggestion, Mr. I. Garland Penn, of Lynchburg, Virginia, was selected to be at the head of the Negro department. I gave him all the aid that I could. The Negro exhibit, as a whole, was large and creditable. The two exhibits in this department which attracted the greatest amount of attention were those from the Hampton Institute and the Tuskegee Institute. The people who seemed to be the most surprised, as well as pleased, at what they saw in the Negro Building were the Southern white people.

As the day for the opening of the exposition drew near, the board of directors began preparing the program for the opening exercises. In the discussion from day to day of the various features of this program, the question came up as to the advisability of putting a member of the Negro race on for one of the opening addresses, since the Negroes had been asked to take such a prominent part in the exposition. It was argued, further, that such recognition would mark the good feeling prevailing between the two races. Of course there were those who were opposed to any such recognition of the rights of the Negro, but the board of directors, composed of men who represented the best and most progressive element in the South, had their way, and voted to invite a black man to speak on the opening day. The next thing was to decide upon the person who was thus to represent the Negro race. After the question had been canvassed for several days, the directors voted unanimously to ask me to deliver one of the opening-day addresses, and in a few days after that I received the official invitation.

The receiving of this invitation brought to me a sense of responsibility that it would be hard for any one not placed in my position to appreciate. What were my feelings when this invitation came to me? I remembered that I had been a slave; that my early years had been spent in the lowest depths of poverty and ignorance, and that I had had little opportunity to prepare me for such a responsibility as this. It was only a few years before that time that any white man in the audience might have claimed me as his slave; and it was easily possible that some of my former owners might be present to hear me speak.

I knew, too, that this was the first time in the entire history of the Negro that a member of my race had been asked to speak from the same platform with white Southern men and women on any important national occasion. I was asked now to speak to an audience composed of the wealth and culture of the white South, the representatives of my former masters. I knew, too, that while the greater part of my audience would be composed of Southern people, yet there would be present a large number of Northern whites, as well as a great many men and women of my own race.

I was determined to say nothing that I did not feel from the bottom of my heart to be true and right. When the invitation came to me, there was not one word of intimation as to what I should say or as to what I should omit. In this I felt that the board of directors had paid a tribute to me. They knew that by one sentence I could have blasted, in a large degree, the success of the exposition. I was also painfully conscious of the fact that, while I must be true to my own race in my utterances, I had it in my power to make such an ill-timed address as would result in preventing any similar invitation being extended to a black man again for years to come. I was equally determined to be true to the North, as well as to the best element of the white South, in what I had to say.

The papers, North and South, had taken up the discussion of my coming speech, and as the time for it drew near this discussion became more and more widespread. Not a few of the Southern white papers were unfriendly to the idea of my speaking. From my own race I received many suggestions as to what I ought to say. I prepared myself as best I could for the address, but as the eighteenth of September drew nearer, the heavier my heart became, and the more I feared that my effort would prove a failure and a disappointment.

The invitation had come at a time when I was very busy with my school work, as it was the beginning of our school year. After preparing my address, I went through it, as I usually do with all those utterances which I consider particularly important, with Mrs. Washington, and she approved of what I intended to say. On the sixteenth of September, the day before I was to start for Atlanta, so many of the Tuskegee teachers expressed a desire to hear my address that I consented to read it to them in a body. When I had done so, and had heard their criticisms and comments, I felt somewhat relieved, since they seemed to think well of what I had to say.

On the morning of September 17, together with Mrs. Washington and my three children, I started for Atlanta. I felt a good deal as I suppose a man feels when he is on his way to the gallows. In passing through the town of Tuskegee I met a white farmer who lived some distance out in the country. In a jesting manner this man said: "Washington, you have spoken before the Northern white people, the Negroes in the South, and to us country white people in the South; but in Atlanta, to-morrow, you will have before you the Northern whites, the Southern whites, and the Negroes all together. I am afraid that you have got yourself into a tight place." This farmer diagnosed the situation correctly, but his frank words did not add anything to my comfort.

In the course of the journey from Tuskegee to Atlanta both colored and white people came to the train to point me out, and discussed with perfect freedom, in my hearing, what was going to take place the next day. We were met by a committee in Atlanta. Almost the first thing that I heard when I got off the train in that city was an expression something like this, from an old colored man near by: "Dat's de man of my race what's gwine to make a speech at de Exposition tomorrow. I'se sho' gwine to hear him."

Atlanta was literally packed, at the time, with people from all parts of this country, and with representatives of foreign governments, as well as with military and civic organizations. The afternoon papers had forecasts of the next day's proceedings in flaring headlines. All this tended to add to my burden. I did not sleep much that night. The next morning, before day, I went carefully over what I intended to say. I also kneeled down and asked God's blessing upon my effort. Right here, perhaps, I ought to add that I make it a rule never to go before an audience, on any occasion, without asking the blessing of God upon what I want to say.

I always make it a rule to make especial preparation for each separate address. No two audiences are exactly like. It is my aim to reach and talk to the heart of each individual audience, taking it into my confidence very much as I would a person. When I am speaking to an audience, I care little for how what I am saying is going to sound in the newspapers, or to another audience, or to an individual. At the time, the audience before me absorbs all my sympathy, thought, and energy.

Early in the morning a committee called to escort me to my place in the procession which was to march to the exposition grounds. In this procession were prominent colored citizens in carriages, as well as several Negro military organizations. I noted that the exposition officials seemed to go out of their way to see that all of the colored people in the procession were properly placed and properly treated. The procession was about three hours in reaching the exposition grounds, and during all of this time the sun was shining down upon us disagreeably hot. When we reached the grounds, the heat, together with my nervous anxiety, made me feel as if I were about ready to collapse, and to feel that my address was not going to be a success. When I entered the audience room, I found it packed with humanity from bottom to top, and there were thousands outside who could not get in.

The room was very large, and well suited to public speaking.

When I entered the room, there were vigorous cheers from the colored portion of the audience, and faint cheers from some of the white people. I had been told, while I had been in Atlanta, that while many white people were going to be present to hear me speak, simply out of curiosity, and that others who would be present would be in full sympathy with me, there was a still larger element of the audience which would consist of those who were going to be present for the purpose of hearing me make a fool of myself, or, at least, of hearing me say some foolish thing, so that they could say to the officials who had invited me to speak, "I told you so!"

One of the trustees of the Tuskegee Institute, as well as my personal friend, Mr. William H. Baldwin, Jr. was at the time general manager of the Southern Railroad, and happened to be in Atlanta on that day. He was so nervous about the kind of reception that I would have, and the effect that my speech would produce, that he could not persuade himself to go into the building, but walked back and forth in the grounds outside until the opening exercises were over.

The Atlanta Exposition, at which I had been asked to make an address as a representative of the Negro race . . . was opened with a short address from Governor Bullock. After other interesting exercises, including an invocation from Bishop Nelson, of Georgia, a dedicatory ode by Albert Howell, Jr., and addresses by the president of the exposition and Mrs. Joseph Thompson, the president of the woman's board, Governor Bullock introduced me with the words, "We have with us to-day a representative of Negro enterprise and Negro civilization."

When I arose to speak, there was considerable cheering, especially from the colored people. As I remember it now, the thing that was uppermost in my mind was the desire to say something that would cement the friendship of the races and bring about hearty cooperation between them. So far as my outward surroundings were concerned, the only thing that I recall distinctly now is that when I got up, I saw thousands of eyes looking intently into my face. The following is the address which I delivered:

Mr. President and Gentlemen of the Board of Directors and Citizens: One-third of the population of the South is of the Negro race. No enterprise seeking the material, civil, or moral welfare of this section can disregard this element of our population and reach the highest success. I but convey to you, Mr. President and Directors, the sentiment of the masses of my race when I say that in no way have the value and manhood of the American Negro been more fittingly and generously recognized than by the managers of this magnificent Exposition at every stage of its progress. It is a recognition that will do more to cement the friendship of the two races than any occurrence since the dawn of our freedom.

Not only this, but the opportunity here afforded will awaken among us a new era of industrial progress. Ignorant and inexperienced, it is not strange that in the first years of our new life we began at the top instead of at the bottom; that a seat in Congress or the state legislature was more sought than real estate or industrial skill; that the political convention or stump speaking had more attractions than starting a dairy farm or truck garden.

A ship lost at sea for many days suddenly sighted a friendly vessel. From the mast of the unfortunate vessel was seen a signal, "Water, water; we die of thirst!" The answer from the friendly vessel at once came back, "Cast down your bucket where you are." A second time the signal, "Water, water; send us water!" ran up from the distressed vessel, and was answered, "Cast down your bucket where you are." And a third and fourth signal for water was answered, "Cast down your bucket where you are." The Captain of the distressed vessel, at last heeding the injunction, cast down his bucket, and it came up full of fresh, sparkling water from the mouth of the Amazon River. To those of my race who depend on bettering their condition in a foreign land or who underestimate the importance of cultivating friendly relations with the Southern white man, who is their nextdoor neighbor, I would say: "Cast down your bucket where you are"—cast it down in making friends in every manly way of the people of all races by whom we are surrounded.

Cast it down in agriculture, mechanics, in commerce, in domestic service, and in the professions. And in this connection it is well to bear in mind that whatever other sins the South may be called to bear, when it comes to business, pure and simple, it is in the South that the Negro is given a man's chance in the commercial world, and in nothing is this exposition more eloquent than in emphasizing this chance. Our greatest danger is that in the great leap from slavery to freedom we may overlook the fact that the masses of us are to live by the productions of our hands, and fail to keep in mind that we shall prosper in proportion as we learn to dignify and glorify comman labor and put brains and skill into the common occupations of life; shall prosper in proportion as we learn to draw the line between the superficial and the substantial, the ornamental gewgaws of life and the useful. No race can prosper till it learns that there is as much dignity in tilling a field as in writing a poem. It is at the bottom of life we must begin, and not at the top. Nor should we permit our grievances to overshadow our opportunities.

To those of the white race who look to the incoming of those of foreign birth and strange tongue and habits for the prosperity of the South, were I permitted I would repeat what I say to my own race, "Cast down your bucket where you are." Cast it down among the 8 millions of Negroes whose habits you know, whose fidelity and love you have tested in days when to have proved treacherous meant the ruin of your firesides. Cast down your bucket among these people who have, without strikes and labor wars, tilled your fields, cleared your forests, builded your railroads and cities, and brought forth treasures from the bowels of the earth, and helped make possible this magnificent representation of the progress of the South. Casting down your bucket among my people, helping and encouraging them as you are doing on these grounds, and to education of head, hand, and heart, you will find that they will buy your surplus land, make blossom the waste places in your fields, and run your factories. While doing this, you can be sure in the future, as in the past, that you and your families will be surrounded by the most patient, faithful, law-abiding, and unresentful people that the world has seen. As we have proved our loyalty to you in the past, in nursing your children, watching by the sickbed of your mothers and fathers, and often following them with tear-dimmed eyes to their graves, so in the future, in our humble way, we shall stand by you with a devotion that no foreigner can approach, ready to lay down our lives, if need be, in defense of yours, interlacing our industrial, commercial, civil, and religious life with yours in a way that shall make the interests of both races one. In all things that are purely social we can be as separate as the fingers, yet one as the hand in all things essential to mutual progress.

There is no defense or security for any of us except in the highest intelligence and development of all. If anywhere there are efforts tending to curtail the fullest growth of the Negro, let these efforts be turned into stimulating, encouraging, and making him the most useful and intelligent citizen. Effort or means so invested will pay a thousand percent interest. These efforts will be twice blessed—"blessing him that gives and him that takes."

There is no escape through law of man or God from the inevitable:

The laws of changeless justice bind
Oppressor with oppressed;
And close as sin and suffering joined
We march to fate abreast.

Nearly 16 millions of hands will aid you in pulling the load upward, or they will pull against you the load downward. We shall constitute one-third and more of the ignorance and crime of the South, or one-third its intelligence and progress; we shall contribute one-third to the business and industrial prosperity of the South, or we shall prove a veritable body of death, stagnating, depressing, retarding every effort to advance the body politic.

Gentlemen of the Exposition, as we present to you our humble effort at an exhibition of our progress, you must not expect overmuch. Starting thirty years ago with ownership here and there in a few quilts and pumpkins and chickens (gathered from miscellaneous sources), remember the path that has led from these to the inventions and production of agricultural implements, buggies, steam engines, newspapers, books, statuary, carving, paintings, the management of drugstores and banks, has not been trodden without contact with thorns and thistles. While we take pride in what we exhibit as a result of our independent efforts, we do not for a moment forget that our part in this exhibition would fall far short of your expectations but for the constant help that has come to our educational life, not only from the Southern states, but especially from Northern philanthropists, who have made their gifts a constant stream of blessing and encouragement.

The wisest among my race understand that the agitation of questions of social equality is the extremest folly, and that progress in the enjoyment of all the privileges that will come to us must be the result of severe and constant struggle rather than of artificial forcing. No race that has anything to contribute to the markets of the world is long in any degree ostracized. It is important and right that all privileges of the law be ours, but it is vastly more important that we be prepared for the exercises of these privileges. The opportunity to earn a dollar in a factory just now is worth infinitely more than the opportunity to spend a dollar in an opera house.

In conclusion, may I repeat that nothing in thirty years has given us more hope and encouragement, and drawn us so near to you of the white race, as this opportunity offered by the exposition; and here bending, as it were, over the altar that represents the results of the struggles of your race and mine, both starting practically empty-handed three decades ago, I pledge that in your effort to work out the great and intricate problem which God has laid at the doors of the South, you shall have at all times the patient, sympathetic help of my race; only let this be constantly in mind, that, while from representations in these buildings of the product of field, of forest, of mine, of factory, letters, and art, much good will come, yet far above and beyond material benefits will be that higher good, that, let us pray God, will come, in a blotting out of sectional differences and racial animosities and suspicions, in a determination to administer absolute justice, in a willing obedience among all classes to the mandates of law. This, this, coupled with our material prosperity, will bring into our beloved South a new heaven and a new earth.

The first thing that I remember, after I had finished speaking, was that Governor Bullock rushed across the platform and took me by the hand, and that others did the same. I received so many and such hearty congratulations that I found it difficult to get out of the building. I did not appreciate to any degree, however, the impression which my address seemed to have made, until the next morning, when I went into the business part of the city. As soon as I was recognized, I was surprised to find myself pointed out and surrounded by a crowd of men who wished to shake hands with me. This was kept up on every street on to which I went, to an extent which embarrassed me so much that I went back to my boarding place. The next morning I returned to Tuskegee. At the station in Atlanta, and at almost all of the stations at which the train stopped between that city and Tuskegee, I found a crowd of people anxious to shake hands with me.

The papers in all parts of the United States published the address in full, and for months afterward there were complimentary editorial references to it. Mr. Clark Howell, the editor of the Atlanta *Constitution,* telegraphed to a New York paper, among other words, the following, "I do not exaggerate when I say that Professor Booker T. Washington's address yesterday was one of the most notable speeches, both as to character and as to the warmth of its reception, ever delivered to a Southern audience. The address was revelation. The whole speech is a platform upon which blacks and whites can stand with full justice to each other."

The Boston *Transcript* said editorially: "The speech of Booker T. Washington at the Atlanta Exposition, this week, seems to have dwarfed all the other proceedings and the Exposition itself. The sensation that it has caused in the press has never been equalled."

I very soon began receiving all kinds of propositions from lecture bureaus, and editors of magazines and papers, to take the lecture platform, and to write articles. One lecture bureau offered me $50,000, or $200 a night and expenses, if I would place my services at its disposal for a given period. To all these communications I replied that my lifework was at Tuskegee; and that whenever I spoke it must be in the interests of the Tuskegee school and my race, and that I would enter into no arrangements that seemed to place a mere commercial value upon my services.

Some days after its delivery I sent a copy of my address to the president of the United States, the Hon. Grover Cleveland. I received from him the following autograph reply:

Gray Gables, Buzzard's Bay, Mass.,
October 6, 1895.

Booker T. Washington, Esq.:

My dear Sir: I thank you for sending me a copy of your address delivered at the Atlanta Exposition.

I thank you with much enthusiasm for making the address. I have read it with intense interest, and I think the Exposition would be fully justified if it did not do more than furnish the opportunity for its delivery. Your words cannot fail to delight and encourage all who wish well for your race; and if our colored fellow-citizens do not from your utterances gather new hope and form new determinations to gain every valuable advantage offered them by their citizenship, it will be strange indeed.

Yours very truly,
Grover Cleveland.

Later I met Mr. Cleveland, for the first time, when, as president, he visited the Atlanta Exposition. At the request of myself and others he consented to spend an hour in the Negro Building, for the purpose of inspecting the Negro exhibit and of giving the colored people in attendance an opportunity to shake hands with him. As soon as I met Mr. Cleveland I became impressed with his simplicity, greatness, and rugged honesty. I have met him many times since then, both at public functions and at his private residence in Princeton, and the more I see of him the more I admire him. When he visited the Negro Building in Atlanta he seemed to give himself up wholly, for that hour, to the colored people. He seemed to be as careful to shake hands with some old colored "auntie" clad partially in rags, and to take as much pleasure in doing so, as if he were greeting some millionaire. Many of the colored people took advantage of the occasion to get him to write his name in a book or on a slip of paper. He was as careful and patient in doing this as if he were putting his signature to some great state document.

Mr. Cleveland has not only shown his friendship for me in many personal ways, but has always consented to do anything I have asked of him for our school. This he has done, whether it was to make a personal donation or to use his influence in securing the donations of others. Judging from my personal acquaintance with Mr. Cleveland, I do not believe that he is conscious of possessing any color prejudice. He is too great for that. In my contact with people I find that, as a rule, it is only the little, narrow people who live for themselves, who never read good books, who do not travel, who never open up their souls in a way to permit them to come into contact with other souls—with the great outside world. No man whose vision is bounded by color can come into contact with what is highest and best in the world. In meeting men, in many places, I have found that the happiest people are those who do the most for others; the most miserable are those who do the least. I have also found that few things, if any, are capable of making one so blind and narrow as race prejudice. I often say to our students, in the course of my talks to them on Sunday evenings in the chapel, that the longer I live and the more experience I have of the world, the more I am convinced that, after all, the one thing that is most worth living for—and dying for, if need be—is the opportunity of making some one else more happy and more useful.

The colored people and the colored newspapers at first seemed to be greatly pleased with the character of my Atlanta address, as well as with its reception. But after the first burst of enthusiasm began to die away, and the colored people began reading the speech in cold type, some of them seemed to feel that they had been hypnotized. They seemed to feel that I had been too liberal in my remarks toward the Southern whites, and that I had not spoken out strongly enough for what they termed the "rights" of the race. For a while there was a reaction, so far as a certain element of my own race was concerned, but later these reactionary ones seemed to have been won over to my way of believing and acting. . . .

I am often asked to express myself more freely than I do upon the political condition and the political future of my race. These recollections of my experience in Atlanta give me the opportunity to do so briefly. My own belief is, although I have never said so in so many words, that the time will come when the Negro in the South will be accorded all the political rights which his ability, character, and material possessions entitle him to. I think, though, that the opportunity to freely exercise such political rights will not come in any large degree through outside or artificial forcing, but will be accorded to the Negro by the Southern white people themselves, and that they will protect him in the exercise of those rights. Just as soon as the South gets over the old feeling that it is being forced by "foreigners," or "aliens," to do something which it does not want to do, I believe that the change in the direction that I have indicated is going to begin. In fact, there are indications that it is already beginning in a slight degree.

Let me illustrate my meaning. Suppose that some months before the opening of the Atlanta Exposition there had been a general demand from the press and public platform outside the South that a Negro be given a place on the opening program, and that a Negro be placed upon the board of jurors of award. Would any such recognition of the race have taken place? I do not think so. The Atlanta officials went as far as they did because they felt it to be a pleasure, as well as a duty, to reward what they considered merit in the Negro race. Say what we will, there is something in human nature which we cannot blot out, which makes one man, in the end, recognize and reward merit in another, regardless of color or race.

I believe it is the duty of the Negro—as the greater part of the race is already doing—to deport himself modestly in regard to political claims, depending upon the slow but sure influences that proceed from the possession of property, intelligence, and high character for the full recognition of his political rights. I think that the according of the full exercise of political rights is going to be a matter of natural, slow growth, not an overnight gourdvine affair. I do not believe that the Negro should cease voting, for a man cannot learn the exercise of self-government by ceasing to vote, any more than a boy can learn to swim by keeping out of the water, but I do believe that in his voting he should more and more be influenced by those of intelligence and character who are his nextdoor neighbors.

I know colored men who, through the encouragement, help, and advice of Southern white people, have accumulated thousands of dollars' worth of property, but who, at the same time, would never think of going to those same persons for advice concerning the casting of their ballots. This, it seems to me, is unwise and unreasonable, and should cease. In saying that I do not mean that the Negro should truckle, or not vote from principle, for the instant he ceases to vote from principle he loses the confidence and respect of the Southern white man even.

I do not believe that any state should make a law that permits an ignorant and poverty-stricken white man to vote, and prevents a black man in the same condition from voting. Such a law is not only unjust, but it will react, as all unjust laws do, in time; for the effect of such a law is to encourage the Negro to secure education and property, and at the same time it encourages the white man to remain in ignorance and poverty. I believe that in time, through the operation of intelligence and friendly race relations, all cheating at the ballot box in the South will cease. It will become apparent that the white man who begins by cheating a Negro out of his ballot soon learns to cheat a white man out of his, and that the man who does this ends his career of dishonesty by the theft of property or by some equally serious crime. In my opinion, the time will come when the South will encourage all of its citizens to vote. It will see that it pays better, from every standpoint, to have healthy, vigorous life than to have that political stagnation which always results when one-half of the population has no share and no interest in the government.

As a rule I believe in universal, free suffrage, but I believe that in the South we are confronted with peculiar conditions that justify the protection of the ballot in many of the states, for a while at least, either by an educational test, a property test, or by both combined; but whatever tests are required, they should be made to apply with equal and exact justice to both races.

Emmett J. Scott and Lyman Beecher Stowe

BOOKER T. WASHINGTON: BUILDER OF A CIVILIZATION

Shortly after his death, this defense of Washington was published by two of his firmest supporters, one black, one white. Emmett J. Scott was Washington's private secretary and adviser from 1897 on. Lyman Beecher Stowe, a grandson of the author of Uncle Tom's Cabin, *represented the Northern philanthropists who staunchly supported the Tuskegee program. In spite of its defensive tone, their biography is richly informative about Washington's manner and method.*

From Emmett J. Scott and Lyman Beecher Stowe, *Booker T. Washington: Builder of a Civilization* (Garden City, N. Y.: Doubleday, Page & Company, 1916), pp. 22–26, 29–31, 82–84, 90–93, 95–102, 104–106.

It was not to be expected . . . that such a radically new note in Negro leadership [as the Atlanta Exposition address] could be struck without some discord. As was perfectly natural, some more or less prominent Negroes, whose mental processes followed the line of cleavage between the races engendered by the embittering experiences of the Reconstruction period, looked with suspicion upon a Negro leader who had won the approbation of the South, of leading white citizens, press, and public. In the days of slavery it was a frequent custom on large plantations to use one of the slaves as a kind of stool pigeon to spy upon the others and report their misdeeds. Naturally such persons were hated and despised and looked upon as traitors to their race. Hence, it came about that the praise of a white man was apt to throw suspicion upon the racial loyalty of a black man. This habit of mind, like all mental habits, long survived the system and circumstances which occasioned it. Therefore, it was inevitable that the fact that the white press throughout the South rang with his praises for days and weeks after the sensationally enthusiastic reception of his speech at the exposition should not be accepted as a desirable endorsement of the new leader by at least a few of his own people.

A more or less conspicuous colored preacher summed up this slight undertow of dissent when he said:

> *I want to pay my respects next to a colored man. He is a great man, too, but he isn't our Moses, as the white people are pleased to call him. I allude to Booker T. Washington. He has been with the white people so long that he has learned to throw sop with the rest. He made a speech at Atlanta the other day, and the newspapers of all the large cities praised it and called it the greatest speech ever delivered by a colored man. When I heard that, I said, "There must be something wrong with it, or the white people would not be praising it so." I got the speech and read it. Then I said, "Ah, here it is," and I read his words, "the colored people do not want social equality." [This man's interpretation of this sentence in the speech, "The wisest among my race understand that the agitation of questions of social equality is the extremest folly, and that progress in the enjoyment of all the privileges that will come to us must be the result of severe and constant struggle rather than of artificial forcing."] I tell you that is a lie. We do want social equality. Why, don't you want your manhood recognized? Then Mr. Washington said that our emancipation and enfranchisement were untimely and a mistake; that we were not ready for it. [Naturally, Mr. Washington said no such thing.] What did he say that for*

but to tickle the palates of the white people? Oh, yes, he was shrewd. He will get many hundreds of dollars for his school by it.

Let it not be thought that this attitude represented any large or important body of opinion among the Negroes. The great majority both of the leaders and the rank and file enthusiastically accepted both the new leader and his new kind of leadership. The small minority, however, holding the view of the preacher quoted, continued to cause Booker Washington some annoyance, which, although continuously lessening, persisted in some degree throughout his life. This numerically small and individually unimportant element of the Negroes in America would hardly warrant even passing mention except that the always carping and sometimes bitter criticisms of these persons are apt to confuse the well-wishers of the race who do not understand the situation.

The Negroes holding this point of view are sometimes pleased to refer to themselves as the Talented Tenth. They are largely city dwellers who have had more or less of what they term "higher education"—Latin, Greek, theology, and the like. A number of these persons make all or a part of their living by publicly bewailing the wrongs and injustices of their race and demanding their redress by immediate means. Mr. Washington's emphasis upon the advantages of Negroes in America and the debt of gratitude which they owe to the whites, who have helped them to make more progress in fifty years than any other race ever made in a like period, is naturally very annoying to this type of person. In spite of their constant abuse of him Mr. Washington some years ago agreed to confer with the leaders of this faction to see if a program could not be devised through which all could work together instead of at cross purposes. In spite of the fact that the chief exponent of this group opened the first meeting with a bitter attack upon Mr. Washington, such a program was adopted, to which, before the conferences were over, all duly and amicably agreed to adhere. Some of the more restless spirits among the leaders of the Talented Tenth soon, however, broke their pledges, repudiated the whole arrangement, and started in as before to denounce Mr. Washington and those who thought and acted with him.

After the Atlanta speech Mr. Washington's task was a dual one. While the active head of his great and rapidly growing institution, he was also the generally accepted leader of his race. It is with his leadership of his race that we are concerned [here]. His duties in this capacity were vast and ill defined, and his responsibility exceedingly heavy. He said, himself, that when he first came to be talked of as the leader of his race he was somewhat at a loss to know what was expected of him in that capacity. His tasks in this direction, however, were thrust upon him so thick and fast that he had not long to remain in this state of mind. After the Atlanta speech he was in almost daily contact with what was befalling his people in all parts of the country and to some extent all over the world. Through his press clipping service, supplemented by myriads of letters and personal reports, practically every event of any significance to his race came to his notice. When he heard of rioting, lynching, or serious trouble in any community he sent a message of advice, encouragement, or warning to the leading Negroes of the locality and sometimes to the whites whom he knew to be interested in the welfare of the Negroes. When the trouble was sufficiently serious to warrant it he went in person to the scene. When he heard of a Negro winning a prize at a county fair, or being placed in some position of unusual trust and distinction, he wrote him a letter of congratulation and learned the circumstances so that he might cite the incident by way of encouragement to others.

After the riots in Atlanta, Georgia, some years ago, when infuriated white mobs foiled in their efforts to lynch a Negro murderer, burned, killed, and laid waste right and left in the Negro section of the town, Mr. Washington, who was in the North at the time, boarded the first train for the city, arrived just after the bloody scenes, gathered together his frightened people amid the smoking ruins of their homes, soothed, calmed, and cheered them. He then went to the leading city officials, secured from them a promise of succor for the stricken people and protection against further attack. Next he went to the governor of the state, secured his sympathy and cooperation, and with him organized a conference of leading state and city officials and other representative men who there and then mapped out a program tending to prevent the recurrence of such race riots—a program which up to the present time has successfully fulfilled its purpose. It is characteristic of Mr. Washington's methods that he turned this disaster into an ultimate blessing for the very community that was afflicted. . . .

He never told a story, however good, for its own sake. He told it only when it would most effectively drive home whatever point he happened to be making. [In a speech he once said] that a Negro who is lazy and unreliable and does nothing to accumulate property or improve his earning capacity deserves no consideration from whites or blacks and has no right to say that the color line is drawn against him. By way of illustration he told this story: "A shiftless Southern poor white asked a self-respecting old black man for three cents with which to pay his ferry fare across a river. The old black man replied: 'I's sorry not to commerdate yer, boss, but der fac' is dat a man what ain't got three cents is jest as bad off on one side ob der ribber as der udder.' "

At another point in this speech he was telling his people not to be discouraged because their race has less to point to than other races in the way of past achievements. He said that after all it was the future that was of vital concern and not the past, and that the future was theirs to a peculiar degree because they were a young race. And to illustrate their situation he told of meeting old Aunt Caroline one evening striding along with a basket on her head. He said, "Where are you going, Aunt Caroline?" And she replied: "Lor' bless yer, Mister Washin'ton, I dun bin where I's er goin'." "And so," he concluded, "some of the races of the earth have dun bin where dey was er goin'!" but fortunately the Negro race was not among them.

In making the point that, in spite of race prejudice, the handicaps to which his people were subjected in the South were after all superficial and did not interfere with their chance to work and earn a living, he told the experience of an old Negro who was accompanying him on one of his Southern educational tours. At a certain city they were obliged to wait several hours between trains, so this old man took advantage of the opportunity to stroll about and see the sights of the place. After a while he pulled out his watch and found he had barely time to get back to the station before the train was due to leave. Accordingly he rushed to a hack stand and called out to the first driver he came to, who happened to be a white man: "Hurry up an' take me to the station, I's gotta get the 4:32 train!" To which the white hack driver replied: "I ain't never drove a nigger in my hack yit an' I ain't goin' ter begin now. You can git a nigger driver ter take ye down!"

To this the old colored man replied with perfect good nature: "All right, my frien', we won't have no misunderstanding or trouble; I'll tell you how we'll settle it: you jest hop in on der back seat an' do der ridin' and I'll set in front an' do der drivin'." In this way they reached the station amicably and the old man caught his train. Like this old Negro, Mr. Washington always devoted his energies to catching the train, and it made little difference to him whether he sat on the front or the back seat. . . .

Booker Washington was occasionally accused both by agitators in his own race and by a certain type of Northern white men who pose as the special champions of the "downtrodden" black man as encouraging a policy of submission to injustice on the part of his people. He was, for example, charged with tame acquiescence in the practical disfranchisement of the Negro in a number of the Southern states. As a matter of fact, when these disfranchising measures were under consideration and before they were enacted, he in each case earnestly pleaded with the legislators that whatever restrictions in the use of the ballot they put upon the statute books should be applied with absolute impartiality to both races. This he urged in fairness to the white man as well as the black man.

In an article entitled, "Is the Negro Having a Fair Chance?" published in the *Century Magazine* five years ago [1912], Booker Washington said in illustrating the evil consequences of discrimination in the application of ballot regulations:

> *In a certain county of Virginia, where the county board had charge of registering those who were to be voters, a colored man, a graduate of Harvard University, who had long been a resident of the county, a quiet, unassuming man, went before the board to register. He was refused on the ground that he was not intelligent enough to vote. Before this colored man left the room a white man came in who was so intoxicated that he could scarcely tell where he lived. This white man was registered, and by a board of intelligent white men who had taken an oath to deal justly in administering the law.*
>
> *Will any one say that there is wisdom or statesmanship in such a policy as that? In my opinion it is a fatal mistake to teach the young black man and the young white man that the dominance of the white race in the South rests upon any other basis than absolute justice to the weaker man. It is a mistake to cultivate in the mind of any individual or group of individuals the feeling and belief that their happiness rests upon the misery of some one else, or that their intelligence is measured by the ignorance of some one else; or their wealth by the poverty of some one else. I do not advocate that the Negro make politics or the holding of office an im-*

portant thing in his life. I do urge, in the interest of fair play for everybody, that a Negro who prepares himself in property, in intelligence, and in character to cast a ballot, and desires to do so, should have the opportunity.

While Booker Washington did not believe that political activities should play an important part among the Negroes as a whole he did believe that the exceptional Negro who was particularly qualified for holding public office should be given the opportunity just as he believed in the higher academic education for the relatively small minority capable of profiting by such an education.

In concluding a letter in which he asks Booker Washington to recommend a member of his race for a federal office in Vicksburg, Mississippi, President Roosevelt said: "The question of the political importance of the colored man is really of no consequence. I do not care to consider it, and you must not consider it. Give me the very best colored man that you know of for the place, upon whose integrity and capacity we can surely rely."

The man, T. V. McAlister, whom Mr. Washington "gave" the president for this office was of such character and reputation that the white citizens of Vicksburg actually welcomed his appointment. Certainly neither Vicksburg nor any other portion of Mississippi can be accused of overenthusiasm for conferring civil and political privileges upon Negroes. . . .

[M]embers of the Georgia legislature, seeking political preferment for themselves through the familiar means of anti-Negro agitation, introduced a bill which aimed to discriminate against the Negroes of Georgia by legislative enactment just as the Negroes of Louisiana had been discriminated against by a constitutional amendment. This time Mr. Washington went personally to Atlanta and appealed directly to a number of the members of the legislature and to the editors of the leading papers in opposition to this bill. In an interview published in the Atlanta *Constitution* at the time he said:

I cannot think that there is any large number of white people in the South who are so ignorant or so poor that they cannot get education and property enough to enable them to stand the test by the side of the Negro in these respects. I do not believe that these white people want it continually advertised to the world that some special law must be passed by which they will seem to be given an unfair advantage over the Negro by reason of their ignorance or their poverty. It is unfair to blame the Negro

> *for not preparing himself for citizenship by acquiring intelligence, and then when he does get education and property, to pass a law that can be so operated as to prevent him from being a citizen, even though he may be a large taxpayer. The Southern white people have reached the point where they can afford to be just and generous; where there will be nothing to hide and nothing to explain. It is an easy matter, requiring little thought, generosity or statesmanship to push a weak man down when he is struggling to get up. Any one can do that. Greatness, generosity, statesmanship are shown in stimulating, encouraging every individual in the body politic to make of himself the most useful, intelligent, and patriotic citizen possible. Take from the Negro all incentive to make himself and his children useful property-holding citizens, and can any one blame him for becoming a beast capable of committing any crime?*

This time the immediate object was attained. The Atlanta *Constitution* and other leading Georgia papers endorsed Booker Washington's appeal and the legislature voted down its anti-Negro members. Be it said to the credit of the Georgia legislature that it has resisted several similar attempts to discriminate against the Negro citizens of the state, and it was not till 1908, ten years after the Louisiana law was passed, that Georgia finally passed a law disfranchising Negro voters.

Booker Washington has been accused of not protesting against the lynching of Negroes. In the article published in the *Century Magazine* in 1912, from which we have previously quoted, he said on this subject:

> *When he was Governor of Alabama, I heard Governor Jelks say in a public speech that he knew of five cases during his administration of innocent colored people having been lynched. If that many innocent people were known to the governor to have been lynched, it is safe to say that there were other innocent persons lynched whom the governor did not know about. What is true of Alabama in this respect is true of other states. In short, it is safe to say that a large proportion of the colored persons lynched are innocent. . . . Not a few cases have occurred where white people have blackened their faces and committed a crime, knowing that some Negro would be suspected and mobbed for it. In other cases it is known that where Negroes have committed crimes, innocent men have been lynched and the guilty ones have escaped and gone on committing more crimes.*
>
> *Within the last twelve months there have been seventy-one cases of lynching, nearly all of colored people. Only seventeen were charged with the crime of rape. Perhaps they are wrong to do so, but colored people*

do not feel that innocence offers them security against lynching. They do feel, however, that the lynching habit tends to give greater security to the criminal, white or black.

Mr. Washington often pointed out how the lynching of blacks leads inevitably to the lynching of whites and how the lynching of guilty persons of either race inevitably leads to the lynching of innocent persons of both races. . . .

Booker Washington also protested that in the matter of public education his people are not given a square deal in parts of the South, particularly in the country districts. He continually emphasized the relation between education and crime. Other things being equal the more and the better the education provided the less the number and seriousness of the crimes committed. Also he pointed out that the neglect of Negro school facilities injures the white citizens almost if not quite as much as the Negroes themselves. And conversely that good school facilities for the colored children benefit the whites almost as much as the Negroes. He also insisted that quite aside from all moral and ethical considerations Negro education pays in dollars and cents. As illustrating the relation between Negro education and crime or rather lack of Negro education and crime he related this incident in an article entitled, "Black and White in the South," published in the *Outlook* of March 14, 1914:

A few weeks ago three of the most prominent white men in Mississippi were shot and killed by two colored boys. Investigation brought to light that the two boys were rough and crude, that they had never been to school, hence that they were densely ignorant. While no one had taught these boys the use of books, some one had taught them, as mere children, the use of cocaine and whiskey. In a mad fit, when their minds and bodies were filled with cheap whiskey and cocaine, these two ignorant boys created a "reign of murder," in the course of which three white men, four colored men, and one colored woman met death. As soon as the shooting was over a crazed mob shot the two boys full of bullet-holes and then burned their bodies in the public streets.

Now this is the kind of thing, more or less varied in form, that takes place too often in our country. Why? The answer is simple: it is dense ignorance on the part of the Negro and indifference arising out of a lack of knowledge of conditions on the part of the white people.

He then pointed out that the last enumeration in Mississippi, where this crime was committed, indicated that 64 percent of the colored children had had no schooling during the past year. That in Charleston County, South Carolina, another backward state in Negro education, there was expended on the public education of each white child $20.20; for the colored child $3.12; in Abbeville County $11.17 for the white, 69 cents for the colored child. This 69 cents per capita expense was incurred by maintaining a one-room school for two and one-half months, with a teacher paid at the rate of $15 a month. In another county the Negro school was in session but one month out of the twelve. Throughout the state, outside the cities and large towns, the school term for the colored children is from two to four months. Thus 200,000 colored children in South Carolina are given only three or four months of schooling a year. "Under these conditions it would require twenty-eight years for a child to complete the eight grades of the public school. . . . But South Carolina is by no means the only State that has these breeding spots for ignorance, crime, and filth which the nation will sooner or later have to reckon with." . . .

In the matter of passenger transportation facilities Booker Washington protested that injustice is done his people by most of the railroads of the South, not in providing separate accommodations for blacks and whites, but in furnishing the Negroes with inferior accommodations while charging them the same rates. This injustice causes, he believes, more resentment and bitterness among his people than all the other injustices to which they are subjected combined. The Negro or "Jim Crow" compartment is usually half of the baggage car which is usually inadequate for the traffic, badly lighted, badly ventilated, and dirty. The newsdealer of the train uses this coach and increases the congestion by spreading his wares over several seats. White men frequently enter this compartment to buy papers and almost always smoke in it, thus requiring the colored women to ride in what is virtually a smoker. Aside from these matters the Negroes rarely have through cars and no sleeping, parlor, or buffet cars, and frequently no means of securing food on long journeys since many if not most of the station restaurants refuse to serve them.

In the *Century* article Mr. Washington thus quoted the experience of a sensible and conservative Negro friend of his from Austin, Texas —a man of education and good reputation among both races in his native city:

At one time [he said, in describing some of his traveling experiences,] I got off at a station almost starved. I begged the keeper of the restaurant to sell me a lunch in a paper and hand it out of the window. He refused, and I had to travel a hundred miles farther before I could get a sandwich. At another time I went to a station to purchase my ticket. I was there thirty minutes before the ticket office was opened. When it did finally open I at once appeared at the window. While the ticket agent served the white people at one window, I remained waiting at the other until the train pulled out. I was compelled to jump aboard the train without my ticket and wire back to get my trunk expressed. Considering the temper of the people, the separate coach law may be wisest plan for the South, but the statement that the two races have equal accommodations is all bosh. I pay the same money, but I cannot have a chair or a lavatory, and rarely a through car. I must crawl out at all times of night, and in all kinds of weather, in order to catch another dirty "Jim Crow" coach to make my connections. I do not ask to ride with white people. I do ask for equal accommodations for the same money.

Booker Washington was of course obliged to travel in the South almost constantly and to a great extent at night. He nearly always traveled on a Pullman car, and so when not an interstate passenger usually "violated" the law of whatever state he happened to be passing through. The conductors, brakemen, and other trainmen, as a rule, treated him with great respect and consideration and oftentimes offered him a compartment in place of the berth which he had purchased.

Pullman cars in the South are not as a rule open to members of the Negro race. It is only under more or less unusual conditions that a black man is able to secure Pullman accommodations. Dr. Washington, however, was generally treated with marked consideration whenever he applied for Pullman car reservations. He was sometimes criticized, not only by members of his own race, but by the unthinking of the white race who accused him of thus seeking "social equality" with the white passengers.

The work he was compelled to do, however, in constantly traveling from place to place, and dictating letters while traveling, made it necessary that he conserve his strength as much as possible. He never believed that he was defying Southern traditions in seeking the comfort essential to his work. . . .

The injustices mentioned and all others connected with railway passenger service for Negroes Booker Washington sought in characteristic fashion to mitigate by instituting, through the agency of the National Negro Business League, what are known as Railroad Days. On these days each year colored patrons of railroads lay before the responsible officials the respects in which they believe they are unfairly treated and request certain definite changes. Although started only a few years ago these Railroad Days have already accomplished a number of the improvements desired in various localities. . . .

Constantly as he labored for the rights of his people he never sought to obtain for them any special privileges. Unlike most leaders of groups, classes, or races of people he never sought any exclusive or special advantages for his followers. He did not want the Negro to receive any favors by reason of his race any more than he wanted him to be discriminated against on that account. He wanted all human beings, Negroes among the rest, to receive their deserts as individuals regardless of their race, color, religion, sex, or any other consideration which has nothing to do with the individual's merits. One of his favorite figures was that "one cannot hold another in a ditch without himself staying in the ditch." There is not a single right for which he contended for his people which if won would not directly or indirectly benefit all other people. Were they in all the states admitted to the franchise on equal terms with white citizens what Mr. Washington termed the "encouragement of vice and ignorance among white citizens" would cease.

Were the lynching of Negroes stopped the lynching of white men would also cease. Both the innocent black man and the innocent white man would feel a greater sense of security while the guilty black man as well as the guilty white man would be less secure. Were the Negroes given their full share of public education the whites would gain not only more reliable and intelligent Negro labor, but would be largely freed so far as Negroes are concerned from the menace of the crimes of violence which are committed almost exclusively by ignorant persons. Finally, were Negro travelers given equal accommodations and treatment for equal rates on all the Southern railways the volume of Negro travel would more rapidly increase, thus increasing the prosperity of the railways and their shareholders which would in turn promote the prosperity of the entire South.

True to his policy of always placing the emphasis upon those things which are encouraging instead of upon those things which are discouraging, Mr. Washington concluded the already much-quoted article, "Is the Negro Having a Fair Chance?" with these observations: "Notwithstanding all the defects in our system of dealing with him, the Negro in this country owns more property, lives in better houses, is in a larger measure encouraged in business, wears better clothes, eats better food, has more schoolhouses and churches, and more teachers and ministers, than any similar group of Negroes anywhere in the world."

II W. E. B. DU BOIS AND THE REEMERGENCE OF PROTEST

W. E. Burghardt Du Bois

MY EARLY RELATIONS WITH BOOKER T. WASHINGTON

Born in Great Barrington, Massachusetts, W. E. Burghardt Du Bois (1868–1963) was educated at Fisk, Harvard, and Berlin. With unusually fine academic credentials, he hoped that his scholarly activities could improve the condition of his fellow blacks. In the following autobiographical selection, he recalls the time when he was a young professor of social sciences at Atlanta University. Describing the opposition of black intellectuals to Washington, Du Bois argues that although they did not oppose all of Washington's ideas, they feared the oppressive power of the "Tuskegee Machine." He includes an intriguing description of the man Booker T. Washington, as he appeared during interviews between the two. (Du Bois pronounced his name DuBOYCE.)

Since the controversy between myself and Mr. Washington has become historic, it deserves more careful statement than it has had hitherto, both as to the matters and the motives involved. There was first of all the ideological controversy. I believed in the higher education of a Talented Tenth who through their knowledge of modern culture could guide the American Negro into a higher civilization. I knew that without this the Negro would have to accept white leadership, and that such leadership could not always be trusted to guide this group into self-realization and to its highest cultural possibilities. Mr. Washington, on the other hand, believed that the Negro as an efficient worker could gain wealth and that eventually through his ownership of capital he would be able to achieve a recognized place in American culture and could then educate his children as he might wish and develop his possibilities. For this reason he proposed to put the emphasis at present upon training in the skilled trades and encouragement in industry and common labor.

These two theories of Negro progress were not absolutely contradictory. I recognized the importance of the Negro gaining a foothold in trades and his encouragement in industry and common labor. Mr. Washington was not absolutely opposed to college training, and sent his own children to college. But he did minimize its importance,

From *Dusk of Dawn: An Essay toward an Autobiography of a Race Concept,* pp. 70–80, by W. E. Burghardt Du Bois, copyright, 1940, by Harcourt, Brace and Company, Inc. Reprinted by permission of Shirley Graham Du Bois.

and discouraged the philanthropic support of higher education; while I openly and repeatedly criticized what seemed to me the poor work and small accomplishment of the Negro industrial school. Moreover, it was characteristic of the Washington statesmanship that whatever he or anybody believed or wanted must be subordinated to dominant public opinion and that opinion deferred to and cajoled until it allowed a deviation toward better ways. This is no new thing in the world, but it is always dangerous.

But beyond this difference of ideal lay another and more bitter and insistent controversy. This started with the rise at Tuskegee Institute, and centering around Booker T. Washington, of what I may call the Tuskegee Machine. Of its existence and work, little has ever been said and almost nothing written. The years from 1899 to 1905 marked the culmination of the career of Booker T. Washington. In 1899 Mr. Washington, Paul Laurence Dunbar, and myself spoke on the same platform at the Hollis Street Theatre, Boston, before a distinguished audience. Mr. Washington was not at his best and friends immediately raised a fund which sent him to Europe for a three months' rest. He was received with extraordinary honors: he had tea with the aged Queen Victoria, but two years before her death; he was entertained by two dukes and other members of the aristocracy; he met James Bryce and Henry M. Stanley; he was received at the Peace Conference at The Hague and was greeted by many distinguished Americans, like ex-President Harrison, Archbishop Ireland and two justices of the Supreme Court. Only a few years before he had received an honorary degree from Harvard; in 1901, he received a LL.D. from Dartmouth and that same year he dined with President Roosevelt to the consternation of the white South.

Returning to America he became during the administrations of Theodore Roosevelt and William Taft, from 1901 to 1912, the political referee in all federal appointments or action taken with reference to the Negro and in many regarding the white South. In 1903 Andrew Carnegie made the future of Tuskegee certain by a gift of $600,000. There was no question of Booker T. Washington's undisputed leadership of the 10 million Negroes in America, a leadership recognized gladly by the whites and conceded by most of the Negroes.

But there were discrepancies and paradoxes in this leadership. It did not seem fair, for instance, that on the one hand Mr. Washington should decry political activities among Negroes, and on the other

FIGURE 2. W. E. Burghardt Du Bois (1868–1963). *(Historical Pictures Service, Chicago)*

hand dictate Negro political objectives from Tuskegee. At a time when Negro civil rights called for organized and aggressive defense, he broke down that defense by advising acquiescence or at least no open agitation. During the period when laws disfranchising the Negro were being passed in all the Southern states, between 1890 and 1909, and when these were being supplemented by "Jim Crow" travel laws and other enactments making color caste legal, his public speeches, while they did not entirely ignore this development, tended continually to excuse it, to emphasize the shortcomings of the Negro, and were interpreted widely as putting the chief onus for his condition upon the Negro himself.

All this naturally aroused increasing opposition among Negroes and especially among the younger classes of educated Negroes, who were beginning to emerge here and there, especially from Northern institutions. This opposition began to become vocal in 1901 when two men, Monroe Trotter, Harvard 1895, and George Forbes, Amherst 1895, began the publication of the Boston *Guardian*. The *Guardian* was bitter, satirical, and personal; but it was well edited, it was earnest, and it published facts. It attracted wide attention among colored people; it circulated among them all over the country; it was quoted and discussed. I did not wholly agree with the *Guardian*, and indeed only a few Negroes did, but nearly all read it and were influenced by it.

This beginning of organized opposition, together with other events, led to the growth at Tuskegee of what I have called the Tuskegee Machine. It arose first quite naturally. Not only did presidents of the United States consult Booker Washington, but governors and congressmen; philanthropists conferred with him, scholars wrote to him. Tuskegee became a vast information bureau and center of advice. It was not merely passive in these matters but, guided by a young unobtrusive minor official who was also intelligent, suave and far-seeing, active efforts were made to concentrate influence at Tuskegee. After a time almost no Negro institution could collect funds without the recommendation or acquiescence of Mr. Washington. Few political appointments were made anywhere in the United States without his consent. Even the careers of rising young colored men were very often determined by his advice and certainly his opposition was fatal. How much Mr. Washington knew of this work of the Tuskegee Machine and was directly responsible, one cannot say, but of its general activity and scope he must have been aware.

Moreover, it must not be forgotten that this Tuskegee Machine was not solely the idea and activity of black folk at Tuskegee. It was largely encouraged and given financial aid through certain white groups and individuals in the North. This Northern group had clear objectives. They were capitalists and employers and yet in most cases sons, relatives, or friends of the abolitionists who had sent teachers into the new Negro South after the war. These younger men believed that the Negro problem could not remain a matter of philanthropy. It must be a matter of business. These Negroes were not to be encouraged as voters in the new democracy, nor were they to be left at the mercy of the reactionary South. They were good laborers and they might be better. They could become a strong labor force and properly guided they would restrain the unbridled demands of white labor, born of the Northern labor unions and now spreading to the South.

One danger must be avoided and that was to allow the silly idealism of Negroes, half-trained in Southern missionary "colleges," to mislead the mass of laborers and keep them stirred up by ambitions incapable of realization. To this school of thought, the philosophy of Booker Washington came as a godsend and it proposed by building up his prestige and power to control the Negro group. The control was to be drastic. The Negro intelligentsia was to be suppressed and hammered into conformity. The process involved some cruelty and disappointment, but that was inevitable. This was the real force back of the Tuskegee Machine. It had money and it had opportunity, and it found in Tuskegee tools to do its bidding.

There were some rather pitiful results in thwarted ambition and curtailed opportunity. I remember one case which always stands in my memory as typical. There was a young colored man, one of the most beautiful human beings I have ever seen, with smooth brown skin, velvet eyes of intelligence, and raven hair. He was educated and well-to-do. He proposed to use his father's Alabama farm and fortune to build a Negro town and independent economic unit in the South. He furnished a part of the capital but soon needed more and he came North to get it. He struggled for more than a decade; philanthropists and capitalists were fascinated by his personality and story; and when, according to current custom, they appealed to Tuskegee for confirmation, there was silence. Mr. Washington would not say a word in favor of the project. He simply kept still. Will Benson struggled on with ups and downs, but always balked by a whispering galley of suspicion, because his plan was never endorsed by Tuskegee. In the midst of what seemed to us who looked on the beginnings of certain success, Benson died of overwork, worry, and a broken heart.

From facts like this, one may gauge the bitterness of the fight of young Negroes against Mr. Washington and Tuskegee. Contrary to most opinion, the controversy as it developed was not entirely against Mr. Washington's ideas, but became the insistence upon the right of other Negroes to have and express their ideas. Things came to such a pass that when any Negro complained or advocated a course of action, he was silenced with the remark that Mr. Washington did not agree with this. Naturally the bumptious, irritated, young black intelligentsia of the day declared, "I don't care a damn what Booker Washington thinks! This is what I think, and *I have a right to think.*"

It was this point, and not merely disagreement with Mr. Washington's plans, that brought eventually violent outbreak. It was more than opposition to a program of education. It was opposition to a system and that system was part of the economic development of the United States at the time. The fight cut deep: it went into social relations; it divided friends; it made bitter enemies. I can remember that years later, when I went to live in New York and was once invited to a social gathering among Brooklyn colored people, one of the most prominent Negroes of the city refused to be present because of my former attitude toward Mr. Washington.

When the *Guardian* began to increase in influence, determined effort was made to build up a Negro press for Tuskegee. Already Tuskegee filled the horizon so far as national magazines and the great newspapers were concerned. In 1901 the *Outlook,* then the leading weekly, chose two distinguished Americans for autobiographies. Mr. Washington's "Up from Slavery" was so popular that it was soon published and circulated all over the earth. Thereafter, every magazine editor sought articles with his signature and publishing houses continued to ask for books. A number of talented "ghost writers," black and white, took service under Tuskegee, and books and articles poured out of the institution. An annual letter "To My People" went out from Tuskegee to the press. Tuskegee became the capital of the Negro nation. Negro newspapers were influenced and finally the oldest and largest was bought by white friends of Tuskegee. Most of the other papers found it to their advantage certainly not to oppose Mr. Washington, even if they did not wholly agree with him. Negroes who sought high positions groveled for his favor.

I was greatly disturbed at this time, not because I was in absolute opposition to the things that Mr. Washington was advocating, but because I was strongly in favor of more open agitation against wrongs and above all I resented the practical buying up of the Negro press and choking off of even mild and reasonable opposition to Mr. Washington in both the Negro press and the white.

Then, too, during these years there came a series of influences that were brought to bear upon me personally, which increased my discomfort and resentment. I had tried to keep in touch with Hampton and Tuskegee, for I regarded them as great institutions. I attended the conferences which for a long time were held at Hampton, and at one of them I was approached by a committee. It consisted of Walter Hines Page, editor of the *Atlantic Monthly;* William McVickar, Episcopal bishop of Rhode Island; and Dr. Frissel, principal of Hampton. They asked me about the possibilities of my editing a periodical to be published at Hampton. I told them of my dreams and plans, and afterwards wrote them in detail. But one query came by mail: that was concerning the editorial direction. I replied firmly that editorial decisions were to be in my hands, if I edited the magazine. This was undiplomatic and too sweeping; and yet, it brought to head the one real matter in controversy: would such a magazine be dominated by and subservient to the Tuskegee philosophy, or would it have freedom of thought and discussion? Perhaps if I had been more experienced, the question could have been discussed and some reasonable outcome obtained; but I doubt it. I think any such magazine launched at the time would have been seriously curtailed in its freedom of speech. At any rate, the project was dropped.

Beginning in 1902 considerable pressure was put upon me to give up my work at Atlanta University and go to Tuskegee. There again I was not at first adverse in principle to Tuskegee, except that I wanted to continue what I had begun and if my work was worth support, it was worth support at Atlanta University. Moreover, I was unable to be assured that my studies would be continued at Tuskegee, and that I would not sink to the level of a "ghost writer." I remember a letter came from Wallace Buttrick late in 1902, asking that I attend a private conference in New York with Felix Adler, William H. Baldwin, Jr., George Foster Peabody, and Robert Ogden. The object of the conference was ostensibly the condition of the Negro in New York City. I went to the conference and I did not like it. Most of the more distinguished persons named were not present. The conference itself amounted to little, but I was whisked over to William H. Baldwin's beautiful Long Island home and there what seemed to me to be the real object of my coming was disclosed. Mr. Baldwin was at that time president of the Long Island Railroad and slated to be president of the Pennsylvania. He was the rising industrial leader of America; also he was a prime mover of the Tuskegee board of trustees. Both he and his wife insisted that my place was at Tuskegee; that Tuskegee was not yet a good school, and needed the kind of development that I had been trained to promote.

This was followed by two interviews with Mr. Washington himself. I was elated at the opportunity and we met twice in New York City. The results to me were disappointing. Booker T. Washington was not an easy person to know. He was wary and silent. He never expressed himself frankly or clearly until he knew exactly to whom he was talking and just what their wishes and desires were. He did not know me, and I think he was suspicious. On the other hand, I was quick, fast-speaking, and voluble. I found at the end of the first interview that I had done practically all the talking and that no clear and definite offer or explanation of my proposed work at Tuskegee had been made. In fact, Mr. Washington had said about as near nothing as was possible.

The next interview did not go so well because I myself said little. Finally, we resorted to correspondence. Even then I could get no clear understanding of just what I was going to do at Tuskegee if I went. I was given to understand that the salary and accommodations would be satisfactory. In fact, I was invited to name my price. Later in the year I went to Bar Harbor for a series of speeches in behalf of Atlanta University, and while there met Jacob Schiff, the Schieffelins, and Merriam of Webster's dictionary. I had dinner with the Schieffelins and again was urged to go to Tuskegee.

Early in the next year I received an invitation to join Mr. Washington and certain prominent white and colored friends in a conference to be held in New York. The conference was designed to talk over a common program for the American Negro and evidently it was hoped that the growing division of opinion and opposition to Mr. Washington within the ranks of Negroes would thus be overcome. I was enthusiastic over the idea. It seemed to me just what was needed to clear the air.

There was difficulty, however, in deciding what persons ought to be invited to the conference, how far it should include Mr. Washington's extreme opponents, or how far it should be composed principally of his friends. There ensued a long delay and during this time it seemed to me that I ought to make my own position clearer than I had hitherto. I was increasingly uncomfortable under the statements of Mr. Washington's position: his depreciation of the value of the vote; his evident dislike of Negro colleges; and his general attitude which seemed to place the onus of blame for the status of Negroes upon the Negroes themselves rather than upon the whites. And above all, I resented the Tuskegee Machine.

I had been asked sometime before by A. C. McClurg and Company of Chicago if I did not have some material for a book; I planned a social study which should be perhaps a summing up of the work of the Atlanta Conferences, or at any rate, a scientific investigation. They asked, however, if I did not have some essays that they might put together and issue immediately, mentioning my articles in the *Atlantic Monthly* and other places. I demurred because books of essays almost always fall so flat. Nevertheless, I got together a number of my fugitive pieces. I then added a chapter, "Of Mr. Booker T. Washington and Others," in which I sought to make a frank evaluation of Booker T. Washington. I left out the more controversial matter: the bitter resentment which young Negroes felt at the continued and increasing activity of the Tuskegee Machine. I concentrated my thought and argument on Mr. Washington's general philosophy. As I read that statement now, a generation later, I am satisfied with it. I see no word that I would change. The *Souls of Black Folk* was published in 1903 and is still selling today.

W. E. Burghardt Du Bois

OF MR. BOOKER T. WASHINGTON AND OTHERS

This justly famous essay, adequately introduced by Du Bois's comments in the preceding selection, is here reprinted in its entirety.

Easily the most striking thing in the history of the American Negro since 1876 is the ascendancy of Mr. Booker T. Washington. It began at the time when war memories and ideals were rapidly passing; a

From W. E. Burghardt Du Bois, *The Souls of Black Folk: Essays and Sketches* (Chicago: A. C. McClurg & Co., 1903), pp. 41–59.

day of astonishing commercial development was dawning; a sense of doubt and hesitation overtook the freedmen's sons,—then it was that his leading began. Mr. Washington came, with a simple definite program, at the psychological moment when the nation was a little ashamed of having bestowed so much sentiment on Negroes, and was concentrating its energies on Dollars. His program of industrial education, conciliation of the South, and submission and silence as to civil and political rights, was not wholly original; the Free Negroes from 1830 up to wartime had striven to build industrial schools, and the American Missionary Association had from the first taught various trades; and Price and others had sought a way of honorable alliance with the best of the Southerners. But Mr. Washington first indissolubly linked these things; he put enthusiasm, unlimited energy, and perfect faith into this program, and changed it from a by-path into a veritable Way of Life. And the tale of the methods by which he did this is a fascinating study of human life.

It startled the nation to hear a Negro advocating such a program after many decades of bitter complaint; it startled and won the applause of the South, it interested and won the admiration of the North; and after a confused murmer of protest, it silenced if it did not convert the Negroes themselves.

To gain the sympathy and cooperation of the various elements comprising the white South was Mr. Washington's first task; and this, at the time Tuskegee was founded, seemed, for a black man, well-nigh impossible. And yet ten years later it was done in the word spoken at Atlanta: "In all things purely social we can be as separate as the five fingers, and yet one as the hand in all things essential to mutual progress." This "Atlanta Compromise" is by all odds the most notable thing in Mr. Washington's career. The South interpreted it in different ways: the radicals received it as a complete surrender of the demand for civil and political equality; the conservatives, as a generously conceived working basis for mutual understanding. So both approved it, and today its author is certainly the most distinguished Southerner since Jefferson Davis, and the one with the largest personal following.

Next to this achievement comes Mr. Washington's work in gaining place and consideration in the North. Others less shrewd and tactful had formerly essayed to sit on these two stools and had fallen between them; but as Mr. Washington knew the heart of the South from birth and training, so by singular insight he intuitively grasped the spirit of the age which was dominating the North. And so thoroughly did he learn the speech and thought of triumphant commercialism, and the ideals of material prosperity, that the picture of a lone black boy poring over a French grammar amid the weeds and dirt of a neglected home soon seemed to him the acme of absurdities. One wonders what Socrates and St. Francis of Assisi would say to this.

And yet this very singleness of vision and thorough oneness with his age is a mark of the successful man. It is as though Nature must needs make men narrow in order to give them force. So Mr. Washington's cult has gained unquestioning followers, his work has wonderfully prospered, his friends are legion, and his enemies are confounded. Today he stands as the one recognized spokesman of his 10 million fellows, and one of the most notable figures in a nation of 70 millions. One hesitates, therefore, to criticize a life which, beginning with so little, has done so much. And yet the time is come when one may speak in all sincerity and utter courtesy of the mistakes and shortcomings of Mr. Washington's career, as well as of his triumphs, without being thought captious or envious, and without forgetting that it is easier to do ill than well in the world.

The criticism that has hitherto met Mr. Washington has not always been of this broad character. In the South especially has he had to walk warily to avoid the harshest judgments,—and naturally so, for he is dealing with the one subject of deepest sensitiveness to that section. Twice—once when at the Chicago celebration of the Spanish-American War he alluded to the color prejudice that is "eating away the vitals of the South," and once when he dined with President Roosevelt—has the resulting Southern criticism been violent enough to threaten seriously his popularity. In the North the feeling has several times forced itself into words, that Mr. Washington's counsels of submission overlooked certain elements of true manhood, and that his educational program was unnecessarily narrow. Usually, however, such criticism has not found open expression, although, too, the spiritual sons of the abolitionists have not been prepared to acknowledge that the schools founded before Tuskegee, by men of broad ideals and self-sacrificing spirit, were wholly failures or worthy of ridicule. While, then, criticism has not failed to follow Mr. Washington, yet the prevailing public opinion of the land has been but too willing to deliver the solution of a wearisome problem into his hands, and say, "If that is all you and your race ask, take it."

Among his own people, however, Mr. Washington has encountered the strongest and most lasting opposition, amounting at times to bitterness, and even today continuing strong and insistent even though largely silenced in outward expression by the public opinion of the nation. Some of this opposition is, of course, mere envy; the disappointment of displaced demagogues and the spite of narrow minds. But aside from this, there is among educated and thoughtful colored men in all parts of the land a feeling of deep regret, sorrow, and apprehension at the wide currency and ascendancy which some of Mr. Washington's theories have gained. These same men admire his sincerity of purpose, and are willing to forgive much to honest endeavor which is doing something worth the doing. They cooperate with Mr. Washington as far as they conscientiously can; and, indeed, it is no ordinary tribute to this man's tact and power that, steering as he must between so many diverse interests and opinions, he so largely retains the respect of all.

But the hushing of the criticism of honest opponents is a dangerous thing. It leads some of the best of the critics to unfortunate silence and paralysis of effort, and others to burst into speech so passionately and intemperately as to lose listeners. Honest and earnest criticism from those whose interests are most nearly touched, —criticism of writers by readers, of government by those governed, of leaders by those led,—this is the soul of democracy and the safeguard of modern society. If the best of the American Negroes receive by outer pressure a leader whom they had not recognized before, manifestly there is here a certain palpable gain. Yet there is also irreparable loss,—a loss of that peculiarly valuable education which a group receives when by search and criticism it finds and commissions its own leaders. The way in which this is done is at once the most elementary and the nicest problem of social growth. History is but the record of such group leadership; and yet how infinitely changeful is its type and character! And of all types and kinds, what can be more instructive than the leadership of a group within a group?—that curious double movement where real progress may be negative and actual advance be relative retrogression. All this is the social student's inspiration and despair.

Now in the past the American Negro has had instructive experience in the choosing of group leaders, founding thus a peculiar dynasty which in the light of present conditions is worthwhile studying. When sticks and stones and beasts form the sole environment of a people, their attitude is largely one of determined opposition to and conquest of natural forces. But when to earth and brute is added an environment of men and ideas, then the attitude of the imprisoned group may take three main forms,—a feeling of revolt and revenge; an attempt to adjust all thought and action to the will of the greater group; or, finally, a determined effort at self-realization and self-development despite environing opinion. The influence of all of these attitudes at various times can be traced in the history of the American Negro, and in the evolution of his successive leaders.

Before 1750, while the fire of African freedom still burned in the veins of the slaves, there was in all leadership or attempted leadership but the one motive of revolt and revenge,—typified in the terrible Maroons, the Danish blacks, and Cata of Stono, and veiling all the Americas in fear of insurrection. The liberalizing tendencies of the latter half of the eighteenth century brought, along with kindlier relations between black and white, thoughts of ultimate adjustment and assimilation. Such aspiration was especially voiced in the earnest songs of Phyllis, in the martyrdom of Attucks, the fighting of Salem and Poor, the intellectual accomplishments of Banneker and Derham, and the political demands of the Cuffes.

Stern financial and social stress after the war cooled much of the previous humanitarian ardor. The disappointment and impatience of the Negroes at the persistence of slavery and serfdom voiced itself in two movements. The slaves in the South, aroused undoubtedly by vague rumors of the Haitian revolt, made three fierce attempts at insurrection,—in 1800 under Gabriel in Virginia, in 1822 under Vesey in Carolina, and in 1831 again in Virginia under the terrible Nat Turner. In the free states, on the other hand, a new and curious attempt at self-development was made. In Philadelphia and New York color prescription led to a withdrawal of Negro communicants from white churches and the formation of a peculiar socioreligious institution among the Negroes known as the African church,—an organization still living and controlling in its various branches over a million of men.

Walker's wild appeal against the trend of the times showed how the world was changing after the coming of the cotton gin. By 1830 slavery seemed hopelessly fastened on the South, and the slaves thoroughly cowed into submission. The free Negroes of the North, inspired by the mulatto immigrants from the West Indies, began to change the basis of their demands; they recognized the slavery of slaves, but insisted that they themselves were freemen, and sought assimilation and amalgamation with the nation on the same terms with other men. Thus, Forten and Purvis of Philadelphia, Shad of Wilmington, Du Bois of New Haven, Barbadoes of Boston, and others, strove singly and together as men, they said, not as slaves; as "people of color," not as "Negroes." The trend of the times, however, refused them recognition save in individual and exceptional cases, considered them as one with all the despised blacks, and they soon found themselves striving to keep even the rights they formerly had of voting and working and moving as freemen. Schemes of migration and colonization arose among them; but these they refused to entertain, and they eventually turned to the abolition movement as a final refuge.

Here, led by Remond, Nell, Wells-Brown, and Douglass, a new period of self-assertion and self-development dawned. To be sure, ultimate freedom and assimilation was the ideal before the leaders, but the assertion of the manhood rights of the Negro by himself was the main reliance, and John Brown's raid was the extreme of its logic. After the war and emancipation, the great form of Frederick Douglass, the greatest of American Negro leaders, still led the host. Self-assertion, especially in political lines, was the main program, and behind Douglass came Elliot, Bruce, and Langston, and the Reconstruction politicians, and, less conspicuous but of greater social significance Alexander Crummell and Bishop Daniel Payne.

Then came the Revolution of 1876, the suppression of the Negro votes, the changing and shifting of ideals, and the seeking of new lights in the great night. Douglass, in his old age, still bravely stood for the ideals of his early manhood,—ultimate assimilation *through* self-assertion, and on no other terms. For a time Price arose as a new leader, destined, it seemed, not to give up, but to restate the old ideals in a form less repugnant to the white South. But he passed away in his prime. Then came the new leader. Nearly all the former ones had become leaders by the silent suffrage of their fellows, had sought to lead their own people alone, and were usually, save Douglass, little known outside their race. But Booker T. Washington arose as essentially the leader not of one race but of two,—a compromiser between the South, the North, and the Negro. Naturally the Negroes resented, at first bitterly, signs of compromise which surrendered their civil and political rights, even though this was to be exchanged for larger chances of economic development. The rich and dominating North, however, was not only weary of the race problem, but was investing largely in Southern enterprises, and welcomed any method of peaceful cooperation. Thus, by national opinion, the Negroes began to recognize Mr. Washington's leadership; and the voice of criticism was hushed.

Mr. Washington represents in Negro thought the old attitude of adjustment and submission; but adjustment at such a peculiar time as to make his program unique. This is an age of unusual economic development, and Mr. Washington's program naturally takes an economic cast, becoming a gospel of Work and Money to such an extent as apparently almost completely to overshadow the higher aims of life. Moreover, this is an age when the more advanced races are coming in closer contact with the less developed races, and the race feeling is therefore intensified; and Mr. Washington's program practically accepts the alleged inferiority of the Negro races. Again, in our own land, the reaction from the sentiment of wartime has given impetus to race prejudice against Negroes, and Mr. Washington withdraws many of the high demands of Negroes as men and American citizens. In other periods of intensified prejudice all the Negro's tendency to self-assertion has been called forth; at this period a policy of submission is advocated. In the history of nearly all other races and peoples the doctrine preached at such crises has been that manly self-respect is worth more than lands and houses, and that a people who voluntarily surrender such respect, or cease striving for it, are not worth civilizing.

In answer to this, it has been claimed that the Negro can survive only through submission. Mr. Washington distinctly asks that black people give up, at least for the present, three things,

First, political power.
Second, insistence on civil rights,
Third, higher education of Negro youth,

and concentrate all their energies on industrial education, the accumulation of wealth, and the conciliation of the South. This policy has been courageously and insistently advocated for over fifteen years, and has been triumphant for perhaps ten years. As a result of this tender of the palm branch, what has been the return? In these years there have occurred:

1. The disfranchisement of the Negro.
2. The legal creation of a distinct status of civil inferiority for the Negro.
3. The steady withdrawal of aid from institutions for the higher training of the Negro.

These movements are not, to be sure, direct results of Mr. Washington's teachings; but his propaganda has, without a shadow of doubt, helped their speedier accomplishment. The question then comes: Is it possible, and probable, that millions of men can make effective progress in economic lines if they are deprived of political rights, made a servile caste, and allowed only the most meager chance for developing their exceptional men? If history and reason give any distinct answer to these questions, it is an emphatic *No.* And Mr. Washington thus faces the triple paradox of his career:

1. He is striving nobly to make Negro artisans businessmen and property owners; but it is utterly impossible, under modern competitive methods, for workingmen and property owners to defend their rights and exist without the right of suffrage.
2. He insists on thrift and self-respect, but at the same time counsels a silent submission to civic inferiority such as is bound to sap the manhood of any race in the long run.
3. He advocates common-school and industrial training, and depreciates institutions of higher learning; but neither the Negro common schools, nor Tuskegee itself, could remain open a day were it not for teachers trained in Negro colleges, or trained by their graduates.

This triple paradox in Mr. Washington's position is the object of criticism by two classes of colored Americans. One class is spiritually descended from Toussaint the Savior, through Gabriel, Vesey, and Turner, and they represent the attitude of revolt and revenge; they hate the white South blindly and distrust the white race generally, and so far as they agree on definite action, think that the Negro's only hope lies in emigration beyond the borders of the

United States. And yet, by the irony of fate, nothing has more effectually made this program seem hopeless than the recent course of the United States toward weaker and darker peoples in the West Indies, Hawaii, and the Philippines,—for where in the world may we go and be safe from lying and brute force?

The other class of Negroes who cannot agree with Mr. Washington has hitherto said little aloud. They deprecate the sight of scattered counsels, of internal disagreement; and especially they dislike making their just criticism of a useful and earnest man an excuse for a general discharge of venom from small-minded opponents. Nevertheless, the questions involved are so fundamental and serious that it is difficult to see how men like the Grimkes, Kelly Miller, J. W. E. Bowen, and other representatives of this group, can much longer be silent. Such men feel in conscience bound to ask of this nation three things:

1. The right to vote.
2. Civic equality.
3. The education of youth according to ability.

They acknowledge Mr. Washington's invaluable service in counseling patience and courtesy in such demands; they to not ask that ignorant black men vote when ignorant whites are debarred, or that any reasonable restrictions in the suffrage should not be applied; they know that the low social level of the mass of the race is responsible for much discrimination against it, but they also know, and the nation knows, that relentless color prejudice is more often a cause than a result of the Negro's degradation; they seek the abatement of this relic of barbarism, and not its systematic encouragement and pampering by all agencies of social power from the Associated Press to the Church of Christ. They advocate, with Mr. Washington, a broad system of Negro common schools supplemented by thorough industrial training; but they are surprised that a man of Mr. Washington's insight cannot see that no such educational system ever has rested or can rest on any other basis than that of the well-equipped college and university, and they insist that there is a demand for a few such institutions throughout the South to train the best of the Negro youth as teachers, professional men, and leaders.

This group of men honor Mr. Washington for his attitude of conciliation toward the white South; they accept the "Atlanta Compromise" in its broadest interpretation; they recognize, with him, many signs of promise, many men of high purpose and fair judgment, in this section; they know that no easy task has been laid upon a region already tottering under heavy burdens. But, nevertheless, they insist that the way to truth and right lies in straightforward honesty, not in indiscriminate flattery; in praising those of the South who do well and criticizing uncompromisingly those who do ill; in taking advantage of the opportunities at hand and urging their fellows to do the same, but at the same time in remembering that only a firm adherence to their higher ideals and aspirations will ever keep those ideals within the realm of possibility. They do not expect that the free right to vote, to enjoy civic rights, and to be educated, will come in a moment; they do not expect to see the bias and prejudices of years disappear at the blast of a trumpet; but they are absolutely certain that the way for a people to gain their reasonable rights is not by voluntarily throwing them away and insisting that they do not want them; that the way for a people to gain respect is not by continually belittling and ridiculing themselves; that, on the contrary, Negroes must insist continually, in season and out of season, that voting is necessary to modern manhood, that color discrimination is barbarism, and that black boys need education as well as white boys.

In failing thus to state plainly and unequivocally the legitimate demands of their people, even at the cost of opposing an honored leader, the thinking classes of American Negroes would shirk a heavy responsibility,—a responsibility to themselves, a responsibility to the struggling masses, a responsibility to the darker races of men whose future depends so largely on this American experiment, but especially a responsibility to this nation,—this common Fatherland. It is wrong to encourage a man or a people in evildoing; it is wrong to aid and abet a national crime simply because it is unpopular not to do so. The growing spirit of kindliness and reconciliation between the North and South after the frightful differences of a generation ago ought to be a source of deep congratulation to all, and especially to those whose mistreatment caused the war; but if that reconciliation is to be marked by the industrial slavery and civic death of those same black men, with permanent legislation into a position of inferiority, then those black men, if they are really men, are called upon by every consideration of patriotism and loyalty to oppose such a course by all civilized methods, even though such opposition involves disagreement with Mr. Booker T. Washington. We have no right to sit silently by while the inevitable seeds are sown for a harvest of disaster to our children, black and white.

First, it is the duty of black men to judge the South discriminately. The present generation of Southerners are not responsible for the past, and they should not be blindly hated or blamed for it. Furthermore, to no class is the indiscriminate endorsement of the recent course of the South toward Negroes more nauseating than to the best thought of the South. The South is not "solid"; it is a land in the ferment of social change, wherein forces of all kinds are fighting for supremacy; and to praise the ill the South is today perpetrating is just as wrong as to condemn the good. Discriminating and broad-minded criticism is what the South needs,—needs it for the sake of her own white sons and daughters, and for the insurance of robust, healthy mental and moral development.

Today even the attitude of the Southern whites toward the blacks is not, as so many assume, in all cases the same; the ignorant Southerner hates the Negro, the workingmen fear his competition, the moneymakers wish to use him as a laborer, some of the educated see a menace in his upward development, while others—usually the sons of the masters—wish to help him to rise. National opinion has enabled this last class to maintain the Negro common schools, and to protect the Negro partially in property, life, and limb. Through the pressure of the moneymakers, the Negro is in danger of being reduced to semislavery, especially in the country districts; the workingmen, and those of the educated who fear the Negro, have united to disfranchise him, and some have urged his deportation while the passions of the ignorant are easily aroused to lynch and abuse any black man. To praise this intricate whirl of thought and prejudice is nonsense; to inveigh indiscriminately against "the South" is unjust; but to use the same breath in praising Governor Aycock, exposing Senator Morgan, arguing with Mr. Thomas Nelson Page, and denouncing Senator Ben Tillman, is not only sane, but the imperative duty of thinking black men.

It would be unjust to Mr. Washington not to acknowledge that in several instances he has opposed movements in the South which were unjust to the Negro; he sent memorials to the Louisiana and

Alabama constitutional conventions, he has spoken against lynching, and in other ways has openly or silently set his influence against sinister schemes and unfortunate happenings. Notwithstanding this, it is equally true to assert that on the whole the distinct impression left by Mr. Washington's propaganda is, first, that the South is justified in its present attitude toward the Negro because of the Negro's degradation; secondly, that the prime cause of the Negro's failure to rise more quickly is his wrong education in the past; and, thirdly, that his future rise depends primarily on his own efforts. Each of these propositions is a dangerous half-truth. The supplementary truths must never be lost sight of: first, slavery and race prejudice are potent if not sufficient causes of the Negro's position; second, industrial and common-school training were necessarily slow in planting because they had to await the black teachers trained by higher institutions,—it being extremely doubtful if any essentially different development was possible, and certainly a Tuskegee was unthinkable before 1880; and, third, while it is a great truth to say that the Negro must strive and strive mightily to help himself, it is equally true that unless his striving be not simply seconded, but rather aroused and encouraged, by the initiative of the richer and wiser environing group, he cannot hope for great success.

In his failure to realize and impress this last point, Mr. Washington is especially to be criticized. His doctrine has tended to make the whites, North and South, shift the burden of the Negro problem to the Negro's shoulders and stand aside as critical and rather pessimistic spectators; when in fact the burden belongs to the nation, and the hands of none of us are clean if we bend not our energies to righting these great wrongs.

The South ought to be led, by candid and honest criticism, to assert her better self and do her full duty to the race she has cruelly wronged and is still wronging. The North—her copartner in guilt—cannot salve her conscience by plastering it with gold. We cannot settle this problem by diplomacy and suaveness, by "policy" alone. If worse come to worst, can the moral fiber of this country survive the slow throttling and murder of 9 millions of men?

The black men of America have a duty to perform, a duty stern and delicate,—a forward movement to oppose a part of the work of their greatest leader. So far as Mr. Washington preaches Thrift, Patience, and Industrial Training for the masses, we must hold up his hands and strive with him, rejoicing in his honors and glorying in the strength of this Joshua called of God and of man to lead the headless host. But so far as Mr. Washington apologizes for injustice, North or South, does not rightly value the privilege and duty of voting, belittles the emasculating effects of caste distinctions, and opposes the higher training and ambition of our brighter minds,—so far as he, the South, or the Nation, does this,—we must unceasingly and firmly oppose them. By every civilized and peaceful method we must strive for the rights which the world accords to men, clinging unwaveringly to those great words which the sons of the Fathers would fain forget: "We hold these truths to be self-evident: That all men are created equal; that they are endowed by their Creator with certain unalienable rights; that among these are life, liberty, and the pursuit of happiness."

Francis L. Broderick

THE FIGHT AGAINST BOOKER T. WASHINGTON

Du Bois was so complex a human being and his long life so rich in intellectual and ideological development that it is fair to say he will escape the full grasp of any biographer. After he was ninety Du Bois joined the Communist party, and he died in Ghana, having shortly before become a citizen of that African nation. By focusing on his opposition to Washington, this anthology inevitably underplays the ambivalences of the man. The following excerpt from the biography by Francis L. Broderick, of the University of Massachusetts, Boston, offers an informed and fair-minded account of a difficult subject. It traces the rising discontent over Washington among educated blacks and Du Bois's gradual emergence as its leading spokesman. Included are evocative pen portraits of the two men and appraisal of Du Bois's theory of the "Talented Tenth."

Reprinted from *W. E. B. Du Bois: Negro Leader in a Time of Crisis*, pp. 62–77, by Francis L. Broderick with the permission of the publishers, Stanford University Press.

Footnotes abridged.

Booker T. Washington's vogue among influential white men and his prestige among Negroes made an outspoken statement of the Negro's cause urgent. As Du Bois saw it, Washington was leading his people into a blind alley: in exchange for paltry support of industrial education, Washington was bartering away the claim to political and civil rights; indeed he was even surrendering their manhood. Every concession Washington won from the white man, Du Bois thought, yielded essential ground which would have to be retaken by hard fighting.

Though nominally a debate over educational systems, the Washington-Du Bois controversy actually arose from Du Bois's attack on Washington's whole program. Washington focused on the Negro masses. He favored industrial education because he thought that technical skills would make Negroes invaluable and therefore welcome in an industrial economy. In seeking support for industrial education, Washington was willing to postpone political and social rights, and in appealing to white philanthropy, he maintained a friendly, accommodating attitude toward all white men, Southerners and Northerners alike. He felt that the temporary suspension of political and social rights was not too high a price for the attainment of this economic shelf.

Washington first gained wide attention by a speech at the Atlanta Exposition in 1895. . . . When his autobiography, *Up from Slavery,* was serialized in *Outlook* in 1900 and published in book form in 1901, his national position was confirmed.

In a subsequent autobiography, *My Larger Education* (1911), Washington made explicit his acceptance of the dominant industrial movement of the age. With praise for industrialists like Andrew Carnegie who were contributing generously to Tuskegee and to similar schools, Washington repeated the familiar aphorisms of nineteenth-century American progress: advancement through self-help, thrift as a path to riches, the importance of responsibilities over rights. In a speech to a Negro audience, Washington even made Christianity the servant of industry: "Nothing pays so well in producing efficient labor as Christianity."

Washington's soothing statements to white audiences won him prestige as the spokesman of his race. Because of his influence with white men and his access to white capital, prominent Negroes supported him and sought his favor. Much of the Negro press fell into line: it shouted down criticism of Tuskegee and its principal and branded Du Bois as a jealous upstart.

As J. Saunders Redding says:

> *From white America's point of view, the situation was ideal. White America had raised this man [Washington] up because he espoused a policy which was intended to keep the Negro docile and dumb in regard to civil, social and political rights and privileges. Having raised him to power, it was in white America's interest to keep him there. All race matters could be referred to him, and all decisions affecting the race would seem to come from him. In this there was much pretense and, plainly, not a little cynicism. There was pretense, first, that Washington was leader by sanction of the Negro people; and there was the pretense, second, that speaking in the name of his people, he spoke for them.*

Washington's ideas did not go unchallenged. To educated Negroes, particularly those who lived in cities outside the South, the traditionally servile position of Negroes in America was abhorrent. Some, whose skin was pale enough, passed over into the white race and, by leaving the area where they were known, cut themselves loose from their past. Others drew into their own tight little group, avoiding contact with the poorer, less educated elements which they thought were responsible for awakening anti-Negro feelings, especially in the North. One articulate group, however, the heirs of Frederick Douglass, channeled their resentment at second-class citizenship into an active fight for equality. Some, like Kelly Miller of Howard University and Charles W. Chesnutt, the novelist, spoke with quiet voices. Some, like Harry C. Smith, the editor of the Cleveland *Gazette,* were more insistent. A few, like Ida B. Wells-Barnett, the chairman of the Anti-Lynching League, and William Monroe Trotter, who with George W. Forbes, edited the Boston *Guardian,* threw restraint to the winds in their attacks on American discrimination and on Booker Washington's soft words. (Trotter had been a contemporary of Du Bois's at Harvard, but they had hardly known each other.) In the early years of the century, Du Bois gradually moved into the position of leader of this articulate group.

The notoriety of the Washington-Du Bois controversy has obscured the similarity of their views for at least six or seven years after the Atlanta speech. The picture of Washington created by partisans of Du Bois has shown him as toadying to the whites, acknowledging Negro disfranchisement without a murmur, and selling out Negro aspiration for a mess of economic pottage. Actually Kelly Miller was probably right in 1903 when he wrote that Washington "would not disclaim, in distinct terms, a single plank in the platform of Douglass." Though he ordinarily spoke in cautious diplomatic terms, he did on occasion take a position against white prejudice, even without the prodding of the Negro press. He spoke out boldly against the "grandfather" clause in the Louisiana constitution of 1898, and though unwilling to associate himself publicly with the move, he asked Francis J. Garrison, William Lloyd Garrison's son, to help raise money to aid responsible colored men in Louisiana in testing it in the courts. The previous year, in Atlanta, he had condemned the violence which had culminated in the lynching of a Negro named Same Hose, and, in private, he had expressed his fear of associating on a public platform with a Negro whose reputation of toadying to the whites might have compromised his own position. Off the record, he offered to help Du Bois to press an action against the Pullman Company for alleged discrimination. In 1903, just before the publication of *The Souls of Black Folk,* he joined Du Bois in protesting to the Rhodes Trust the exclusion of Negro candidates from consideration in the Atlanta area.

Furthermore, until the publication of *The Souls of Black Folk,* Washington maintained cordial personal relations with Du Bois. In 1900, Washington, apparently at Du Bois's request, recommended him for a position as superintendent of the Negro schools in Washington, D.C., and the following year Du Bois accepted a social invitation to Washington's summer camp in West Virginia. At the 1902 Atlanta conference, Washington praised Du Bois's work as a "monument to his ability, wisdom and faithfulness." Until the break in 1903 Washington and his white backers continued to urge Du Bois to join the staff of Tuskegee. Though Washington equivocated, compromised, and frequently kept silent, he differed with Du Bois on method rather than on final goals. And even in the choice of method, they shared some ground.

Conversely, Du Bois had at various times moved closer to the Tuskegee ideology than his partisans would admit. In a letter to the New York *Age,* he had greeted Washington's Atlanta speech as the basis for a real settlement if the South would open the doors of economic activity to the Negroes and if the Negroes would cooperate with the white South in "political sympathy." . . . In the mid-nineties, when Washington was telling a Brooklyn audience that it was more important that the Negro be *prepared* for voting, office holding, and the highest recognition than that he vote, hold office, and be recognized, Du Bois was scoffing at the Negro's "wail" of complaint against his lack of privilege: "Bah—what of that! what does man who has the world in his grasp care for the meteors that escape him—and what does the monarch of the sphere, of the 7 stars and solar years care if some little stars of the universe shine not for him? Turn your back on evils you can not right, & press to work that is calling so loudly and clearly."

Du Bois's speech on the "Meaning of Business" in 1898 reflected the mercantile spirit of the age so characteristic of Washington's teachings. Business organization and economic development must claim the major energies of the people, he said. The task was therefore to accumulate capital and to use it wisely: "The day the Negro race courts and marries the savings-bank will be the day of its salvation."

On universal suffrage Du Bois was no more outspoken than Washington. When Georgia considered the Hardwick bill for effective Negro disfranchisement in 1899, Du Bois endorsed educational and property qualifications for voting, thus protecting the ballot for the few at the expense of the many. Du Bois was more insistent than Washington in applying the standard equally to both races, but on the basic issue of universal suffrage, neither took a particularly democratic view.

Du Bois always regarded industrial education and college work as complementary. About 1899 he outlined a plan of cooperation between the investigative conferences at Hampton and Atlanta. In the same years he assured Washington of his "best sympathy for the Tuskegee work" and predicted that eventually it would "undoubtedly bear fruit." In 1901, he publicly praised Tuskegee's ten-year battle against the crop-lien system, one-room cabin, and poor and short-termed public schools. The next year, in inviting Washington to the annual Atlanta conference, Du Bois emphasized his anxiety to minimize the break between colleges and industrial schools and to cooperate with Tuskegee. Even in *The Negro Artisan* (1902), where his comments were more explicitly critical of industrial education, he was also on record as a member of the resolutions committee which stated: "We especially commend Trades Schools as a means of imparting skill to Negroes, and manual training as a means of general education. We believe the movements in this line, especially in the last ten years, have been of inestimable benefit to the freedmen's sons."

This atmosphere of mutual cordiality, however, was deceptive, for the pressures which led to the explosion in 1903 had been building up for three years. In 1900 Du Bois spoke very generally of the Negro who forgot too easily that "life is more than meat and the body more than raiment." Such a person was likely to be "a traitor to right and a coward before force." The following year, in reviewing Washington's autobiography for the *Dial,* Du Bois ascribed two great achievements to him: gaining the sympathy and cooperation of the white South and learning so thoroughly "the speech and thought of triumphant commercialism and the ideals of material prosperity" that he gained equal consideration in the North. Opposition to his ideals of material prosperity at the expense of social and political advance, Du Bois explained, arose from the "spiritual sons of the abolitionists" and from a large and important group in Washington's own race "who, without any single definite program, and with complex aims, seek nevertheless that self-development and self-realization in all lines of human endeavor which they believe will eventually place the Negro beside the other races. While these men respect the Hampton-Tuskegee idea to a degree, they believe it falls short of a complete program. They believe, therefore, also in the higher education of Fisk and Atlanta Universities; they believe in self-assertion and ambition; they believe in the right of suffrage for blacks on the same terms with whites." These opponents were silenced, he said, only by "Mr. Washington's very evident sincerity of purpose. We forgive much to honest purpose which is achieving something. We may not agree with the man at all points, but we admire him and cooperate with him as far as we conscientiously can. It is no ordinary tribute to this man's tact and power, that, steering as he must amid so many diverse interests and opinions, he to-day commands not simply the applause of those who believe in his theories, but also the respect of those who do not."

The tone of the essay aligned Du Bois with this latter group, in which he included some of the most important Negro intellectuals—the educator Kelly Miller, the poet Paul Laurence Dunbar, . . . and the novelist Charles W. Chesnutt. Even in the role of critic, Du Bois remained fair: the criticisms of Washington were vigorous, but Washington's own position was presented with understanding.

The essay on Washington in *The Souls of Black Folk* the following year still retained much of Du Bois's balanced appraisal of Washington—respect for the "most distinguished Southerner since Jefferson Davis" together with sharp criticism of his overemphasis on industrial education. . . .

A substantial gulf had come to separate the two men. But the gulf was not new. Why did the differences develop into open warfare at the time? It is hard to say. Perhaps the favorable reception of Du Bois's early work gave him sufficient security to challenge the champion. Perhaps the hammering attacks on Washington by Trotter in the Boston *Guardian* and the more restrained criticism elsewhere appealed to Du Bois's pride in his race. Perhaps Atlanta's failure to share in the white philanthropy at Washington's command convinced Du Bois of the hostility behind Washington's diplomatic cordiality. Perhaps Du Bois already had suspicions that his path of scholarship would not lead to advancement of the Negro and that a more aggressive policy of agitation was required. All these factors undoubtedly contributed in varying degrees to the decision, and Du Bois's publication of a collection of his fugitive essays seemed like the appropriate occasion for a firm challenge.

Behind the conflict in ideas were two discordant personalities. Both possessed titanic ambition. Washington, thick-set and slow-moving, had the assurance of a self-trained man. A shrewd, calculating judge of people, he had the soft speech and the accommodating manner that made him equally at home among sharecroppers and at the president's table. A master of equivocation, he made platitudes pass as earthly wisdom, and he could take unnoticed with one hand what he had given with the other. Du Bois, slight, nervous in his movements, never forgot for a moment his educational background. Proud and outspoken, he held aloof from the Negro masses, but felt at home with a small company of his peers with whom he could be witty and convivial. Washington had the appearance of a sturdy farmer in his Sunday best; Du Bois, with his well-trimmed goatee, looked like a Spanish aristocrat. Where Washington was accommodating, Du Bois was fretful and aggressive. The conflicting personalities of these two men supplied the rallying points for two groups of articulate Negroes. James Weldon Johnson observed years later that one unfamiliar with the twelve-year period after 1903 could not imagine "the bitterness of the antagonism between these two wings."

Once the fire had broken out within the race, it created its own fuel. On the one hand, Washington was frightened by the attacks and apprehensive for his role as leader. On the other hand, the adverse criticism which greeted Du Bois's moderate essay may well have provoked his proud spirit. His comments against Washington grew ever more vehement until mutual recriminations blocked compromise. In the Negro press the partisans of both parties egged Du Bois into even blunter criticism. The *Colored American* chided Du Bois as a "hanger-on at a place created by white people"; seeing little chance to sell *The Souls of Black Folk* on "its own bottom," Du Bois tried to sell it by a sensational attack. The *Southern Workman,* noting that "pessimism is never helpful," found Du Bois unfair to Washington: the latter had his eye on the Negro masses, Du Bois on the few more favored than the rest yet shut out from social and political equality with the white man. At the same time the Cleveland *Gazette* labeled Du Bois's essay a "proper estimate," and the *Guardian,* which had been singing Du Bois's praises even before the essay appeared, gladly welcomed its new ally. Du Bois responded to this last bit of adulation directly. After the "Boston riot," a meeting in July 1903 at which heckling of Washington led to Trotter's arrest for disorderly conduct, Du Bois wrote to Clement Morgan: "While I have not always agreed with Mr. Trotter's methods, I have had the greatest admiration for his singlehearted earnestness & devotion to a great cause and I am the more minded to express this respect publicly when I see him the object of petty persecution & dishonest attack." Du Bois thus aligned himself with the "radicals."

Once committed to battle, Du Bois continued to attack. Under a thin veil of praising Washington as part of the "advance guard of the race," he subordinated Washington's work as an educator and moral leader to his skill in political maneuver. He referred to the "marvelous facility" with which Washington "so manipulated the forces of a strained political and social situation as to bring about . . . the greatest consensus of opinion in this country since the Missouri Compromise." Washington, Du Bois continued, "kept his hand on the pulse of the North and South, advancing with every sign of good will and generosity, and skillfully retreating to silence or shrewd disclaimer at any sign of impatience or turmoil." Few readers could miss the object of Du Bois's remarks the following year: What are personal humiliation and denial of civil rights against a chance to earn a living, or filthy Jim Crow cars next to bread and butter? he asked sarcastically. "Earn a living; get rich, and all these things shall be added unto you. Moreover, conciliate your neighbors, because they are more powerful and wealthier, and the price you must pay to earn a living in America is that of humiliation and inferiority." One of his addresses to the Washington, D.C., colored school children included a warning against the humiliating program which sought "to train black boys and girls forever to be hewers of wood and drawers of water for the cowardly people who seek to shackle our minds as they shackled our hands yesterday." "Loose yourselves," he told them, "from that greater temptation to curse and malign your own people and surrender their rights for the sake of applause and popularity and cash." Moving directly into the camp of the enemy, he spoke at Hampton in 1906 and attacked the "heresy" of industrial education: "Take the eyes of these millions off the stars and fasten them in the soil and if their young men will dream dreams, let them be dreams of corn bread and molasses." He admitted the necessity of training most men to provide the world's physical wants, but he begged the teachers attending the summer session at Hampton to release their most able students for higher education, "the training of a self whose balanced trained assertion will mean as much as possible for the great ends of civilization."

Even before *The Souls of Black Folk* appeared, Washington had called a conference of outstanding Negroes to consider the present condition and future of the race. The conference purportedly sought a reconciliation of views, but Du Bois told Kelly Miller that he was afraid the meeting would become a "B. T. W. ratification meeting." Yet Du Bois accepted the opportunity to confront Washington with his equivocal stands on such questions as civil rights, and organized a caucus of the opposition. He proposed that these men stand on the following platform: full political rights on the same terms as other Americans; higher education of selected Negro youth; industrial education for the masses; common school training for every

Negro child; stoppage of the campaign of self-deprecation; careful study of the real condition of the Negro; a national Negro periodical; thorough and efficient federation of Negro societies and activities; raising of a defense fund; judicious fight in the courts for civil rights. "Finally the general watch word must be, not to put further dependence on the help of the whites but to organize for self-help, encouraging 'manliness without defiance, conciliation with servility.' " As the meeting approached, a circular letter, probably put out by Du Bois, warned that "the main issue of this meeting is *Washington,* refuse to be side-tracked."

Washington never lost mastery of the conference. He controlled the invitations and travel allowances. Lyman Abbott and Andrew Carnegie were on hand to praise him abundantly. After he and Du Bois had spoken, a committee of three was selected to appoint a larger committee as the steering group for the Negro race in America. The committee of three included both principals, and the third member, Hugh M. Browne, was so responsive to Washington that Du Bois was overruled on every major point, including the membership of the permanent Committee of Twelve for the Advancement of the Interests of the Negro Race—a sort of Negro general staff. When Washington was named chairman of this group, Du Bois resigned to avoid responsibility for statements over which he would have little personal control.

The failure of the 1904 conference solidified Du Bois's opposition to Washington. In January 1905, Du Bois's article in *The Voice of the Negro,* "Debit and Credit (The American Negro in account with the Year of Grace 1904)" listed in its debit column "$3,000 of 'hush money' used to subsidize the Negro press in 5 leading cities." This was the first open attack on the "Tuskegee Machine," the elusive organization through which Washington influenced Negro life in America by his power over appointments, both political and educational, by his manipulation of white capital, and by his control over a part of the Negro press. William H. Ward of the *Independent* and Oswald Garrison Villard of the New York *Evening Post* urged Du Bois either to withdraw his statement or to substantiate it with factual proof. But though evidence in the Booker T. Washington papers backs up Du Bois's charge, the charge could not be proved: advertisements from Tuskegee in friendly journals were hard to brand as bribery, and proof of direct bribery—if it existed—lay hidden in the files of givers and takers. Privately, on a confidential basis, Du Bois assembled a substantial portfolio to convince Villard, but Villard legitimately rejected this hearsay evidence as insufficient; he retained his faith in Washington's "purity of purpose and absolute freedom from selfishness and personal ambition," though he admitted that Emmett J. Scott, Washington's confidential secretary, had been "extremely injudicious."[1]

Washington's program gave Du Bois an anvil on which to hammer out his own ideas. At the core of Du Bois's philosophy was the role assigned to the Talented Tenth because, like all races, Du Bois said, the Negro race would be saved by its exceptional men, trained to the knowledge of the world and man's relation to it. As teachers, ministers, professional men, spokesmen, the exceptional few must come first: "To attempt to establish any sort of system of common and industrial school training, without *first* (and I say *first* advisedly) without *first* providing for the higher training of the very best teachers, is simply throwing your money to the winds." Du Bois did not deprecate the importance of industrial training, but "it is industrialism drunk with its vision of success, to imagine that its own work can be accomplished without providing for the training of broadly cultured men and women to teach its own teachers, and to teach the teachers of the public school." Du Bois pointed to the thirty college-trained teachers on Washington's own staff as an effective argument for training in the liberal arts.

Du Bois's theory of the Talented Tenth was the striking product of his own total experience and training. It singled out a select minority, enriched it with the finest education, and then bade it lead the masses. They were to be the thinkers, educators, ministers, lawyers, editors, political leaders. To the ears of Du Bois's opponents, this theory, from the mouth of one who was undoubtedly a member of the Talented Tenth, had a selfish, self-serving ring, and its echoes of the heroic vitalism of Carlyle and Nietzsche do not

[1] The list of charges and the correspondence relating to it are in the Oswald Garrison Villard Papers, Houghton Library, Harvard University. August Meier's article, "Booker T. Washington and the Negro Press: With Special Reference to the *Colored American Magazine*," has put beyond historical question the fact that Washington attempted to buy support in the Negro press. *Journal of Negro History* 38 (January 1953): 67–90. In a friendly biography of Washington, Samuel R. Spencer, Jr., acknowledges that "in some cases" Washington and his staff encouraged the printing of Tuskegee press releases "by occasional 'contributions' to Negro editors." *Booker T. Washington and the Negro's Place in American Life* (Boston, 1955), p. 163.

recommend it to modern ears. Booker Washington was able to score constantly against Du Bois by charging that Du Bois was interested only in a handful of Negroes, while Washington concerned himself with the masses. There was some truth in Washington's charge, but not much. An essential part of Du Bois's idea was that the tenth was to be trained as the servants of the other 90 percent. Their special privileges were justified by the benefits which they could confer on their fellow men, and Du Bois never asked for special privileges on any other terms. Du Bois himself had had as fine an education as any man in America; was he not using his entire energy to raise his people? With a thousand, or ten thousand, Negroes similarly trained, similarly devoted to duty, how long would American Negroes remain in poverty and degradation?

The training of the Talented Tenth was a means to an end: political and civil rights equal to those of other Americans. In 1899, Du Bois had acknowledged the propriety of proscribing ignorance and bribery; by 1901, skeptical of Georgia's avowed intention to disfranchise the ignorant, he asked in an unpublished article: *"Do you propose to disfranchise ignorant white people? Do you propose to leave the ballot in the hands of intelligent Negroes and protect them in its exercise?"* Three years later he withdrew his acceptance of partial Negro disfranchisement and argued in favor of universal suffrage free from arbitrary educational requirements, for, he said, in losing the ballot, Negro workingmen faced a hostile South unprotected and powerless. In March 1905, Du Bois and four other Negroes petitioned President Theodore Roosevelt to instruct his attorney general to help in testing the validity of state constitutions which deprived the Negro of his vote by constitutional trickery and to support the passage of the Morrill bill, then pending, which forbade racial discrimination of any kind in vehicles in interstate commerce.

To help in the fight to secure Negro rights, Du Bois committed himself to a program of direct agitation. He denounced Negro silence during the previous decade: the absence of complaint had permitted white America to assume that the Negro was satisfied. If Negroes sat "in courteous and dumb self-forgetting silence" until others came to their rescue, he said, degeneration and destruction might come first. In a preoccupied world, people had to take care of themselves.

From 1903 until 1910, Du Bois took some time from his duties at the university to devote himself to his new program of direct agitation. As professor of sociology, he continued to train part of the Talented Tenth and to issue sociological reports. But as spokesman for the "radical" wing of the Negro race, he took on new responsibilities.

To mobilize articulate Negroes ready to fight for their rights, Du Bois in 1905 sent out a summons for the first convention of what became known as the Niagara Movement. Several of Du Bois's "radical" associates had for some time been urging him to organize a national committee of Negroes representing their views. Two of them, F. L. McGhee and C. C. Bentley, drew up a plan for the new group: a nationwide organization with committees assigned to definite Negro problems, local organizations of militant Negroes, and an annual convention to plan and to generate enthusiasm. In response to Du Bois's appeal, twenty-nine professional men from thirteen states and the District of Columbia met at Niagara Falls, Ontario. These were to be the nucleus of the "very best class of Negro Americans." For Du Bois, the movement's executive officer, the Niagara Movement was to serve two functions: in the white world, its annual manifestoes would periodically call attention to the Negro's complaint; among Negroes, the movement would whip up indignation against the injustices of white America. Both purposes hinged on Booker T. Washington: the steady barrage of protest would contradict his soothing assurances to the whites, and the movement would offer dissident Negroes a medium for opposition to him.

A "Declaration of Principles," largely written by Trotter and Du Bois, was dramatically "submitted to the American people, and Almighty God" after the first convention. It indicated the broad sweep of the Negro "radical" protest with which Du Bois now associated himself. Demands for suffrage and civil rights headed the list, followed by complaints against "peonage and virtual slavery" in the rural South and against the prejudice "helped often by iniquitous laws" that created difficulties in earning a decent living. Two classes of men deserved public excoriation, it said: employers who imported ignorant Negro American laborers in emergencies, and then afforded them "neither protection nor permanent employment" (an elaborate circumlocution for "strike breakers"); and labor unions which excluded "their fellow toilers, simply because they are black." Free and compulsory education through the high-school level was set as a universal minimum, and college training, instead of being the "monopoly" of any class or race, should, the statement continued, be open to talent. Trade schools and higher education were both listed as essential. In the courts the Negro wanted upright judges, juries selected without reference to color, and equal treatment both in punishment and in efforts at reformation. Some of Du Bois's old complaints appeared: "We need orphanages and farm schools for dependent children, juvenile reformatories for delinquents, and the abolition of the dehumanizing convict-lease system." Any discrimination along the color line was said to be a relic of "unreasoning human savagery of which the world is, and ought to be, thoroughly ashamed." The Niagara group expressed astonishment at the increase of prejudice in the Christian church, and labeled the third-class accommodations of Jim Crow cars as an attempt "to crucify wantonly our manhood, womanhood, and self-respect." They pleaded for health—the opportunity to live in decent localities with a chance to raise children in "physical and moral cleanliness."

To right the wrongs, the small band urged national aid to education, especially in the South, a return to the "faith of the fathers," and legislation to secure proper enforcement of the War Amendments. Rejecting the "cowardice and apology" of the current Negro leadership, it called for "persistent manly agitation" as the road to liberty, for "to ignore, overlook, or apologize for these wrongs is to prove ourselves unworthy of freedom." To accomplish its ends, the Niagara group appealed for the cooperation of men of all races.

The past decade, the Niagara band said, had shown "undoubted evidences of progress": the increase in intelligence and in the ownership of property, the decrease in crime, the uplift in home life, the advance in literature and art, and the demonstration of executive ability in religious, economic, and educational institutions. However, in the face of the "evident retrogression of public opinion on human brotherhood," only loud and insistent complaint could hold America to its professed ideals.

Ray Stannard Baker

AN OSTRACIZED RACE IN FERMENT

In the muckraking tradition, the journalist Ray Stannard Baker traveled throughout the United States in 1906–1907 to learn the effects of the increasingly rigid "color line." He described, first in magazine articles and then in book form, the shocking oppression and poverty that he found. In the following passage, he reports the division over strategy among blacks. He conceived of two sharply differentiated approaches, one symbolized by Washington, the other by Du Bois. As a white observer, Baker inevitably wrote as an outsider. Perhaps nothing indicates this more clearly than his use of the dubious cliché that blacks shared no historical consciousness which could give them a separate identity from other Americans.

One of the things that has interested me most of all in studying Negro communities, especially in the North, has been to find them so torn by cliques and divided by such wide differences of opinion.

No other element of our population presents a similar condition; the Italians, the Jews, the Germans, and especially the Chinese and Japanese are held together not only by a different language, but by ingrained and ancient national habits. They group themselves naturally. But the Negro is an American in language and customs; he knows no other traditions and he has no other conscious history; a large proportion, indeed, possess varying degrees of white American blood (restless blood!) and yet the Negro is not accepted as an American. Instead of losing himself gradually in the dominant race, as the Germans, Irish, and Italians are doing, adding those traits or qualities with which Time fashions and modifies this human mosaic called the American nation, the Negro is set apart as a peculiar people.

With every Negro, then, an essential question is: "How shall I meet this attempt to put me off by myself?"

That question in one form or another—politically, industrially, socially—is being met daily, almost hourly, by every Negro in this country. It colors his very life.

"You don't know, and you can't know," a Negro said to me, "what it is to be a problem, to understand that everyone is watching you and studying you, to have your mind constantly on your own actions. It has made us think and talk about ourselves more than other people do. It has made us self-conscious and sensitive."

It is scarcely surprising, then, that upon such a vital question there should be wide differences of opinion among Negroes. As a matter of fact, there are almost innumerable points of view and suggested modes of conduct, but they all group themselves into two great parties which are growing more distinct in outline and purpose every day. Both parties exist in every part of the country, but it is in the North that the struggle between them is most evident. I have found a sharper feeling and a bitterer discussion of race relationships among the Negroes of the North than among those of the South. If you want to hear the race question discussed with fire and fervor, go to Boston! . . .

Now, the Negroes of the country are meeting the growing discrimination against them in two ways, out of which have grown the two great parties to which I have referred. One party has sprung, naturally, from the thought of the Northern Negro and is a product of the freedom which the Northern Negro has enjoyed; although, of course, it finds many followers in the South.

The other is the natural product of the far different conditions in the South, where the Negro cannot speak his mind, where he has never realized any large degree of free citizenship. Both are led by able men, and both are backed by newspapers and magazines. It has come, indeed, to the point where most Negroes of any intelligence at all have taken their place on one side or the other.

The second-named party, which may best, perhaps, be considered first, is made up of the great mass of the colored people both South and North; its undisputed leader is Booker T. Washington.

Nothing has been more remarkable in the recent history of the Negro than Washington's rise to influence as a leader, and the spread of his ideals of education and progress. It is noteworthy that he was born in the South, a slave, that he knew intimately the common struggling life of his people and the attitude of the white race toward them. He worked his way to education in Southern schools and was graduated at Hampton—a story which he tells best himself in his book, *Up from Slavery*. He was and is Southern in feeling and point of view. When he began to think how he could best help his people the same question came to him that comes to every Negro: "What shall we do about this discrimination and separation?"

And his was the type of character which answered, "Make the best of it; overcome it with self-development."

The very essence of his doctrine is this: "Get yourself right, and the world will be all right."

His whole work and his life have said to the white man: "You've set us apart. You don't want us. All right; we'll be apart. We can succeed as Negroes."

It is the doctrine of the opportunist and and optimist: peculiarly, indeed, the doctrine of the man of the soil, who has come up fighting, dealing with the world, not as he would like to have it, but as it overtakes him. Many great leaders have been like that: Lincoln was one. They have the simplicity and patience of the soil, and the immense courage and faith. To prevent being crushed by circumstances they develop humor; they laugh off their troubles. Washington has all of these qualities of the common life: he possesses in high degree what some one has called "great commonness." And finally he has a simple faith in humanity, and in the just purposes of the Creator of humanity.

Being a hopeful opportunist Washington takes the Negro as he finds him, often ignorant, weak, timid, surrounded by hostile forces, and tells him to go to work at anything, anywhere, but go to work, learn how to work better, save money, have a better home, raise a better family.

The central idea of his doctrine, indeed, is work. He teaches that if the Negro wins by real worth a strong economic position in the country, other rights and privileges will come to him naturally. He should get his rights, not by gift of the white man, but by earning them himself.

> *I noticed* [he says] *when I first went to Tuskegee to start the Tuskegee Normal and Industrial Institute, that some of the white people about there looked rather doubtfully at me. I thought I could get their influence by telling them how much algebra and history and science and all those things I had in my head, but they treated me about the same as they did before. They didn't seem to care about the algebra, history, and science that were in my head only. Those people never even began to have confidence in me until we commenced to build a large three-story brick build-*

ing; and then another and another, until now we have eighty-six buildings which have been erected largely by the labour of our students, and to-day we have the respect and confidence of all the white people in that section.

There is an unmistakable influence that comes over a white man when he sees a black man living in a two-story brick house that has been paid for.

In another place he has given his ideas of what education should be: "How I wish that, from the most cultured and highly endowed university in the great North to the humblest log cabin schoolhouse in Alabama, we could burn, as it were, into the hearts and heads of all that usefulness, that service to our brother is the supreme end of education."

It is, indeed, to the teaching of service in the highest sense that Washington's life has been devoted. While he urges every Negro to reach as high a place as he can, he believes that the great masses of the Negroes are best fitted today for manual labor; his doctrine is that they should be taught to do that labor better: that when the foundations have been laid in sound industry and in business enterprise, the higher callings and honors will come of themselves.

His emphasis is rather upon duties than upon rights. He does not advise the Negro to surrender a single right: on the other hand, he urges his people to use fully every right they have or can get—for example, to vote wherever possible, and vote thoughtfully. But he believes that some of the rights given the Negro have been lost because the Negro had neither the wisdom nor the strength to use them properly.

I have not said much thus far in these articles about Booker T. Washington, but as I have been traveling over this country, South and North, studying Negro communities, I have found the mark of him everywhere in happier human lives. Wherever I found a prosperous Negro enterprise, a thriving business place, a good home, there I was almost sure to find Booker T. Washington's picture over the fireplace or a little framed motto expressing his gospel of work and service. I have heard bitter things said about Mr. Washington by both colored people and white. I have waited and investigated many of these stories, and I am telling here what I have seen and known of his influence among thousands of common, struggling human beings. Many highly educated Negroes, especially, in the North, dislike him and oppose him, but he has brought new hope and given new courage to the masses of his race. He has given them a working plan of life. And is there a higher test of usefulness? Measured by any standard, white or black, Washington must be regarded today as one of the great men of this country: and in the future he will be so honored.

The party led by Washington is made up of the masses of the common people; the radical party, on the other hand, represents what may be called the intellectuals. The leading exponent of its point of view is unquestionably Professor W. E. B. Du Bois of Atlanta University—though, like all minority parties, it is torn with dissension and discontent. Dr. Du Bois was born in Massachusetts of a family that had no history of Southern slavery. He has a large intermixture of white blood. Broadly educated at Harvard and in the universities of Germany, he is today one of the able sociologists of this country. His economic studies of the Negro made for the United States government and for the Atlanta University conference (which he organized) are works of sound scholarship and furnish the student with the best single source of accurate information regarding the Negro at present obtainable in this country. And no book gives a deeper insight into the inner life of the Negro, his struggles and his aspirations, than *The Souls of Black Folk.*

Dr. Du Bois has the temperament of the scholar and idealist—critical, sensitive, unhumorous, impatient, often covering its deep feeling with sarcasm and cynicism. When the question came to him: "What shall the Negro do about discrimination?" his answer was the exact reverse of Washington's: it was the voice of Massachusetts: "Do not submit! agitate, object, fight."

Where Washington reaches the hearts of his people, Du Bois appeals to their heads. Du Bois is not a leader of men, as Washington is: he is rather a promulgator of ideas. While Washington is building a great educational institution and organizing the practical activities of the race, Du Bois is the lonely critic holding up distant ideals. Where Washington cultivates friendly human relationships with the white people among whom the lot of the Negro is cast, Du Bois, sensitive to rebuffs, draws more and more away from white people.

Several years ago Du Bois organized the Niagara Movement for the purpose of protesting against the drawing of the color line. It is important, not so much for the extent of its membership, which is small, but because it represents, genuinely, a more or less prevalent point of view among many colored people.

Its declaration of principles says:

> *We refuse to allow the impression to remain that the Negro-American assents to inferiority, is submissive under oppression and apologetic before insults. Through helplessness we may submit, but the voice of protest of ten million Americans must never cease to assail the ears of their fellows, so long as America is unjust.*
>
> *Any discrimination based simply on race or color is barbarous, we care not how hallowed it be by custom, expediency, or prejudice. Differences made on account of ignorance, immorality, or disease are legitimate methods of fighting evil, and against them we have no word of protest, but discriminations based simply and solely on physical peculiarities, place of birth, color of skin, are relics of that unreasoning human savagery of which the world is, and ought to be, thoroughly ashamed.*

The object of the movement is to protest against disfranchisement and Jim Crow laws and to demand equal rights of education, equal civil rights, equal economic opportunities, and justice in the courts. Taking the ballot from the Negro they declare to be only a step to economic slavery; that it leaves the Negro defenseless before his competitor—that the disfranchisement laws in the South are being followed by all manner of other discriminations which interfere with the progress of the Negro.

"Persistent manly agitation is the way to liberty," says the declaration, "and toward this goal the Niagara movement has started."

The annual meeting of the movement was held last August in Boston, the chief gathering being in Faneuil Hall. Every reference in the speeches to Garrison, Phillips, and Sumner was cheered to the echo. "It seemed," said one newspaper report, "like a revival of the old spirit of abolitionism—with the white man left out."

Several organizations in the country, like the New England Suffrage League, the Equal Rights League of Georgia, and others, take much the same position as the Niagara Movement.

The party led by Dr. Du Bois is, in short, a party of protest which endeavors to prevent Negro separation and discrimination against Negroes by agitation and political influence.

These two points of view, of course, are not peculiar to Negroes; they divide all human thought. The opportunist and optimist on the one hand does his great work with the world as he finds it: he is resourceful, constructive, familiar. On the other hand, the idealist, the agitator, who is also a pessimist, performs the function of the critic, he sees the world as it should be and cries out to have it instantly changed.

Thus with these two great Negro parties. Each is working for essentially the same end—better conditions of life for the Negro—each contains brave and honest men, and each is sure, humanly enough, that the other side is not only wrong, but venally wrong, whereas both parties are needed and both perform a useful function.

Kelly Miller

WASHINGTON'S POLICY

Son of a South Carolina tenant farmer, at the time he wrote this essay Kelly Miller was professor of mathematics at Howard University, where he later became dean of the College of Arts and Sciences. Other blacks sometimes criticized him as a "straddler," and as this selection shows, he tried hard to find merit in both Washington and the "anti-Bookerites." He writes most favorably of Washington when judging him in the context of time and place. Washington does not come off well in the extended comparison with Frederick Douglass (1817?–1895), runaway slave, abolitionist orator and editor, and political activist. In contrast to Baker's view, Miller sees the black masses as not particularly strong in support of Washington. When Miller republished this essay in 1908 in his book Race Adjustment, *he revised it to include a more favorable judgment of Washington.*

When a distinguished Russian was informed that some American Negroes were radical and some conservative, he could not restrain his laughter. The idea of conservative Negroes was more than the Cossack's risibilities could endure. "What on earth," he exclaimed with astonishment, "have they to conserve?"

According to a strict construction of terms, a conservative is one

From Kelly Miller, "Washington's Policy," Boston *Evening Transcript*, September 18–19, 1903.

who is satisfied with, and advocates the continuance of existing conditions; while a radical clamors for amelioration through change. No thoughtful Negro is satisfied with the present status of his race, whether viewed in its political, civil or general aspect. He labors under an unfriendly public opinion which is being rapidly crystallized into rigid caste and enacted into unrighteous law. How can he be expected to contemplate such oppressive conditions with satisfaction and composure? Circumstances render it imperative that his attitude should be dissentient rather than conformatory. Every consideration of enlightened self-respect impels to unremitting protest, albeit the manner of protestation may be mild or pronounced, according to the dictates of prudence. Radical and conservative Negroes agree as to the end in view, but differ as to the most effective means of attaining it. The difference is not essentially one of principle or purpose, but point of view. All antislavery advocates desired the downfall of the iniquitous institution, but some were more violent than others in the expression of this desire. Disagreement as to method led to personal estrangement, impugnment of motive, and unseemly factional wrangle. And so, colored men who are zealous alike for the betterment of their race, lose half their strength in internal strife, because of variant methods of attack upon the citadel of prejudice. The recent regrettable "Boston riot" is a striking case in point. Mr. Booker T. Washington is the storm center about which the controversy rages. Contending forces have aligned themselves, in hostile array, as to the wisdom or folly of the doctrine of which he is the chief exponent. Two recent occurrences have served to accentuate this antagonism.

1. About two years ago, a group of Boston colored men, exotics, as some would say, of New England colleges, who had grown restive under the doctrine of the famous Tuskegeean, founded the Boston *Guardian* as a journal of protest. These men believe that the teachings of Mr. Washington are destructive of the rights and liberties of the race, and are pledged to spare no effort to combat what they deem his damaging doctrine. Mr. William Monroe Trotter, a Harvard graduate, and who is said to have maintained a higher scholastic average than any other colored student at that famous institution, is head and front of the movement. Mr. Trotter possesses considerable

independent means, and is as uncompromising as William Lloyd Garrison.

2. The recent publication of *The Souls of Black Folk,* by Professor W. E. B. Du Bois, also a Harvard graduate, has added new emphasis to the prevailing controversy. Dr. Du Bois is not an agitator, nor a carping critic of another's achievements, but a scholar, a painstaking, accurate investigator, a writer of unusual lucidity and keenness, and a fearless advocate of the higher aspirations of his race. He has stated in pointed, incisive terms, the issue between Mr. Washington and his critics, and has given the controversy definiteness and cast. Du Bois and Washington are being held up to public view as contrasted types of Negro leadership.

The radical and conservative tendencies cannot be better described than by comparing, or rather contrasting, the two superlative colored men in whom we find their highest embodiment—Frederick Douglass and Booker Washington. The two men are in part products of their times, but are also natural antipodes. Douglass lived in the day of moral giants; Washington in the era of merchant princes. The contemporaries of Douglass emphasized the rights of man; those of Washington his productive capacity. The age of Douglass acknowledged the sanction of the Golden Rule; that of Washington worships the Rule of Gold. The equality of men was constantly dinned into Douglass's ears; Washington hears nothing but the inferiority of the Negro and the dominance of the Saxon. Douglass could hardly receive a hearing today; Washington would have been hooted off the stage a generation ago. Thus all truly useful men must be, in a measure, time-servers; for unless they serve their time, they can scarcely serve at all. But great as was the diversity of formative influences that shaped these two great lives, there is no less opposability in their innate bias of souls. Douglass was like a lion, bold and fearless; Washington is lamblike, meek and submissive. Douglass escaped from personal bondage, which his soul abhorred; but for Lincoln's proclamation, Washington would probably have arisen to esteem and favor in the eyes of his master as a good and faithful servant. Douglass insisted upon rights; Washington upon duty. Douglass held up to public scorn the sins of the white man; Washington portrays the faults of his own race. Douglass spoke what he thought the world should hear; Washington only what he feels it is disposed to listen to. Douglass's conduct was actuated by principle; Washington's by prudence. Douglass had no limited, copyrighted program for his race, but appealed to the decalogue, the Golden Rule, the Declaration of Independence, the Constitution of the United States; Washington, holding these great principles in the shadowy background, presents a practical expedient applicable to present needs. Douglass was a moralist, insisting upon the application of righteousness to public affairs; Washington is a practical statesman, accepting the best terms which he thinks it possible to secure.

Washington came upon the stage at the time when the policies which Douglass embodied had seemed to fail. Reconstruction measures had proved abortive. Negro politicians, like Othello, had lost their occupation, and had sought asylum in the government departments at Washington. The erstwhile advocates of the Negro's cause had grown indifferent or apologetic. The plain intent of the Constitution had been overborne in the South with the connivance of the North. The idea of lifting the Negro to the plane of equality with the white race, once so fondly cherished, found few remaining advocates. Mr. Washington sized up the situation with the certainty and celerity of a genius. He based his policy upon the ruins of the one that had been exploited. He avoided controverted issues, and moved, not along the line of least resistance, but of no resistance at all. He founded his creed upon construction rather than criticism. He urged his race to do the things possible rather than whine and pine over things prohibited. According to his philosophy, it is better to build even upon the shifting sands of expediency than not to build at all, because you cannot secure a granite foundation. He thus hoped to utilize whatever residue of good feeling there might be in the white race for the betterment of the Negro. Tuskegee Institute, which is of itself a marvelous achievement, is only the pulpit from which Mr. Washington proclaims his doctrine. Industrial education has become so intricately interwoven into his policy that his critics are forced into the ridiculous attitude of opposing a form of training essential to the welfare of any people. For reasons of policy, Mr. Washington is provokingly silent as to the claim of higher education, although his personal actions proclaim loudly enough the belief that is in his heart. The subject of industrial and higher education is merely one of ratio and proportion and not one of fundamental controversy.

Mr. Washington's bitterest opponents cannot gainsay his sincerity or doubt that the welfare of his race is the chief burden of his soul. He follows the leading of his own light. Few men of this generation have shown such signal devotion, self-abnegation and strenuous endeavor for an altruistic cause.

One of the chief complaints against the Tuskegeean is lack of definitive statement upon questions of vital concern. Mr. Washington is a diplomat of the first water. He sinks into sphinxlike silence when the demands of the situation seem to require emphatic utterance. His carefully studied deliverances upon disputed issues often possess the equivocalness of a Delphic oracle. While he does not openly avow, yet he would not disclaim, in distinct terms, a single plank in the platform of Douglass. The white race saddles its own notions and feelings upon him, and yet he opens not his mouth. His sagacious silence and shrewdly measured assertions must be taken, if not with the traditional grain of salt, at least with a goodly lump of diplomatic allowance. We do not usually associate deep moral conviction with the guileful arts of diplomacy, but we must remember that the delicate role of race statesmanship cannot be played without rare caution and tactful prudence.

Mr. Washington's popularity and prominence depend largely upon the fact that his putative policy is acceptable to the Southern whites, because he allows them to believe that he accepts their estimate of the Negro's inferior place in the social scheme. He is quiescent if not acquiescent as to the white man's superior claims. He shuts his eyes to many of the wrongs and outrages heaped upon the race. He never runs against the Southerner's traditional prejudices. Even when he protests against his practices the protestation is so palliatory that, like a good conscience, it is void of offense. Equality between the races, whether social, political or civil, is an unsavory term to the white man's palate, and, therefore, Mr. Washington obliterates it from his vocabulary. The higher education of the Negro is in general disfavor, so Mr. Washington gives the approval of his silence to the charge that such pure and devoted philanthropists as President Ware of Atlanta, Patton of Howard, Tupper of Shaw, and Cravath of Fisk, who did more than all others to quicken and inspire the Negro race, have lived, loved, labored and died in vain. Nor is he objectionable to white men by reason of his self-assertive personality. He is an exact modern counterpart of Chaucer's knight: "Curteys he was, lowly, and servysable." Even when he violates their sacred code by dining with the president or mingling on easy terms with ultra-fashionable circles, they lash themselves into momentary fury, but straightway proceed to laud and glorify his policy. The North applauds and sustains his propagandism because he strives to be at peace with all men. He appeals to the amity and not the enmity of both races. We are in the midst of an era of good feeling, and must have peace at any price. It is interesting to witness how many of the erstwhile loud-voiced advocates of the Negro's rights have seized upon Mr. Washington's pacific policy as a graceful recession from their former position. The whites have set up Booker Washington as the divinely appointed and anointed leader of his race, and regard as sacrilege all criticism or even candid discussion on the part of those whom he had been sent to guide. They demand for him an exemption which they have never accorded their own leaders, from George Washington to Theodore Roosevelt. Nothing could be further from Mr. Washington's thoughts than the assumption of divine commission which the whites seek to impose upon him. He makes no claim to have received a revelation, either from burning bush or mountain top; but is a simple, sincere, unsophisticated co-laborer with his brethren, as a single, though signal, agency for the betterment of his race.

Mr. Washington is not a leader of the people's own choosing. He does not command an enthusiastic and spontaneous following. He lacks that magnetic personality that would cause men to love and women to adore him. His method is rather that of a missionary seeking the material and moral betterment of an unfortunate people, than a spontaneous leader voicing their highest self-expression. He is deficient in the fearlessness, self-assertion, aggressiveness and heroic spirit necessary to quicken and inspire. Such a leader must not hold up for painful contemplation or emphasize to the outside world the repugnant, grotesque and ludicrous faults and foibles of his own people, but must constantly direct attention to higher and better ideals. His dominant note must be pitched in the major, and not the minor key. He must not be of the earth earthy, with range of vision limited to the ugliness of untoward conditions, but must have the power of idealization and spiritual vista. Exaggerated self-importance is deemed an individual fault, but a racial virtue. It is the chief incentive of every race or nation that has ever gained prominence in the world's affairs. The triumphant, God-sent leader of any people must be the exponent and expounder of their highest aspirations and feelings, and must evoke their manhood and self-esteem, yea, even their vanity and pride.

Mr. Washington's following is very largely prudential and constrained: it lacks spontaneousness and joyance. He is not hailed with glad acclaim as the deliverer of his people. He brings good gifts rather than glad tidings. Many believe in him for his works' sake; some acquiesce rather than antagonize one who has gained so large a measure of public confidence; others are willing to cooperate in the accomplishment of good deeds, though they inwardly detest his doctrine; while those of political instinct seek his favor as a passkey to prestige and place. Few thoughtful colored men espouse what passes as Mr. Washington's policy, without apology or reserve.

The so-called radical Negroes are wholly wanting in organization and leadership. They have no commanding personality or concrete achievement as a basis and background for their propagandism. Their plea is sought to be silenced by the cry that they have founded no institution and projected no practical project. The same might have been said of Garrison and Phillips. It is difficult to found an effective organization upon a protest. There is little constructive possibility in negation. These men believe in the doctrine of Douglass, who has become their prototype and patron saint. They have learned well the lesson which Northern statesmanship and philanthropy taught them a generation ago, although they are sought to be derided and belittled for adhering to their teachings.

Mr. Washington's critics assert that his leadership has been barren of good results to the race. Under his regnancy the last vestige of political power has been swept away. Civil privileges have been restricted, educational opportunities, in some states at least, have been curtailed; the industrial situation, the keynote of his policy, has become more ominous and uncertain, while the feeling between the races is constantly growing more acute and threatening. To this it is averred that no human power could stay the wave of race hatred now sweeping over the country, but that the Tuskegeean's pacific policy will serve to relieve the severity of the blow. The majority of thoughtful men range between these wide-apart views. They believe neither in surrender nor revolution. Both forces have their place and function in the solution of the race problem. While it would be unseemly for those who breathe the free air of New England to remain silent as to the heavy burden borne by their brethren in the South, yet we must not forget that Frederick Douglass could not today build up an institution in Alabama, nor do the imperative constructive work in that section. The progress of all peoples is marked by alternations of combat and contention on the one hand, and compromise and concession on the other. Progress is the resultant of the play and counterplay of these forces. Colored men should have a larger tolerance for the widest latitude of opinion and method. Too frequently what passes as an irrepressible conflict is merely difference in point of view. A striking illustration of harmony of aim with variance of method is furnished by the close alliance and friendly co-operation of Thomas Fortune and Booker Washington. It would be impossible to find two Negroes who are farther apart in temper and spirit, and yet we find them working together for the good of the race.

The Negro's lot would be sad indeed if, under allurement of material advantage and temporary easement, he should sink into pliant yieldance to unrighteous oppression; but it would be sadder still if intemperate insistence should engender ill will and strife, when the race is not yet ready to be "battered with the shocks of doom."

III HENRY M. TURNER AND THE BACK-TO-AFRICA MOVEMENT

Henry M. Turner

TWO EDITORIALS

South Carolina-born Henry McNeal Turner (1834–1915) was named the first black chaplain in the United States Army during the Civil War. After engaging in Georgia politics during Reconstruction, he became a bishop of the African Methodist Episcopal Church in 1880. He was one of the first to object to Washington's Atlanta address. A man of many activities and ideas, Turner took the lead in advocating black emigration to Africa. Although he never imagined that all those of African ancestry could leave the United States for Africa, he hoped that many would do so, building up an independent nation which would heighten black pride everywhere. During a period when many poor black farmers showed great enthusiasm for emigration, Turner helped send several hundred to Liberia. He himself visited Africa several times and wrote glowing reports of its economic possibilities, but it was chiefly on grounds of race pride and escape from white domination that he advocated emigration. Although most of Turner's plans were frustrated and many of those who went to Liberia returned in distress, the "back-to-Africa" idea never died out completely and was revived under the leadership of Marcus Garvey in the 1920s. The following documents, from 1898 and 1903, typical of Turner's blistering style, show his skepticism about America.

WAR WITH SPAIN

Being out of the country when the present war with Spain broke out, we could not define our position relative to the part that the colored man should play upon the bloody program.

Since our arrival home we have been asked a thousand times for our opinion, and we have simply replied that the war is now in progress and the black man is in it and it would be useless to say anything; but just as we expected, we see that he is made the butt of ridicule, his faults are magnified and he is still the bone of contention. He is being snubbed while even defending the stars and stripes. This is no news to us, however, for we knew it would be the case before we returned to the country, or before we had even heard a

From *Voice of Missions,* July 1, 1898. Reprinted from *Black Nationalism in America,* edited by John H. Bracey, Jr., August Meier, and Elliott Rudwick, pp. 174–75.

word uttered. We do not see what the Negro is so anxious to fight for anyway, he has no country here and *never will* have.

Much is being said about fighting poor little Spain, the eighth power of the world for the purpose of humanity, that the Spanish are so cruel and brutal in their treatment toward the Cubans. "Physician, heal thyself," very appropriately comes in here. Enough men have been lynched to death to reach a mile high if laid one upon the other, and enough women and children to form the head and foot slab if they could be arranged to stand upon the head of each other. The United States puts more people to death without law than all the other nations of earth combined. So our humanitarianism is too ridiculous to be made a count in the argument of justification.

The Negro will be exterminated soon enough at best, without being overanxious to die in the defense of a country that is decimating his numbers daily.

The colored men would far better be employed in remaining at home, marrying wives and giving the race sons and daughters, and perpetuating our existence, than rushing into a death struggle for a country that cares nothing for their rights or manhood, and wait till they are wanted, and then the nation will feel and know his worth and concede to him the respect due the defenders of a nation.

It is very likely that the Negro will be wanted before this little fuss is over, anyway, for we have but little doubt that the greater part of Europe will have a hand in this affair before it is ended, and should it so turn out the black man will be wanted, and inducements will be offered for his blood and bravery in common with other men. One thing can be said to the everlasting credit of Spain—a man is a man in her domain. We have been from one end of Spain to the other, and we have seen black men and black women enjoying every privilege that was being enjoyed by people of any other color. We have stopped at some of her finest hotels and have enjoyed such respect and honors that some Americans who were there exhibited their disapproval because we were seated at the table in the midst of them. We pretended not to notice it, however, although we *did* notice it. Governor Atkinson of Georgia, who said that he would not enlist Negroes in this war, according to what we saw in the English papers before our arrival home, shows himself a greater friend to the Negro than those governors who are enlisting his aid and service. Governor

FIGURE 3. Henry McNeal Turner (1834–1915). *(Historical Pictures Service, Chicago)*

Atkinson knows that the Negro has nothing for which he should fight, and he has too much respect for the Negro to encourage him to die for nothing.

We endorse Governor Atkinson in toto and tender him our gratitude for the interest he exhibits in behalf of our race.

BOOKER T. WASHINGTON AND BOSTON

The newspapers bring tidings that since our last issue quite a riot was created in A. M. E. Z. church, where Professor Washington was to address a very large assembly of people, colored and white. It appears that hisses, cat squalls, groans, with the cry, "Take him out!" and many kinds of interruptions were indulged in till many got up and left the hall. Police were called for, arrests were made and a general confusion ensued, and perfect order was never restored while strenuous and vehement efforts were put forth to establish harmony. It seems from the papers, that Prof. Washington had used terms, phrases and sentences that were countenancing or excusing, or palliating disfranchisement of our race in Alabama, South Carolina and other states. And from the trend of his discourses, he was educating the white people of the nation to regard the Negro as a simple laborer and scullion, and that he was not fitted or qualified by nature to pursue professions, callings and studies of the higher kind.

We will neither commend or condemn Washington or the Boston rioters or mass meeting disturbers, as neither party meets our idea. Washington's policy is not worth a cent. It accomplishes no racial good, except as it helps about a thousand students at Tuskegee, and while we endorse the manhood of the race and agree with our Boston friends in spitting upon everything that would appear to underrate the value of the Negro in every particular, they are doing no more ultimate good than Washington, as we see. They are all timberheads together, fussing and calling each other fools. Nothing less than a nation owned and controlled by the Negro, will amount to a hill of beans. We are individually friendly with Dr. Washington, and he would do anything he could, we believe, to favor us and we know we are on friendly terms with everybody in Boston. We have spoken in different churches and in Tremont Temple, and we have never seen larger meetings than have come to hear us in Boston. But neither the policy of Washington or of our Boston friends is worth a pinch of snuff. Anything less than separation and the black man relying upon himself is absolutely nonsense. Negro nationality is the only remedy, and time will show it.

From *Voice of the People,* September, 1903. The editor thanks Edwin S. Redkey, who kindly provided a true copy of this document.

Edwin S. Redkey

BLACK EXODUS

The scholar who has done most to revive interest in Turner's racial ideas, Edwin S. Redkey, here analyzes the failure of the back-to-Africa movement of the late nineteenth and early twentieth centuries. A comparison with the Zionist movement that led to the founding of Israel helps show special qualities of black nationalism in America. Redkey is dean of students at the State University of New York at Purchase.

When Bishop Turner died in 1915, W. E. B. Du Bois remembered him as the "last of his clan: mighty men, physically and mentally, men who started at the bottom and hammered their way to the top by sheer brute strength." But it was for his personal ability and churchmanship that Turner was most remembered, not his black nationalism. Most black intellectuals disagreed with the bishop's solution to the American racial problem and were happy to forget his back-to-Africa schemes, which had excited many black peasants. Because black nationalism was overshadowed by the "accommodation" of Booker T. Washington and the civil rights protests of W. E. B. Du Bois, contemporary observers took little notice of it. Even today it is difficult to evaluate Turner's movement.

It is clear that the African emigration movements of 1890–1910 were black in makeup and broad in extent. Some white men, such as those in the American Colonization Society and the International Migration Society, served as auxiliaries by providing transportation. But the leadership, money, and inspiration came from blacks. Just how broad the movement was is difficult to judge with precision, but signs of emigrationism appeared in all the Deep South and Southwestern states, where the vast majority of Afro-Americans lived. Thousands were caught up directly in one or more of the emigration schemes and millions may have shared the black nationalists' pessimism about the United States. Although "African fever" reached its peak in the mid-1890s, it seems never to have died completely, as later movements attest.

Alienation and despair lay at the root of nationalism and emigration: despair of ever realizing the American dream and alienation from land, society, and self. Although the motives of would-be emigrants were vague, and hardly ever explicit, desire for land and economic security clearly played a major role. The 1890s juxtaposed the sharecrop and crop-lien system and a vicious depression, twin specters from which flight seemed the only chance of escape. The abrupt increase in violence while their civil rights rapidly disappeared convinced some of the more thoughtful black farmers that, despite the glorious verbal façade of freedom, liberty, equality, and democracy, the United States was no place for the black man. Bishop Turner drove home the fact that long years of slavery and subservience had subtly convinced the blacks themselves that black was evil and to be despised. Despite their fears to the contrary, Afro-Americans wanted to believe that they were as good as white men, and it appeared to some that the only way they could prove their worth was to establish a black nation.

Individual leaders played a crucial role in the emigration movement. Local organizers and advocates, indispensable but largely anonymous, served as emigration agents and nationalist spokesmen in country churches and lodge halls scattered throughout the South. Bishop Turner, on the other hand, used his high office in a national church to channel the basic peasant unrest and pessimism into African emigrationism. Black bitterness and despair could have led to violent anarchy, as it did with Robert Charles in New Orleans, if a nationalist leader had not provided a convincing analysis of the problems and a clear hope for success through emigration. It took a spokesman of national reputation, moreover, to dare to indict America's oppression of blacks. Much of Turner's popularity lay in his willingness to describe the racial situation as many blacks believed it to be but feared to state publicly.

Not least among Turner's functions was the portrayal of Africa as the promised land. Afro-American pessimism did not necessarily lead to nationalism, nor nationalism to emigrationism, nor emigrationism to Africa. When Turner first decided that Africa was the place to go, it was truly a dark continent, unknown to most of the world. By 1890, however, the Western world knew much more about it. Despite his four visits to "the fatherland," Turner never lost his romantic view of a potentially industrial land where the good life awaited Afro-Americans. By portraying it as such he could excite discouraged blacks into emigration. By describing his promised land in terms of the American dream, which Southern blacks also dreamed, he nurtured their desire for equality and self-government. By reminding them that Africa was their ancestral home and their promised land, Turner tried to prevail over advocates of emigration to other countries and continents.

Despite the popularity of Bishop Turner and Africa among Southern black farmers, middle-class blacks generally opposed nationalism and emigration. Despite their disabilities in the United States, they could see their progress up from slavery much more clearly than the sharecroppers, still in quasi slavery. Even though Liberia cried for their talents and emigrationists urged them to go, few of the "black bourgeoisie" settled in Africa. They compensated for their refusal by sending missionary-teachers to Africa and by protesting against the excesses of European colonialism. Among black college students there was more respect for nationalism, but after graduation the student radicals retreated to more "respectable" protests. The hallmark of the middle class was optimism, American optimism, which made the nationalist emigration movement appear to be folly. Many lower-class blacks joined their betters in rejecting emigration because they shared the aspiration, if not the successes, of the middle class. Quite probably, however, many more blacks approved Bishop Turner's bold, pungent attacks on American society, and perhaps endorsed his call for some kind of black separatism, than supported emigration.

The impact of African emigrationism upon white Americans was minimal. Only when actual migrations took place did most whites suspect that such black sentiment existed. On such occasions, furthermore, they were always caught unawares because customary "Negro spokesmen" had perpetuated the myth of the docile black peasant, content to stay at the bottom of society. While European immigrants by the millions entered the country, the very thought that anyone would want to leave the United States to look for better opportunities elsewhere seemed absurd to most Americans.

Within this general context, white reactions varied. Northern liberals like Tourgee rejected emigration because they believed the American love of justice would overcome the prejudice of race. More conservative whites endorsed the "gospel of wealth," as interpreted by Booker T. Washington, as the proper approach to race relations; they preferred the vision of industrious, uncomplaining workers to the prospect of radical malcontents who might upset the social equilibrium. The few whites who supported the American Colonization Society were either remnants of the pre-Civil War group that pictured emigration as a paternalistic solution to the race problem or representatives of a later generation that was concerned only for the welfare of Liberia. Although reactionaries like Thomas Dixon advocated deportation of blacks from the country, they found little support for the actual removal of Afro-Americans. Most whites simply wanted to keep the blacks at the lowest possible level of American society.

In Africa, however, the Afro-American emigration movement had considerable impact, although the thousand or so black peasants who sailed to Liberia between 1890 and 1910 helped that country but little. But the rhetoric of nationalism and the climate of protest among Afro-Americans reached far, and Bishop Turner's newspapers found avid readers in Sierra Leone, the Gold Coast, and Lagos. His visits to West and South Africa stirred the Africans, to the dismay of colonial officials. Just as important, African students who had studied in American colleges returned home with a newly militant attitude toward the colonial powers. If white Americans considered blacks passive and content, Africans learned otherwise.

Perhaps the most important effect of Bishop Turner's campaign was to foster the hope for a better life in Africa in the memories of black Americans. For the African emigration movement did not stop in 1910; it has continued, in periodic outbursts, well into the twentieth century. The best-known movements were those led by Chief Alfred C. Sam and Marcus Garvey. But if the leaders and organizations changed with time, the blacks who responded so vigorously remained essentially the same. . . .

The African emigration movement of 1890–1910 failed. . . . The troubles in the South were not sufficiently severe to drive the Afro-Americans out of the United States. Nor could the attractions of Africa draw the blacks away from home, especially while there were opportunities to move north or west within the United States. Emigrationist leaders, primarily Bishop Turner, could not generate enough push toward Africa to overcome the pull of the American dream. And, had he succeeded, transportation would have been lacking.

Seen in retrospect, the African emigration movement never had much chance of success.

On the other hand, when viewed as a nationalist movement, Bishop Turner's campaign was more significant. The nationalist or separatist attitude toward race problems has appeared and reappeared frequently in Afro-American history but has not yet succeeded to the extent of establishing separate political units or unifying black Americans behind its objectives. Comparison of Turner's nationalist campaign with "successful" nationalist efforts in nineteenth-century Europe, especially in Germany and Italy, suggests that important nationalist elements were missing from the Afro-American movement.

Nineteenth-century nationalism had for its chief spokesmen the intellectuals and bourgeois leaders of Europe. They brought their talents as thinkers, writers, and teachers to the task of building a national spirit among their people as old empires were overthrown and old disunities mended. In the aristocratic societies of Europe, intellectuals were marginal men but they had abilities and aspirations that brought them success. The Afro-American middle class also consisted of marginal men, but neither they nor the educated black elite endorsed black nationalism; they were still caught up in American individualism. Their best minds protested discrimination, seeking inclusion in the American system, and did not plan or visualize a black nation. Bishop Turner was the only man in the movement who could be considered an intellectual—a leader whose supporters were inarticulate—and there grew up no dialogue within the movement between men who endorsed separation. Without such dialogue there was no sharpening of arguments, no clarification of strategies, no toughening of resolve. Although nationalists have always sought to unite the masses behind them, intellectual leadership has been indispensable. Black nationalism in the 1890s, as well as at other times, did not have that kind of leadership.

Bishop Turner, who built his nationalist appeal not on the culture of black people but on an Africanized American dream, thereby lost one of the basic appeals that has strengthened other nationalisms, the call for a people with a distinct culture to establish a state in which that culture could flourish. European nationalists asserted their claims to political self-determination by delving into the primitive backgrounds of their people, finding tribal legends, fairy tales, mythical heroes, and linguistic origins. By asserting ancient grandeur, the nationalists could not only rationalize modern, self-determined states but could give the people a cultural identity beyond a mere linguistic or geographic identity. American blacks, cut off from most of their African memories and immersed in a nation that refused to acknowledge that blacks could have a cultural background, have had a difficult time fashioning a cultural identity other than the tradition of oppression. Bishop Turner was unable to find or create a mythical structure of the Afro-American past that would inspire his people. Because his African dream was essentially the American dream, he was unable to convince those who saw the discrepancies, particularly economic, between the two. His focus was still on the American goals of elite achievement rather than on the "soul" of the black masses. His movement, to succeed, would have needed more internal cohesion in its vision—a uniqueness that only black folk could give, not just a dark imitation of the United States.

Geography also played an important role in nationalism. In most European and other nationalist movements the people who called for their own state occupied a specific territory on which their government could be based. They would throw off foreign kings, drive out alien residents, and gather in all the dispersed people who shared the national heritage. This, of course, has not been the case with Afro-Americans. Although in Bishop Turner's time the blacks were concentrated in the former Confederate states, they were not the majority element even there. There, more than elsewhere, blacks were continually reminded that they lived in "white man's country." Consequently a black nationalist movement could not realistically call for the independence of a black South. The attempt to make Oklahoma a black state met with no success at all. Therefore one of the basic elements of successful nationalism, a home territory sacred to its people and drenched in their national tradition, a land truly their own, was missing from black nationalism.

That Afro-Americans had no land to call their own explains why black nationalists have usually wanted to leave the United States. The lure of Africa as the ancestral home made it the emotional if not the logical choice for a modern black nation. The only nationalist movement to succeed in repatriating its members to a distant "homeland" has been Zionism. The parallels between Zionism and the black nationalism of Bishop Turner, Marcus Garvey, and other emigrationists are obvious, but the differences between them sum up the weaknesses of African emigration as a solution to the American race problem. The foremost advocates of Zionism were Jewish intellectuals who, after 1896, met frequently to plan a strategy for founding a Jewish state. Without that intellectual leadership the Jewish peasants and refugees who might have wanted a state of their own would have had little chance of success. Not only intellectuals but at least a few wealthy and highly placed Zionists provided leadership, financial aid, and political pressure; without the aid of the Rothschilds or of affluent American Jews, Zionism would have had little success in creating a modern state of Israel. Black nationalists have had no such powerful support. Indeed, Bishop Turner found that financial crises did more to harm his scheme than ideological attacks. Although West Africa, as a potential homeland, was probably more blessed with resources than Palestine, its development needed capital and skilled entrepreneurs. Israel received those benefits, especially after the attempted genocide of European Jews by Nazi Germany. No such outpouring of skilled refugees followed by sympathetic investment capital went to Liberia.

Political Zionism was accompanied, even preceded, by a cultural Zionism whose goal was the revival of a national language and culture. Even though political and cultural Zionists did not agree on priorities, they nevertheless reinforced each other. Black Americans, as different from their surrounding populations as the Jews, and as oppressed, lacked the conscious cultural tradition based on religion and language that gave inner strength to Jews. Afro-Americans did indeed have a culture of their own, but in Turner's time it was not an object of pride. The bishop could urge his followers to "respect black" but the plea was based on elemental humanity and minimal achievements rather than on a unique tradition and cultural pride.

These comparisons between Bishop Turner's black nationalism and other nationalisms point up the serious problems that faced his movement. They also demonstrate that nationalism as a proposed solution to group friction is a widespread phenomenon. Moreover, there are enough similarities between the problems of Afro-Americans and other nationalist minorities to give black nationalists hope that their ideology may achieve similar success. Again, the persistence of black nationalism demonstrates the attractiveness of ethnic solidarity and self-determination as a means of fighting oppression.

Subsequent black nationalist movements have differed from Bishop Turner's in numerous ways, adding some features and shedding others, especially emigration. Still central, however, is the bitter protest against American hypocrisy and white nationalism. This has been accompanied by a call for blacks, who in an individualistic society are oppressed as a group, to face this collective aspect of their situation and to increase their solidarity and power as a group. Finding new ways to apply this principle to the American dilemma occupies many blacks, as it concerned Turner and his followers. The persistence of black nationalism suggests that, even though mass emigration has never been feasible, in his nationalistic reaction to American racism Bishop Turner transmitted an important but unrefined idea which may yet help solve the problems of Afro-Americans.

Booker T. Washington

THE FUTURE OF THE AMERICAN NEGRO

It would be wrong to grant Turner and his followers a monopoly on advocacy of black unity and pride. In the following statement of 1899, where Washington gives his reasons for rejecting the emigrationist program, he sharply attacks white imperialism in Africa and spells out his version of racial pride and solidarity. His call for black support of black businessmen is qualified, but the idea dominated the National Negro Business League, of which Washington was president from its founding in 1900 until his death.

One of the great questions which Christian education must face in the South is the proper adjustment of the new relations of the two races. It is a question which must be faced calmly, quietly, dispas-

From Booker T. Washington, *The Future of the American Negro* (Boston: Small, Maynard & Company, 1899), pp. 157–83.

sionately; and the time has now come to rise above party, above race, above color, above sectionalism, into the region of duty of man to man, of American to American, of Christian to Christian.

I remember not long ago, when about 500 colored people sailed from the port of Savannah bound for Liberia, that the news was flashed all over the country, "The Negro has made up his mind to return to his own country," and that, "in this was the solution of the race problem in the South." But these short-sighted people forgot the fact that before breakfast that morning about 500 more Negro children were born in the South alone.

And then, once in a while, somebody is so bold as to predict that the Negro will be absorbed by the white race. Let us look at this phase of the question for a moment. It is a fact that, if a person is known to have 1 percent of African blood in his veins, he ceases to be a white man. The 99 percent of Caucasian blood does not weigh by the side of the 1 percent of African blood. The white blood counts for nothing. The person is a Negro every time. So it will be a very difficult task for the white man to absorb the Negro.

Somebody else conceived the idea of colonizing the colored people, of getting territory where nobody lived, putting the colored people there, and letting them be a nation all by themselves. There are two objections to that. First, you would have to build one wall to keep the colored people in, and another wall to keep the white people out. If you were to build ten walls around Africa today you could not keep the white people out, especially as long as there was a hope of finding gold there.

I have always had the highest respect for those of our race who, in trying to find a solution for our Southern problem, advised a return of the race to Africa, and because of my respect for those who have thus advised, especially Bishop Henry M. Turner, I have tried to make a careful and unbiased study of the question, during a recent sojourn in Europe, to see what opportunities presented themselves in Africa for self-development and self-government.

I am free to say that I see no way out of the Negro's present condition in the South by returning to Africa. Aside from other insurmountable obstacles, there is no place in Africa for him to go where his condition would be improved. All Europe—especially England, France, and Germany—has been running a mad race for the last twenty years, to see which could gobble up the greater part of

Africa; and there is practically nothing left. Old King Cetewayo put it pretty well when he said, "First come missionary, then come rum, then come traders, then come army"; and Cecil Rhodes has expressed the prevailing sentiment more recently in these words, "I would rather have land than 'niggers.' " And Cecil Rhodes is directly responsible for the killing of thousands of black natives in South Africa, that he might secure their land.

In a talk with Henry M. Stanley, the explorer, he told me that he knew no place in Africa where the Negroes of the United States might go to advantage; but I want to be more specific. Let us see how Africa has been divided, and then decide whether there is a place left for us. On the Mediterranean coast of Africa, Morocco is an independent state, Algeria is a French possession, Tunis is a French protectorate, Tripoli is a province of the Ottoman Empire, Egypt is a province of Turkey. On the Atlantic coast, Sahara is a French protectorate, Adrar is claimed by Spain, Senegambia is a French trading settlement, Gambia is a British crown colony, Sierra Leone is a British crown colony. Liberia is a republic of freed Negroes, Gold Coast and Ashanti are British colonies and British protectorates, Togoland is a German protectorate, Dahomey is a kingdom subject to French influence, Slave Coast is a British colony and British protectorate, Niger Coast is a British protectorate, the Cameroons are trading settlements protected by Germany, French Congo is a French protectorate, Congo Free State is an international African Association, Angola and Benguela are Portuguese protectorates, and the inland countries are controlled as follows: The Niger States, Masina, etc., are under French protection; Land Gandu is under British protection, administered by the Royal Haussan Niger Company.

South Africa is controlled as follows: Damara and Namaqua Land are German protectorates, Cape Colony is a British colony, Basutoland is a crown colony, Bechuanaland is a British protectorate, Natal is a British colony, Zululand is a British protectorate, Orange Free State is independent, the South African Republic is independent, and the Zambesi is administered by the British South African Company. Lourenço Marques is a Portuguese possession.

East Africa has also been disposed of in the following manner: Mozambique is a Portuguese possession, British Central Africa is a British protectorate, German East Africa is in the German sphere of influence, Zanzibar is a sultanate under British protection, British

East Africa is a British protectorate, Somaliland is under British and Italian protection, Abyssinia is independent. East Soudan (including Nubia, Kordofan, Darfur, and Wadai) is in the British sphere of influence. It will be noted that, when one of these European countries cannot get direct control over any section of Africa, it at once gives it out to the world that the country wanted is in the "sphere of its influence,"—a very convenient term. If we are to go to Africa, and be under the control of another government, I think we should prefer to take our chances in the "sphere of influence" of the United States.

All this shows pretty conclusively that a return to Africa for the Negro is out of the question, even provided that a majority of the Negroes wished to go back, which they do not. The adjustment of the relations of the two races must take place here; and it is taking place slowly, but surely. As the Negro is educated to make homes and to respect himself, the white man will in turn respect him.

It has been urged that the Negro has inherent in him certain traits of character that will prevent his ever reaching the standard of civilization set by the whites, and taking his place among them as an equal. It may be some time before the Negro race as a whole can stand comparison with the white in all respects,—it would be most remarkable, considering the past, if it were not so; but the idea that his objectionable traits and weaknesses are fundamental, I think, is a mistake. For, although there are elements of weakness about the Negro race, there are also many evidences of strength.

It is an encouraging sign, however, when an individual grows to the point where he can hold himself up for personal analysis and study. It is equally encouraging for a race to be able to study itself, —to measure its weakness and strength. It is not helpful to a race to be continually praised and have its weakness overlooked, neither is it the most helpful thing to have its faults alone continually dwelt upon. What is needed is downright, straight-forward honesty in both directions; and this is not always to be obtained.

There is little question that one of the Negroes' weak points is physical. Especially is this true regarding those who live in the large cities, North and South. But in almost every case this physical weakness can be traced to ignorant violation of the laws of health or to vicious habits. The Negro, who during slavery lived on the large plantations in the South, surrounded by restraints, at the close of the war came to the cities, and in many cases found the freedom and temptations of the city too much for him. The transition was too sudden.

When we consider what it meant to have four millions of people slaves today and freemen tomorrow, the wonder is that the race has not suffered more physically than it has. I do not believe that statistics can be so marshalled as to prove that the Negro as a race is physically or numerically on the decline. On the other hand, the Negro as a race is increasing in numbers by a larger percentage than is true of the French nation. While the death rate is large in the cities, the birth rate is also large; and it is to be borne in mind that 85 percent of these people in the Gulf states are in the country districts and smaller towns, and there the increase is along healthy and normal lines. As the Negro becomes educated, the high death rate in the cities will disappear. For proof of this, I have only to mention that a few years ago no colored man could get insurance in the large first-class insurance companies. Now there are few of these companies which do not seek the insurance of educated colored men. In the North and South the physical intoxication that was the result of sudden freedom is giving way to an encouraging, sobering process; and, as this continues, the high death rate will disappear, even in the large cities.

Another element of weakness which shows itself in the present stage of the civilization of the Negro is his lack of ability to form a purpose and stick to it through a series of years, if need be,—years that involve discouragement as well as encouragement,—till the end shall be reached. Of course there are brilliant exceptions to this rule; but there is no question that here is an element of weakness, and the same, I think, would be true of any race with the Negro's history.

Few of the resolutions which are made in conventions, etc., are remembered and put into practice six months after the warmth and enthusiasm of the debating hall have disappeared. This, I know, is an element of the white man's weakness, but it is the Negro I am discussing, not the white man. Individually, the Negro is strong. Collectively, he is weak. This is not to be wondered at. The ability to succeed in organized bodies is one of the highest points in civilization. There are scores of colored men who can succeed in any line of business as individuals, or will discuss any subject in a most intelligent manner, yet who, when they attempt to act in an organized body, are utter failures.

But the weakness of the Negro which is most frequently held up to the public gaze is that of his moral character. No one who wants to be honest and at the same time benefit the race will deny that here is where the strengthening is to be done. It has become universally accepted that the family is the foundation, the bulwark, of any race. It should be remembered, sorrowfully withal, that it was the constant tendency of slavery to destroy the family life. All through two hundred and fifty years of slavery, one of the chief objects was to increase the number of slaves; and to this end almost all thought of morality was lost sight of, so that the Negro has had only about thirty years in which to develop a family life; while the Anglo-Saxon race, with which he is constantly being compared, has had thousands of years of training in home life. The Negro felt all through the years of bondage that he was being forcibly and unjustly deprived of the fruits of his labor. Hence he felt that anything he could get from the white man in return for this labor justly belonged to him. Since this was true, we must be patient in trying to teach him a different code of morals.

From the nature of things, all through slavery it was life in the future world that was emphasized in religious teaching rather than life in this world. In his religious meetings in antebellum days the Negro was prevented from discussing many points of practical religion which related to this world; and the white minister, who was his spiritual guide, found it more convenient to talk about heaven than earth, so very naturally that today in his religious meeting it is the Negro's feelings which are worked upon mostly, and it is description of the glories of heaven that occupy most of the time of his sermon.

Having touched upon some of the weak points of the Negro, what are his strong characteristics? The Negro in America is different from most people for whom missionary effort is made, in that he works. He is not ashamed or afraid of work. When hard, constant work is required, ask any Southern white man, and he will tell you that in this the Negro has no superior. He is not given to strikes or to lockouts. He not only works himself, but he is unwilling to prevent other people from working.

Of the forty buildings of various kinds and sizes on the grounds of the Tuskegee Normal and Industrial Institute, in Alabama, as I have stated before, almost all of them are the results of the labor performed by the students while securing their academic education. One day the student is in his history class. The next day the same student, equally happy, with his trowel and in overalls, is working on a brick wall.

While at present the Negro may lack that tenacious mental grasp which enables one to pursue a scientific or mathematical investigation through a series of years, he has that delicate, mental feeling which enables him to succeed in oratory, music, etc.

While I have spoken of the Negro's moral weakness, I hope it will be kept in mind that in his original state his is an honest race. It was slavery that corrupted him in this respect. But in morals he also has his strong points.

Few have ever found the Negro guilty of betraying a trust. There are almost no instances in which the Negro betrayed either a Federal or a Confederate soldier who confided in him. There are few instances where the Negro has been entrusted with valuables when he has not been faithful. This country has never had a more loyal citizen. He has never proven himself a rebel. Should the Southern states, which so long held him in slavery, be invaded by a foreign foe, the Negro would be among the first to come to the rescue.

Perhaps the most encouraging thing in connection with the lifting up of the Negro in this country is the fact that he knows that he is down and wants to get up, he knows that he is ignorant and wants to get light. He fills every schoolhouse and every church which is opened for him. He is willing to follow leaders, when he is once convinced that the leaders have his best interest at heart.

Under the constant influence of the Christian education which began thirty-five years ago, his religion is every year becoming less emotional and more rational and practical, though I, for one, hope that he will always retain in a large degree the emotional element in religion.

During the two hundred and fifty years that the Negro spent in slavery he had little cause or incentive to accumulate money or property. Thirty-five years ago this was something which he had to begin to learn. While the great bulk of the race is still without money and property, yet the signs of thrift are evident on every hand. Especially is this noticeable in the large number of neat little homes which are owned by these people on the outer edges of the towns and cities in the South.

I wish to give an example of the sort of thing the Negro has to contend with, however, in his efforts to lift himself up.

Not long ago a mother, a black mother, who lived in one of our Northern states, had heard it whispered around in her community for years that the Negro was lazy, shiftless, and would not work. So, when her only boy grew to sufficient size, at considerable expense and great self-sacrifice, she had her boy thoroughly taught the machinist's trade. A job was secured in a neighboring shop. With dinner bucket in hand and spurred on by the prayers of the now happy-hearted mother, the boy entered the shop to begin his first day's work. What happened? Every one of the twenty white men threw down his tools, and deliberately walked out, swearing that he would not give a black man an opportunity to earn an honest living. Another shop was tried with the same result, and still another, the result ever the same. Today this once promising, ambitious black man is a wreck,—a confirmed drunkard,—with no hope, no ambition. I ask, Who blasted the life of this young man? On whose hands does his lifeblood rest? The present system of education, or rather want of education, is responsible.

Public schools and colleges should turn out men who will throw open the doors of industry, so that all men, everywhere, regardless of color, shall have the same opportunity to earn a dollar that they now have to spend it. I know of a good many kinds of cowardice and prejudice, but I know none equal to this. I know not which is the worst,—the slaveholder who perforce compelled his slave to work without compensation or the man who, by force and strikes, compels his neighbor to refrain from working for compensation.

The Negro will be on a different footing in this country when it becomes common to associate the possession of wealth with a black skin. It is not within the province of human nature that the man who is intelligent and virtuous, and owns and cultivates the best farm in his county, is the largest taxpayer, shall very long be denied proper respect and consideration. Those who would help the Negro most effectually during the next fifty years can do so by assisting in his development along scientific and industrial lines in connection with the broadest mental and religious culture.

From the results of the war with Spain let us learn this, that God has been teaching the Spanish nation a terrible lesson. What is it? Simply this, that no nation can disregard the interest of any portion of its members without that nation becoming weak and corrupt. The penalty may be long delayed. God has been teaching Spain that for every one of her subjects that she has left in ignorance, poverty, and crime the price must be paid; and, if it has not been paid with the very heart of the nation, it must be paid with the proudest and bluest blood of her sons and with treasure that is beyond computation. From this spectacle I pray God that America will learn a lesson in respect to the ten million Negroes in this country.

The Negroes in the United States are, in most of the elements of civilization, weak. Providence has placed them here not without a purpose. One object, in my opinion, is that the stronger race may imbibe a lesson from the weaker in patience, forbearance, and child-like yet supreme trust in the God of the Universe. This race has been placed here that the white man might have a great opportunity of lifting himself by lifting it up.

Out from the Negro colleges and industrial schools in the South there are going forth each year thousands of young men and women into dark and secluded corners, into lonely log schoolhouses, amidst poverty and ignorance; and though, when they go forth, no drums beat, no banners fly, no friends cheer, yet they are fighting the battles of this country just as truly and bravely as those who go forth to do battle against a foreign enemy.

If they are encouraged and properly supported in their work of educating the masses in the industries, in economy, and in morals, as well as mentally, they will, before many years, get the race upon such an intellectual, industrial, and financial footing that it will be able to enjoy without much trouble all the rights inherent in American citizenship.

Now, if we wish to bring the race to a point where it should be, where it will be strong, and grow and prosper, we have got to, in every way possible, encourage it. We can do this in no better way than by cultivating that amount of faith in the race which will make us patronize its own enterprises wherever those enterprises are worth patronizing. I do not believe much in the advice that is often given that we should patronize the enterprises of our race without regard to the worth of those enterprises. I believe that the best way to bring the race to the point where it will compare with other races is to let it understand that, whenever it enters into any line of business, it will be patronized just in proportion as it makes that business as successful, as useful, as is true of any business enterprise conducted by any other race. The race that would grow strong and powerful must have the element of hero worship in it that will, in the largest degree, make it honor its great men, the men who have succeeded in that race. I think we should be ashamed of the colored man or woman who would not venerate the name of Frederick Douglass. No race that would not look upon such a man with honor and respect and pride could ever hope to enjoy the respect of any other race. I speak of this, not that I want my people to regard themselves in a narrow, bigoted sense, because there is nothing so hurtful to an individual or to a race as to get into the habit of feeling that there is no good except in its own race, but because I wish that it may have reasonable pride in all that is honorable in its history. Whenever you hear a colored man say that he hates the people of the other race, there, in most instances, you will find a weak, narrow-minded colored man. And, whenever you find a white man who expresses the same sentiment toward the people of other races, there, too, in almost every case, you will find a narrow-minded, prejudiced white man.

That person is the broadest, strongest, and most useful who sees something to love and admire in all races, no matter what their color.

If the Negro race wishes to grow strong, it must learn to respect itself, not to be ashamed. It must learn that it will only grow in proportion as its members have confidence in it, in proportion as they believe that it is a coming race.

We have reached a period when educated Negroes should give more attention to the history of their race; should devote more time to finding out the true history of the race, and in collecting in some museum the relics that mark its progress. It is true of all races of culture and refinement and civilization that they have gathered in some place the relics which mark the progress of their civilization, which show how they lived from period to period. We should have so much pride that we would spend more time in looking into the history of the race, more effort and money in perpetuating in some durable form its achievements, so that from year to year, instead of looking back with regret, we can point to our children the rough path through which we grew strong and great.

We have a very bright and striking example in the history of the Jews in this and other countries. There is, perhaps, no race that has suffered so much, not so much in America as in some of the countries in Europe. But these people have clung together. They have had a certain amount of unity, pride, and love of race; and, as the years go on, they will be more and more influential in this country,—a country where they were once despised, and looked upon with scorn and derision. It is largely because the Jewish race has had faith in itself. Unless the Negro learns more and more to imitate the Jew in these matters, to have faith in himself, he cannot expect to have any high degree of success.

IV. THE CHALLENGE FROM THE NAACP

THE NATIONAL NEGRO COMMITTEE ON MR. WASHINGTON, 1910

Shocked by the brutality of a mob that killed black people and burned their homes in Springfield, Illinois, Lincoln's home city, a group of reformers called a conference in 1909 which led to the formation a year later of the National Association for the Advancement of Colored People. In this biracial organization, Du Bois took the position of director of publicity and research. The NAACP soon proved itself more effective than such protest efforts as the Niagara Movement and the Afro-American Council. Although not an official NAACP statement, the following document, dated October 26, 1910, was issued from the NAACP headquarters, signed by Du Bois and twenty-two other black Americans. The new organization was dedicated to attacking racial injustice through agitation and law suits, but these objections to Washington's comments during a lecture tour in England suggest that it was also a direct challenge to his leadership.

To the People of Great Britain and Europe—

The undersigned Negro-Americans have heard, with great regret, the recent attempt to assure England and Europe that their condition in America is satisfactory. They sincerely wish that such were the case, but it becomes their plain duty to say that if Mr. Booker T. Washington, or any other person, is giving the impression abroad that the Negro problem in America is in process of satisfactory solution, he is giving an impression which is not true.

We say this without personal bitterness toward Mr. Washington. He is a distinguished American and has a perfect right to his opinions. But we are compelled to point out that Mr. Washington's large financial responsibilities have made him dependent on the rich charitable public and that, for this reason, he has for years been compelled to tell, not the whole truth, but that part of it which certain powerful interests in America wish to appear as the whole truth. . . .

Our people were emancipated in a whirl of passion, and then left naked to the mercies of their enraged and impoverished ex-masters. As our sole means of defense we were given the ballot, and we used

From Herbert Aptheker, ed., *A Documentary History of the Negro People in the United States* (New York: Citadel Press, 1951), pp. 884–886.

it so as to secure the real fruits of the war. Without it we would have returned to slavery; with it we struggled toward freedom. No sooner, however, had we rid ourselves of nearly two-thirds of our illiteracy, and accumulated $600 million worth of property in a generation, than this ballot, which had become increasingly necessary to the defense of our civil and property rights, was taken from us by force and fraud.

Today in eight states where the bulk of the Negroes live, black men of property and university training can be, and usually are, by law denied the ballot, while the most ignorant white man votes. This attempt to put the personal and property rights of the best of the blacks at the absolute political mercy of the worst of the whites is spreading each day.

Along with this has gone a systematic attempt to curtail the education of the black race. Under a widely advertised system of "universal" education, not one black boy in three today has in the United States a chance to learn to read and write. The proportion of school funds due to black children are often spent on whites, and the burden on private charity to support education, which is a public duty, has become almost intolerable.

In every walk of life we meet discrimination based solely on race and color, but continually and persistently misrepresented to the world as the natural difference due to condition.

We are, for instance, usually forced to live in the worst quarters, and our consequent death rate is noted as a race trait, and reason for further discrimination. When we seek to buy property in better quarters we are sometimes in danger of mob violence, or, as now in Baltimore, of actual legislation to prevent.

We are forced to take lower wages for equal work, and our standard of living is then criticized. Fully half the labor unions refuse us admittance, and then claim that as "scabs" we lower the price of labor.

A persistent caste proscription seeks to force us and confine us to menial occupations where the conditions of work are worst.

Our women in the South are without protection in law and custom, and are then derided as lewd. A widespread system of deliberate public insult is customary, which makes it difficult, if not impossible, to secure decent accommodation in hotels, railway trains, restaurants and theaters, and even in the Christian church we are in most cases given to understand that we are unwelcome unless segregated.

Worse than all this is the wilful miscarriage of justice in the courts. Not only have 3,500 black men been lynched publicly by mobs in the last twenty-five years without semblance or pretense of trial, but regularly every day throughout the South the machinery of the courts is used, not to prevent crime and correct the wayward among Negroes, but to wreak public dislike and vengeance, and to raise public funds. This dealing in crime as a means of public revenue is a system well-nigh universal in the South, and while its glaring brutality through private lease has been checked, the underlying principle is still unchanged.

Everywhere in the United States the old democratic doctrine of recognizing fitness wherever it occurs is losing ground before a reactionary policy of denying preferment in political or industrial life to competent men if they have a trace of Negro blood, and of using the weapons of public insult and humiliation to keep such men down. It is today a universal demand in the South that on all occasions social courtesies shall be denied any person of known Negro descent, even to the extent of refusing to apply the titles of Mr., Mrs., and Miss.

Against this dominant tendency strong and brave Americans, white and black, are fighting, but they need, and need sadly, the moral support of England and of Europe in this crusade for the recognition of manhood, despite adventitious differences of race, and it is like a blow in the face to have one, who himself suffers daily insult and humiliation in America, give the impression that all is well. It is one thing to be optimistic, self-forgetful and forgiving, but it is quite a different thing, consciously or unconsciously, to misrepresent the truth.

Basil Matthews

AN EXCHANGE BETWEEN BOOKER T. WASHINGTON AND OSWALD GARRISON VILLARD

Grandson of William Lloyd Garrison, the most famous American abolitionist, Oswald Garrison Villard was a reformer of wealth and influence and chief editorial writer of the New York Evening Post. *Villard's leadership in the formation of the NAACP strained his long-cordial relations with Washington. The two men explored their differences in an extended correspondence.*

"From my point of view, [Villard wrote to Washington] your philosophy is wrong. You are keeping silent about evils in regard to which you should speak out, and you are not helping the race by portraying all the conditions as favorable. If my grandfather had gone to Europe, say in 1850, and dwelt in his speeches on slavery upon certain encouraging features of it, such as the growing anger and unrest of the poor whites, and stated the number of voluntary liberations and number of escapes to Canada, as evidences that the institution was improving, he never would have accomplished what he did, and he would have hurt, not helped, the cause of freedom. It seems to me that the parallel precisely affects your case. It certainly cannot be unknown to you that a greater and greater percentage of the intellectual colored people are turning from you, and becoming your opponents, and with them a number of white people as well."

In the course of a long letter in reply to Villard (January 10, 1911), Washington revealed clearly the sharp contrast between his philosophy of construction and cooperation and that of aggressive attack; yet, in his restrained way, making an attack on the knowledge and attitude of his opponents.

"My speeches in Europe did not differ from my speeches in this country. When I am in the South speaking to the Southern white people, anyone who hears me speak will tell you that I am frank and direct in my criticism of the Southern white people. I cannot agree with you, or any others, however, that very much or any good is to be gained just now by going out of the South and merely speaking about the Southern white people. . . . I think it pays to do such talking to the people who are most responsible for injustice being inflicted upon us in certain directions. . . .

"There is little parallel between conditions that your grandfather had to confront and those facing us now. Your grandfather faced a great evil which was to be destroyed. Ours is a work of construction rather than a work of destruction. My effort in Europe was to show to the people that the work of your grandfather was not wasted and that the progress the Negro has made in America justified the words and work of your grandfather. . . .

"You, of course, labor under the disadvantage of not knowing as much about the life of the Negro race as if you were a member of that race yourself. Unfortunately, too, I think you are brought into contact with that group of our people who have not succeeded in any large degree—dissatisfied and unhappy. I wish you could come more constantly into contact with that group of our people who are succeeding, who have accomplished something, and are not continually sour and disappointed. I keep pretty closely in touch with the life of my race, and I happen to know that the very same group of people who are opposing me now have done so practically ever since my name became in any way prominent, certainly ever since I spoke at the opening of the Atlanta Exposition. No matter what I would do or refrain from doing, the same group would oppose me. I think you know this. . . .

"I cannot agree with you that there is an increasing number of intellectual colored people who oppose me, or are opposed to me. My experience and observation convince me to the contrary. I do not see how any man could expect or hope to have to a larger extent the good will and cooperation of the members of his race of all classes than I have, and it is this consciousness that makes me feel very humble.

"I confess that I cannot blame anyone who resides in the North or in Europe for not taking the same hopeful view of conditions in the South that I do. The only time I ever become gloomy or despondent regarding the conditions of the Negro in the South is when I am in the North. When I am in the North I hear for the most part only of the most discouraging and disheartening things that take place in the South, but when I leave the North and get right in the South in the midst of the work and see for myself what is being done and how it is being done, and what the actual daily connection between the white man and the black man is, then it is that I become encouraged.

"You say that I ought to speak out more strongly on public questions. I suppose that means such questions as relate to our receiving justice in the matter of public schools, lynchings, etc. In that regard I quote you some sentences which I used only a few days ago in talking to the Southern white people here in Alabama concerning their duty toward the Negro: 'I do not believe that the leading white people, and especially landowners of the Black Belt counties know how little money some Negro schools receive. I actually know of communities where Negro teachers are being paid only from $15 to $17 per month for services for a period of three or four months in the year.... More money is paid for Negro convicts than for Negro teachers. About $46 per month is now being paid for first-class able-bodied Negro convicts, $36 for second class, and $26 for third class for twelve months in the year.... One other element in the situation that drives Negroes from the farms of the Black Belt counties is this. In many of the Black Belt counties, when a Negro is charged with a crime, a mob of wild, excited and often intoxicated people go scouring through the country in search of the Negro.... In my opinion, if the Negroes understand that their public schools in the country districts are gradually going to be improved as fast as the state can do so, and that they will receive police protection in case they are charged with crime in the country districts, as they do in the cities, then the best colored farmers will cease moving from the country districts into the cities.' "

After giving one or two more cases of this kind Washington concluded his letter to Villard with "I am always glad to hear from you."

August Meier

BOOKER T. WASHINGTON AND THE "TALENTED TENTH"

The following comes from a detailed study of racial ideologies during Washington's ascendancy. Its author, August Meier of Kent State University, has pioneered in many areas of black history. The case studies included here indicate that Washington's "opponents" sometimes adopted an ambiguous stance and could be surprisingly inconsistent on the question of Washington and his program. Washington was able through the press, political influence, and personal pressure—and through "intelligence-gathering" by undercover agents—to influence the positions of educated blacks, even some of those active in the NAACP. Yet the often favorable reaction among intellectuals to Washington reflects more than his power. Meier suggests further that Washington appealed to a persisting strain of racial solidarity and self-help among Afro-Americans. In the "Brownsville affair" President Theodore Roosevelt peremptorily discharged, with forfeiture of benefits, three companies of black soldiers after some of their number resorted to violent retaliation against harassment and discrimination in Brownsville, Texas. Washington urged a more moderate course on the president, but refused to condemn his action after it was taken.

An examination of the role of Negro lawyers in the ideological controversies during the ascendancy of Booker T. Washington is especially illuminating. For, even though they formed but a tiny proportion of the professional class, they were particularly influential in the Negro community and were active among the radicals to an extent well out of proportion to their numbers. Among Washington's leading critics in Chicago were lawyers E. H. Morris and Ferdinand Barnett; Archibald Grimké and Clement Morgan were prominent in the Trotter circle in Boston; Niagarite W. Ashbie Hawkins, who represented the NAACP in its fight against the Baltimore municipal segregation ordinance, was a leading radical there; and F. L. McGhee of St. Paul was credited with suggesting the Niagara Movement. And out of twenty-three signers of Du Bois's London circular attacking Washington in 1910, nine were lawyers.

Particularly evident among the lawyers was the contrast between

Northern and Southern leaders in their attitude toward Washington. Due to limited opportunities for legal practice, most of the Southern lawyers—men like the bankers J. T. Settle of Memphis, W. E. Mollison of Vicksburg and J. C. Napier of Nashville—were primarily businessmen or politicians, or both. As Southerners they were likely to agree with the conciliatory tone of Washington's utterances. As businessmen they naturally supported his economic emphasis. As bankers, real estate agents, and professional men dependent upon the support of the Negro community they were sympathetic with Washington's philosophy of economic chauvinism. And as politicians they were compelled to court the favor of the man who held the patronage strings during the administrations of Roosevelt and Taft.

An occasional Southern lawyer was ambivalent toward Washington. However, I have found only two who cared to oppose him openly. One was James H. Hayes of Richmond, who organized a National Negro Suffrage League in 1902 and planned to contest the Virginia disfranchisement laws in the federal courts. Washington objected to the emotional character of Hayes's agitation and through coercion applied by his power over the press, and through the influence of mutual friends, brought Hayes around to his point of view—though only temporarily. The other Southern lawyer who openly opposed Washington was McKinley's register of the Treasury, Judson W. Lyons of Augusta. He had successfully sought Washington's aid for reappointment to his post after Roosevelt became president, but he failed in his bid for a third term in 1905 because he had come to identify himself with Washington's critics.

In contrast to the Southern lawyers, most of the important Northern attorneys and jurists appear to have made law the cornerstone of their careers. Little is known of the lesser lawyers, but it is likely that, like their Southern counterparts, they depended almost entirely on Negroes for their business and eked out a modest living in real estate, insurance, and collecting claims. The more eminent Northern lawyers were, as far as can be ascertained, all men of Northern birth or long Northern residence, often educated at the best Northern colleges, and members of that older upper class that to a considerable extent depended on whites for its livelihood. It would be expected, therefore, that they would be unlikely to champion the doctrines of "no social equality," economic chauvinism, and industrial education, or relegate civil and political rights to a secondary place, as Washington did. Nevertheless, Washington secured the whole-hearted support of some and the half-hearted support of many. Illustrative of the former were Clifford H. Plummer of Boston and Wilford Smith of New York. Trotter hired Plummer as his attorney when Washington sued the editor for the "Boston riot" incident, but the lawyer was secretly in touch with Tuskegee in the case and later acted as Washington's undercover agent in Trotter's New England Suffrage League. Smith represented Washington in the same case, and was attorney for the Alabama test cases on disfranchisement and jury discrimination financed by Washington.

There were no more consistent opponents of Washington than Morris and Barnett of Chicago. Kentucky-born E. H. Morris, graduate of St. Patrick's College in Chicago, was a distinguished and wealthy corporation lawyer, attorney for Cook County, twice a member of the state legislature, chief figure among Negro Oddfellows, and a valiant defender of Negro rights. When, in his address before the Bethel Literary Association in 1904, he accused the Tuskegeean of believing in Negro inferiority, racial segregation, and eschewing politics, the alarm of the Tuskegee group was therefore eminently justified. Ferdinand Barnett, graduate of Northwestern University and founder of the first Negro newspaper in Illinois (the *Conservator,* 1878), and his wife, the noted antilynching crusader, Ida Wells, had both been active in the battle for Negro rights ever since their marriage in 1895. In contrast, Barnett's former law partner, S. Laing Williams, and his wife, the noted club woman, Fannie Barrier Williams, assiduously cultivated Washington. From the time of their marriage in 1887 the Williamses played a leading role in social welfare activities in Chicago's Negro community. During the height of Washington's power, Mrs. Williams was busy writing and talking on the self-help of the Negro women's club movement and other organizations, and the importance of middle-class virtues. Her husband, Washington's closest friend in Chicago, ghostwrote the Tuskegeean's book on Frederick Douglass, and for his loyalty was rewarded with the post of federal assistant district attorney. Nevertheless we find Williams a vice-president of the Chicago NAACP in 1913.

A third couple were the Terrells of Washington. In almost every respect they epitomized Du Bois's concept of Talented Tenth leadership. Raised in Virginia and Washington, D.C., Robert H. Terrell had graduated as commencement orator and the first Negro with an A.B. cum laude from Harvard College in 1884. While teaching classics in Washington he obtained a law degree from Howard University, participated in movements for political and civil rights, and encouraged the development of Negro business enterprise, serving as secretary of the ill-fated Capital Savings Bank. Mary Church Terrell, the daughter of a wealthy Memphis real estate dealer, had been educated at Oberlin and had taught at Wilberforce and in Washington before she married her colleague at the M Street High School in 1891. Subsequently she became the first president of the National Association of Colored Women and for a dozen years (1895–1901 and 1906–1911) a member of the Washington Board of Education. In 1901 at the suggestion of his closest friend in the nation's capital, the real estate dealer Whitefield McKinlay, Washington secured the appointment of Terrell, then principal of the high school, as a magistrate in the District of Columbia. From then on Terrell was a member of the Tuskegee circle; he was among those defending Washington when Morris spoke at the Bethel Literary in 1904, and subsequently Washington's opponents seem to have been his chief obstacle in securing reappointments.

Nevertheless, both Terrell and his wife flirted with the opposition. The judge tailored his addresses to suit his audience. As during the 1880s he could either protest vigorously against discrimination and stress the role of the Talented Tenth and the importance of higher education, or he could enthusiastically endorse the economic formulas of Washington's National Negro Business League. Similarly he tailored his activities in regard to Washington to fit the occasion. By the summer of 1905 Washington felt that Terrell was not behaving as a "supposed friend" should. Soon the exasperating inconsistency of his wife's speeches was arousing Tuskegee ire. On February 19, 1906, Washington wrote Terrell that while he liked her conservative speech at Charlotte, he found it curious that his friends made radical speeches in the North and conservative speeches in the South. In the fall of 1906 Mrs. Terrell was working hand in glove with Washington to prevent Du Bois from securing an appointment as assistant superintendent of schools in the nation's capital—a post awarded to a Tuskegee supporter, Roscoe Conkling Bruce. But the fat was in the fire when she took up the cause of the Brownsville soldiers in cooperation with the Constitution League. Toward the end of 1906 she even indirectly criticized the Tuskegeean by an attack on the race leadership that told dialect stories, counseled an inferior sort of education, and advised accommodation to other discrimination. She was reported as saying privately that this speech was intended to "unshirt" Washington. When Terrell himself was reported shocked at Washington's actions toward the defenders of the discharged soldiers, Collector Anderson thought "Judge Terrell had better take a stitch in his tongue." He accused the judge of posing as a Tuskegee man when Washington was around, and yet managing to support all of Washington's enemies.

Mrs. Terrell further offended Tuskegee by a speech before the American Missionary Association in 1907 in which she caustically criticized the South. R. W. Tyler, fourth auditor of the Treasury, expressed the agitation of the Tuskegee group when he declared that "some one ought to muzzle Mary Church Terrell," and wrote an editorial for the *Age* which closed with the remark that "what we now want as a race, is less agitators and more constructors."

So irritating was her work with the NAACP that Washington wrote Terrell how embarrassing it was to have his wife connected with it. Since the new organization was likely to attack Taft, her activities put those who had worked for Terrell's reappointment in a difficult spot. "Of course," added Washington, "I am not seeking to control anyone's actions, but I simply want to know where we stand." Nevertheless, Mrs. Terrell remained active in the NAACP and became a vice-president of the Washington branch. However, the judge was supported by the Bookerites and was opposed by the anti-Bookerites for appointment to the Howard University Law School. When Anderson called attention to the fact that Terrell was associated with Du Bois in an essay contest sponsored by the NAACP, and commented that it was unfortunate that he was one of "our fellows" who "will not 'shinny on their own side,'" Washington apparently thought it desirable to cultivate Terrell by asking him to give the next commencement address at Tuskegee. Indeed, the judge proved to be an outstanding jurist and a consummate politician, for he remained in office throughout the Wilson administration in the face of opposition from Southern senators and a sharp drop in the number of Negro officeholders.

William H. Lewis, the leading Negro lawyer in metropolitan Boston, was a native of Virginia who had been educated at Amherst and Harvard, and had started out as an ardent agitator and anti-Bookerite. By the time he was elected to the state legislature in 1901, however, he was coming to have respect for Washington to whom he wrote that "while we may differ I trust that we may always be friends." Washington soon recommended Lewis to Roosevelt for the post of assistant district attorney in Boston; Lewis was "very graciously" received by the president, who was glad to hear that the lawyer was more in agreement with Washington than formerly. Lewis was the only one of the five Bostonians at the Louisville Convention of the Afro-American Council who identified himself with Washington, and he further indicated his conservatism by acting as chairman of the "Boston riot" meeting in August 1903. He received the coveted post in the same year, was appointed special attorney in charge of naturalization affairs for the New England states in 1907, and in 1908 he was chosen by Washington to be the Negro to second Taft's nomination. While the evidence suggests that Lewis cultivated Washington for political reasons, he rationalized his behavior with the remark that the Tuskegeean was trying to bring the wooden horse inside the walls of Troy. Though in his public utterances Lewis made eulogistic references to Washington and usually hewed closely to the Tuskegee line, he still collaborated with members of the opposition on occasion. In October 1907, for example, he held a banquet for Du Bois; and this and similar actions led Anderson to resent his behavior in view of all that Washington had done for Lewis. Yet Washington not only failed to break with Lewis, but in 1911 secured for him the highest federal appointment yet accorded a Negro—that of assistant United States attorney general.

Frederick L. McGhee (died 1912) of St. Paul, a leader in the civil rights movement of Minnesota during the 1890s, was on friendly terms with Washington at the opening of the century. A leading Catholic layman, he was employed by the Tuskegeean in 1904 as an emissary to the Maryland hierarchy in an effort to secure its opposition to disfranchisement proposals there, and as a lobbyist with senators on the Crum appointment. Active in the affairs of the Afro-American Council, McGhee had charge first of its legislative committee and then of its legal bureau. He posed as a Washington supporter in council affairs, yet found it necessary to make unconvincing explanations as to why he opposed Fortune's election to the presidency at both the 1902 and 1903 conventions. Though it was in

1904 that he worked for Washington on his political missions, Du Bois already regarded him as "uncompromisingly" anti-Washington, and by 1905 he was openly allied with the radicals, serving as head of the Niagara Movement's Legal Department.

Two older leaders are especially worthy of consideration—D. Augustus Straker and Archibald Grimké. Straker, a successful jurist in Detroit, maintained, as he had done during the 1880s, that the race problem could be solved only by a two-pronged approach of economic self-help on the part of Negroes, and of whites according Negroes economic opportunity and political rights. He unsuccessfully sought Washington's assistance to obtain a consulship in 1901, and a few years later wrote the Tuskegeean that he would "not stand silently by and see you falsely accused or abused, while I may not agree with you in details." Yet until he died in 1906 Washington's critics considered Straker one of their number, one "who never gave up his ideals and never crawled or kow-towed to the 'New South.' "

Archibald H. Grimké illustrates the oscillation in thought characteristic of some of the intellectuals. A graduate of Harvard Law School in 1874, he established himself in Boston where he married a white woman and became a successful lawyer. An independent in politics, he was rewarded with the post of consul in Santo Domingo, 1894–1898, and supported the Progressives in 1912–1913. During the disturbing years at the turn of the century, when the Hampton-Tuskegee philosophy enjoyed its greatest vogue, Grimké urged Negroes to do well whatever work it fell to them to do, no matter how menial, and by success achieved through industry, thrift, intelligence, and the accumulation of wealth, arrest increasing white indifference. But Grimké was soon associated with the Trotter group, and Washington invited him to the Carnegie Hall Conference only after considerable hesitation, as he thought Grimké "a noisy, turbulent and unscrupulous" man "more bent upon notoriety and keeping up discord than any other motive." Unexpectedly Grimké was impressed by Washington's explanation of his policy, and Moton reported the lawyer as saying that Washington was undoubtedly working for the best interests of the race. Though Emmett Scott learned that Grimké did remain friendly with Trotter, Washington took steps to cultivate him. Grimké temporarily endorsed Washington's views on franchise limitations, though by 1905 he was again opposed to them. Moreover, Washington benefited from the irascible personality of Du Bois who insulted Grimké in 1905. The turning point in the relationship between Grimké and Washington may have come as a result of Grimké's stand on the Brownsville affair; he was reliably reported as "savagely denouncing" the president, the secretary of war, and the Tuskegeean on the matter at a meeting in 1908. From then on Grimké was distinctly of the opposition, serving as president of the NAACP's Washington chapter and forthrightly attacking all forms of discrimination.

Of those who adopted a consistently uncompromising philosophy of assimilation and protest, few were more respected than the noted author Charles W. Chesnutt. A successful lawyer, accepted in high political and social circles in Cleveland, Chesnutt championed full equality, advocated intermarriage, opposed doctrines of race pride and race solidarity, and believed the solution to the race problem lay in whites living up to their democratic ideas more than in Negroes improving themselves. Even though the two men were thus decidedly in disagreement Chesnutt and Washington maintained a friendly relationship. Washington assiduously cultivated the prominent writer and lawyer, and Chesnutt for his part was of assistance in arranging philanthropic contacts for Washington's Cleveland visits. Nevertheless, Chesnutt always frankly stated his ideological opposition to Washington. He forthrightly told the Tuskegeean that he disagreed with the latter's support of a restricted franchise, his emphasis on economic accumulation rather than on political and civil rights, his tendency to dwell on Negro weaknesses, his overemphasis on industrial education, and his faith in the good will of the Southern white man. The available Chesnutt correspondence with the anti-Bookerites is incomplete, but he undoubtedly maintained cordial relations with members of the radical group, spoke at the Niagara Movement meeting in 1908, and from 1910 on was actively associated with the NAACP. Thus Chesnutt, courted by both sides, appears to have been a radical by conviction, but one who respected the views of others. He frankly stated his differences with Washington both publicly and privately, but declined to enter the fray.

It is evident that though lawyers played a prominent role in the opposition, it is likely that the majority of them either passively or actively endorsed Washington's leadership. Practically all of the

Southern lawyers did. Though direct evidence is lacking, probably most of the Northern lawyers, who were primarily petty businessmen dependent on the Negro community for their living, also supported Washington, for they would espouse his philosophy of economic accumulation and economic chauvinism. On the other hand, the most distinguished Northern lawyers had been educated at the best Northern universities, and (except for Terrell) appeared to have had their economic and often even their social roots in the white community. These men would therefore, in the normal course of events, be unlikely to favor soft-pedaling political demands, accepting segregation, sneering at "the intellectuals," or emphasizing racial solidarity. And in fact many exhibited strong anti-Bookerite tendencies. It thus is apparent that support of Washington was in part a function of social status and economic interest.

The magnitude of Washington's personal influence cannot be ignored when considering the forces that shaped ideological expression during his ascendancy. People like to be in accord with currently admired figures. Moreover, the evidence is clear that especially after he came to political power, many former critics became supporters. In proportion to their numbers, more eminent lawyers than members of any other professional group dared to publicly oppose Washington. Yet even among those who either opposed him at first, or who might normally have been expected to do so, he wielded a substantial influence. Men such as Grimké and Chesnutt wanted to see value in his program and therefore tried to arrive at a modus vivendi with him. And this desire undoubtedly influenced others such as Terrell, Straker, and Lewis, who were also largely motivated by personal ambition. It would be a mistake to call these individuals insincere, for self-interest and social idealism are inextricably interwoven in human motivation and the power of rationalization is strong. Moreover, almost anyone, white or Negro, who wanted to do anything about the race problem at least tried to work with Washington. Undoubtedly just as Washington advanced his own career and believed he was serving the best interests of the race by his program, so men like Terrell and Lewis probably justified their action in a similar way. The fact is that these men simply never gave up their relationship with the opposition.

Thus among the lawyers the complex motivations entering into the ideological expression of Negro leaders are made particularly evident. For here a group of outstanding men who clearly met every requirement of Du Bois's definition of the Talented Tenth cannot be said to have been in the majority clearly for or consistently opposed to Washington. Not only did those dependent on the Negro community for their livelihood naturally espouse much of Washington's philosophy, but the general drift of opinion, the prestige of Washington, the ambitions of individual men, and the configurations of power all served to incline toward Washington the very men who might have been most expected to oppose him.

In reviewing the data we have presented on the thinking of an illustrative sampling of Negro intellectuals, it is evident that most of them—even those with a college education—were at one time or another (if not all the time) either enthusiastic or lukewarm supporters of Booker T. Washington, and that doctrines of racial pride, economics, solidarity, and self-help loomed large in their thinking, though of course their goal was full citizenship rights. This is true even of Du Bois, the most illustrious intellectual of all.

Support for Washington's program was strongest at the turn of the century, when many who later became outspoken critics espoused his program. By 1903, as Kelly Miller pointed out, few thoughtful men endorsed him and his platform unreservedly, and Washington's recognition of this fact was what prompted the Carnegie Hall Conference. During the last decade of Washington's life more and more of the intellectuals drifted into the ranks of the radicals and the NAACP; and even some of his strongest supporters came to give qualified endorsement to the position of the opposition, and themselves came to take a more radical stand, even while remaining personally loyal to Washington.

It is true that the radicals drew most of their support from the college-educated group (though who was more consistently radical than H. C. Smith, who had only a high school education?). It is also evident that conservatism was, by and large, more prevalent among those educators and ministers who themselves lacked a college training, and that the consistent supporters of Washington were largely concentrated in this group. But it is just as true that most of the college-educated elite were either wholeheartedly or partially in support of Washington, at least for a time, and saw at least temporary value in various forms of group separatism; and that some of the chief radical figures themselves at one time or another approved of these things. To assume that, because the leadership of the opposition came from the college-educated elite, more than a small minority of this group were consistently antagonistic to Washington would then be erroneous.

The reasons for the support accorded to Washington by the intellectuals were several. The discouragement characteristic of the period, especially around 1900, certainly swayed many. Washington's money, prestige, and influence were also important factors. Ambitious lawyers, educators, editors, and even ministers felt it worth their while to cultivate the Tuskegeean. Thus the power structure of the Negro community not only strengthened a conservative tendency that was already gaining popularity, but it also contributed substantially to the instability of the ideological expression of many leaders, most notably among the lawyers, editors, and teachers at liberal arts colleges.

Most radical in their expression, by and large, were the lawyers; the ministers and especially the educators were mostly conservative; while the editors were in between. This correlation is undoubtedly related to the social role of the individuals concerned. The radical lawyers and doctors tended to be Northern men with their economic and sometimes their social connections in the white community, though some men of similar background did support Washington. Ministers with their otherworldly interests quite easily fell into an accommodating position. School administrators depended on white public opinion and philanthropy. Even the ministers, who were more directly responsive to Negro rather than white thought, were more outspoken than the school presidents and principals. The newspapers were influenced by Washington directly, and by the general trends of thought. Their dependence on the Negro market seems to have worked in two ways, however. On the one hand they were ordinarily zealous advocates of economic self-help and economic chauvinism. On the other hand their readers apparently did not intend to forget "the promise of American life," and the editors gave considerable emphasis to protest and agitation.

Finally, it cannot be overlooked that the aspirations of the professional men, no matter how conservative their utterances, included integration and the attainment of citizenship rights; and this aspiration they expressed as an ultimate goal where they did not insist upon it as an immediate one. Therefore, although the temporary advantages of the disadvantages in segregation, disillusionment with protest and politics, and the influence of Washington all served to make Negro thought in this period far more separatist, economically orientated, self-helpish, and accommodating than it has been in more optimistic periods, it must be emphasized that the leaders as a group hoped for ultimate equality and citizenship rights, whatever the tactical advantages that might be derived from a conservative program.

It must be concluded that, broadly speaking, while the intellectuals formed the backbone of the Niagara Movement and the NAACP, most of them for one reason or another were friendly with Washington, or at least gave him greater or lesser support, though they were not always consistent in doing this. Moreover, to the extent that they were forming the new middle class dependent on the Negro market, they espoused the ideas of race pride and economic solidarity. The assimilationist orientation of the anti-Bookerites is central in Negro thinking, but its fundamental importance should not permit one to minimize the rising tide of sentiment favoring a "cultural pluralism" that was developing in the age of Booker T. Washington and which became the ideological basis of the postwar "New Negro."

V. CHANGING PERSPECTIVES ON BOOKER T. WASHINGTON

Horace Mann Bond

THE INFLUENCE OF PERSONALITIES ON THE PUBLIC EDUCATION OF NEGROES IN ALABAMA

For many years dean of the School of Education at Atlanta University, Horace Mann Bond included the following treatment of Washington in a much broader study of the way in which social forces shape educational institutions. Since Bond is primarily interested in how Washington's program and the design of Tuskegee served certain class interests, the title of this chapter is somewhat misleading. But he concludes by raising the question: In what sense, if any, was Washington a "great man," a major historical influence? The author's response suggests the power of personality and myth in human history.

It is . . . impossible to disentangle the role of Tuskegee Institute and Washington as educational agencies, and as self-conscious social forces. Washington himself always indicated that Tuskegee "was built around a problem." The problem included three classes of people: the Negroes, whom he hoped to educate and to aid in achieving progress; the Northern white people, whom he depended upon to finance the school; and the Southern white people whose support was essential, first, in order to permit such an institution as he envisioned to exist in the heart of the South, and, second, to make a success of the demonstration in better race relations which was his ultimate goal. "I saw," he said, "that in order to succeed I must in some way secure the support and sympathy of each of them."

It was a task easily seen to require the most consummate skill, amounting, in Washington's case, to a peculiar genius. Educationally it had the misfortune to depend so much upon his personality and upon a refined technique of racial strategy that whatever educational outcomes were derivative from his work could easily be swallowed up in an ocean of individual and racial deceit. It has an additional disadvantage for the student of educational structures. Since the school was an instrument of a social policy, it is difficult to tell

From Horace Mann Bond, *Negro Education in Alabama: A Study in Cotton and Steel,* pp. 205–219, 224–225. Footnotes omitted.

where it was primarily an educational institution, and where a social device.

One appraisal of Washington disregards the contribution he is ordinarily thought to have made to education. He was important, "not because he became a great man, or a great Negro, or rose from slavery, but because he embodied the survival elements of the Negro race in an environment hostile to its ultimate objectives." From this standpoint his work at Tuskegee is interpreted as that of "a social strategist," giving a common-sense demonstration of what a student of human behavior might prescribe today as the technique of social adaptation in a situation immensely complicated by age-old social structures. Given an acute sense of the power of social and racial attitudes, an indomitable will to achieve ends to which these attitudes were barriers, the attainment of ultimate objectives could follow either the pathway of direct assault upon the interposed barriers, or that of careful, tedious, skillful indirection. Washington is seen as having chosen, with utter clarity of vision, this latter course.

Whether "strategy" or no, the educational work of Washington in Alabama is reflected intelligibly only by reference to the social and economic influences with which he was associated and frequently aligned. When he spoke of "the white people of the South," he appears to have been talking of that social and economic class dominant in the state when Tuskegee Institute was established, and not of the turbulent, discontented folk who were later to figure so largely in the administration of public affairs.

A speech delivered at the Atlanta Exposition on September 18, 1895, is generally credited as the fortuitous circumstance which enabled Washington to project himself before the nation as the recognized representative of his race. Ex-Governor Bullock of Georgia announced in advance of the exposition that its purpose was to prove to Northern capitalists that the "free-silver lunacy" and anti-Negro agitation were "silly hobbies," not truly representative of the South. He explained further to the New York Chamber of Commerce:

> *... one of the good effects of our Exposition will be to dissipate the political usefulness of the color-line bugaboo and set our white people free to form and act upon their best judgment as to governmental policies, uncontrolled by prejudices engendered by issues that are now happily of the past.*

The board of directors was described, with a highly significant sense of values, as "made up of fifty men, who are the best of our city—bank presidents, wholesale dealers, manufacturers and retired capitalists." He concluded by assuring the New York businessmen that all was well in the South, and that "the colored labor in our section is the best, safest and most conservative in the world."

Several incidents given wide national publicity during the month of August 1895 may or may not shed illumination upon Washington's Atlanta speech. On August 1, at the Brookside Mines in Jefferson County, near Birmingham, there was a riot between white and Negro miners. The whites were striking for higher wages; the Negroes refused to quit work. On August 4, at Princeton, Illinois, began a race riot lasting for several days between Italian and Negro coal miners. The Negroes were strikebreakers imported from the South.

Washington said aferward that he felt he "had in some way achieved" his object, which he described as "getting a hearing from the dominant class of the South." In composing the speech, he said, he kept in mind that his audience would be composed largely "of the wealth and culture of the white South."

An examination of the document shows Washington's mastery of the art of opposing shibboleth to shibboleth. "Social Equality" had been the stereotype by which the "dominant class" to which he now addressed himself had won the support of the poorer whites and overturned the Reconstruction governments. Washington met the issue with skillful phrases: "The wisest among my race understand that the agitation of questions of social equality is the extremest folly, and that progress in the enjoyment of all the privileges that will come to us must be the result of severe and constant struggle rather than of artificial forcing. . . . In all things that are purely social we can be as separate as the fingers, yet one as the hands in all things essential to mutual progress."

He invoked the shade of the traditional, paternalistic relationship so dear to the romantic picture of the antebellum South. "As we have proved our loyalty to you in the past, in nursing your children, watching by the sick-bed of your mothers and fathers, and often following them with tear-dimmed eyes to their graves. . . ." Washington said the exposition would introduce "a new era of industrial progress" to the South. The white people were advised to "cast down your bucket where you are," and not to "look to the incoming of those of foreign birth and strange tongue and habits for the prosperity of the South." The Negroes were described as the "most patient, faithful, law-abiding, and unresentful people the world has seen," who could be depended upon to "buy your surplus land, make blossom the waste places in your fields, and run your factories." The Negro would continue to labor "without strikes or labor troubles."

In his speeches before mixed audiences, Washington employed the oratorical device of addressing the white and Negro divisions of his audience alternately. Only one brief paragraph of the Atlanta speech was so directed to the Negroes. They were advised: "We shall prosper in proportion as we learn to dignify and glorify common labor and put brains and skill into the common occupations of life." They were to remember that "there is as much dignity in tilling a field as in writing a poem." Negroes must begin at the bottom and not at the top.

The effect of the speech was as dramatic as the circumstances surrounding its delivery. Clark Howell wired the *New York World* that "the whole speech is a platform upon which blacks and whites can stand with full justice to each other." Grover Cleveland thought that the speech justified holding the exposition. It made Washington the arbiter of matters affecting the Negro, not only in education, but in social, economic, and political affairs as well. It also gave him an opportunity to reach more persons of wealth in the country and obtain more money for Tuskegee Institute.

The Friends of Washington and Tuskegee

As Washington, in his Atlanta speech, frankly addressed himself to "the dominant class in the South," his whole career was bound up with a successful appeal to the sympathies of that class, both in the South and in the North, among white people. His course has significance for the education of Negroes in Alabama because it meant that much depended on the persistence of this class in control of public affairs. It also meant that Washington and the Negroes generally were allied with the dominant social and economic class as they had been, in the thinking of the poorer whites, during slavery. It may have been that Washington believed it was fruitless to cultivate the class of white persons who were on the lower levels of society;

that he thought the antipathy of this class to the Negroes was too thoroughgoing to overcome. Whatever the reason, Washington definitely allied himself to "the better class of white people" incarnated in the powerful and wealthy of his period.

In Alabama Washington sustained relations of the most friendly sort to the leading politicians of the "oligarchy," up to the time when the line was overturned by insurgent Democrats. Governor Thomas Seay (1886–1890) was a "friend and champion of the Negro's rights." Washington is quoted as saying that Seay was "the best friend the Negro race ever had."

Seay's successors, Thomas Goode Jones (1890–1894), and Governor Oates (1894–1898), were elected over Populist opponents by various political devices. Jones was one of the staunch defenders of Negro rights in the Constitutional Convention of 1901. On September 14, 1901, Theodore Roosevelt wrote to Washington, asking him to come to the Capitol for a conference on Southern political appointments. On October 2, 1901, Washington wrote to Roosevelt:

> Judge Bruce, the Judge of the Middle District of Alabama, died yesterday. There is going to be a very hard scramble for his place. I saw ex-Governor Jones yesterday, as I promised, and he is willing to accept the judgeship of the Middle District of Alabama. I am more convinced now than ever that he is the proper man for the place. He has until recently been president of the Alabama State Bar Association. He is a Gold Democrat, and is a clean, pure man in every respect. He stood up in the Constitutional Convention and elsewhere for a fair election law, opposed lynching, and he has been outspoken for the education of both races.
>
> Yours truly,
> Booker T. Washington

Jones's appointment to the position was announced on October 14, 1901. When it became noised about that Booker T. Washington was responsible for the appointment a storm of criticism was leveled at Jones, Washington, and Roosevelt. Jones denied this, saying that he owed his appointment to Grover Cleveland. Under the administration of Governor Comer (1907–1911), the Alabama legislature passed several laws intended to effect rate making on Alabama railroads. Jones ruled in a series of decisions handed down from 1909 to 1911 that the regulatory laws of the Alabama legislation were "confiscatory" and unconstitutional. Each of his several decisions was reversed by the Circuit and United States Supreme Courts.

Now, the same "antirailway" legislature of 1906–1907 promptly passed a joint resolution asking the governor to appoint an accountant to investigate the business affairs of Tuskegee Institute, and all other departments which he saw fit to inspect. The spirit of the proposed investigation was so hostile that Washington was unable to make his "usual Northern trip seeking contributions in the winter of 1907." It was "designed to reveal the shortcomings of the school and thus to bring reproach upon Northern ideas concerning Negro education." Washington succeeded in bringing enough pressure to bear upon Governor Comer, so that the latter appointed as investigator a friend of Tuskegee whose report was favorable to the school.

This incident is an illustration of the possible defect in the appeal of Washington and J. L. M. Curry to "the dominant class of the South." In application to the common schools it meant when that class lost its political dominance the Negroes had no friend at court. It is entirely possible, of course, that no other strategy was feasible for Washington and Curry.

Jones's successor as governor, Oates, was a staunch friend of Booker T. Washington, and, like Jones, defended the rights of the Negroes in the Constitutional Convention of 1901. There is an incident connected with Oates that reflects Washington's invariable skill in handling difficult situations. Washington invited Oates to speak at the Tuskegee Commencement of 1894 and to share the platform with a Negro, John C. Dancey, who was later appointed collector of customs at Wilmington, North Carolina, through Washington's influence. Dancey was an eloquent speaker. He paid "a glowing tribute to the New England men and women who had built up Negro schools in the South." Oates, the next speaker, arose in obvious agitation.

> *I have written this speech for you (waving it at his audience) but I will not deliver it. I want to give you niggers a few words of plain talk and advice. No such address as you have just listened to is going to do you any good; it's going to spoil you. You had better not listen to such speeches. You might just as well understand that this is a white man's country, so far as the South is concerned, and we are going to make you keep your place. Understand that. I have nothing more to say to you.*

The audience, composed for the most part of the teachers and students at Tuskegee, was plainly nettled. Another speaker was scheduled to follow Oates. But Washington arose and said:

> *Ladies and Gentlemen: I am sure you will agree with me that we have had enough eloquence for one occasion. We shall listen to the next speaker at another occasion, when we are not so fagged out. We will now rise, sing the doxology, and be dismissed.*

Oates's speeches in favor of the education of Negroes and for a just treatment of the race in the Constitutional Convention of 1901, might have lacked much of their fervor had Washington been less tactful.

Washington's relations with the Alabama politicians who were themselves so deeply implicated in industrial and financial developments in the state were duplicated by his experience with national leaders of industry. The task of raising money for Tuskegee was said to have consumed two-thirds of his time, "and perhaps even more of his strength and energy." His frank appraisal of the men to whom he appealed, and the methods he employed, may have been either incredibly naive, or as consciously artful. As, when he spoke of the "white people" of the South, he was speaking of the "dominant class," the "best white people" of America were those who had money to give to Tuskegee. The drudgery of raising money had its compensation, he said, in that it gave him an opportunity to meet "some of the best people in the world—to be more correct, I think I should say *the best* people in the world." "My experience in getting money for Tuskegee," he said, "has taught me to have no patience with those who are always condemning the rich because they are rich, and because they do not give more to objects of charity."

In the role of defender of the rich, Washington was superficial both in appraising the nature of criticism directed at them and in his answers to that criticism. "Those who are guilty of such sweeping criticisms do not know how many people would be made poor, and how much suffering would result, if wealthy people were to part all at once with any large proportion of their wealth in a way to disorganize and cripple great business enterprises." His preference as to an audience was for groups of "strong, wide-awake, business men, such, for example, as is found in Boston, New York, Chicago, and Buffalo."

It is probably without significance that the men who contributed most largely to his work at Tuskegee also had, in most instances, large business and industrial interests in Alabama; for they were men who participated in industrial development everywhere in the United States. Andrew Carnegie made numerous gifts to Tuskegee, including a personal donation of $600,000, the interest from which was set aside, at the request of the donor, to free Washington, during his lifetime, from any care or anxiety regarding his personal expenses. Carnegie called Washington "a modern Moses and Joshua combined." "No truer, more self-sacrificing hero ever lived; a man compounded of all the virtues. It makes one better just to know such pure and noble souls—human nature in its highest types is already divine here on earth." . . .

H. H. Rogers, Standard Oil and railroad financier, was another large contributor to the work at Tuskegee. In defining the attitudes of the different wealthy men to whom he appealed for funds Washington said that Rogers regarded Negroes as "part of the resources of the country which he wanted to develop." Like Carnegie, Rogers's first interest in Tuskegee was said to have come from reading *Up from Slavery.* Washington said that he received his first gift from Rogers, amounting to $10,000, on the morning after a New York speech delivered by Washington. The first gift was to aid Negroes in the rural regions surrounding Tuskegee to build schoolhouses, a conditional grant that was later taken up by Rosenwald. While Rogers was building the Virginia Railway from Norfolk, Virginia, to Deepwater, West Virginia, he planned with Washington "a wide reaching work in agricultural education among the Negro farmers living within carting distance of his road." "Booker T. Washington had demonstrated to his satisfaction that by increasing at the same time their wants and their ability to gratify their wants he would be building up business for his railroad." Before his death in 1909 Rogers arranged for a speaking tour by Washington along the line of the railroad, giving him a special train for the purpose. The tour was carried out and Washington, in a climactic address at Suffolk, described the previous arrangement and lauded Mr. Rogers to several thousands of the members of both races. . . .

A list of "exceptional men" that Washington gives as "types" is illuminating. No white farmer or laborer of the lower economic classes is given in this list of his "friends"; a white railroad conductor marks the nadir of the social and economic classification represented. Henry Watterson and J. L. M. Curry are given as representatives of the old aristocratic South. John M. Parker of Louisiana, planter and cotton broker, is described as "a man who has no special sentiment for or against the Negro, but appreciates the importance of the Negro race as a commercial asset." The future of the Negro in the South, thought Washington, depended largely on men like Parker, who "see the close connection between labor, industry, education and political institutions, and have learned to face the race problem in a large and tolerant spirit." Three exceptional men in the North were H. H. Rogers, interested in Negroes as natural resources; Robert C. Ogden, interested in Negroes as "human beings"; and Oswald Garrison Villard, who was interested in Negroes as objects for the application of the principles of abstract justice.

Washington met the problem of the unionization of Negro workers with silence, until just before his death. In 1904, when the effort to organize the Chicago stockyards was defeated by the importation of Negro strikebreakers from the South, the officials of the unions appealed to Washington "to use his influence to prevent Negroes from working in the plants until the strike was settled, and to address a mass meeting of colored citizens in Chicago on the subject: 'Should Negroes become strikebreakers?' " Washington pled a previous engagement in stating his inability to address the mass meeting, and never issued the appeal requested. In 1913 he published an article which by implication discouraged the unionization of Negro workers. Negroes generally, he said, looked to their employers as their friends, and did not understand or like "an organization which seems to be founded on a sort of impersonal enmity to the man by whom he is employed."

Industrial Education

J. L. M. Curry was a firm believer in the virtues both of industrial and manual training in the schools. His election to the position of field agent for the Peabody Fund in 1881, in the same year that Washington came to Tuskegee, may have been responsible for the great vogue this theory of education immediately began to enjoy in schools for Negroes. The Slater Fund for the education of Negroes, incorporated in 1882, was placed in the hands of trustees, two of whom were also on the Peabody Board. Curry was consulted in making plans for the disposition of the fund. A Southern minister, Atticus G. Haygood, was made the general agent. On Haygood's election to the bishopric of the Methodist Episcopal Church, South, in 1890, Curry was given his place. He thus combined, for all practical purposes, the work of the two funds.

The degree to which these foundations were able to effect educational policy in the Negro schools and colleges is obvious. It became a stipulation of both that no aid was to be granted unless the school maintained a department for training in the industries.

At Hampton Institute Washington had become thoroughly imbued with the "practical" educational principles instilled in him by General Armstrong. As Washington described it, the school which he attended from 1872–1875 had no formal courses in the industries. It was a school with an "English" normal curriculum, where students were given an opportunity to work their way through school. In his own account of his education at Hampton, Washington nowhere mentions having studied any specific "industry" or trade. He did learn "a valuable lesson at Hampton by coming into contact with the best breeds of live stock and fowl." This was incidental to the general understanding that every student was supposed to work. Washington's principal job as a student was one as janitor.

At Tuskegee he said that each industry had grown gradually; "We began with farming," he said, "because we wanted something to eat." The students were desperately poor; and, besides, he believed thoroughly that no person should dislike manual work. In his first report he referred to industrial beginnings as follows: "In order to give the students a chance to pay a part of their expenses in work, to teach the dignity of labor, and to furnish agricultural training, the friends of the school have bought a farm." The term "industrial education" appears to have been borrowed by Washington from its current popularity as an innovation in American schools. Washington referred to it first in a speech before the National Educational Association in 1884. Curry took up the phrase in his report for 1882.

The second "industry" was begun in 1882 when bricks were needed for a new building and the school had no money with which to purchase them. A brickyard was started.

Lewis Adams, the Negro trustee and political figure who had helped obtain the appropriation for the school, was a tinsmith. One of the next "trades" started was that of tinsmithing. After the brickyard had begun to produce bricks the trades of carpentry and brick-masonry were begun in conjunction with the building of the proposed structures. "Practical housekeeping" was begun for the benefit of the women. Dormitory life was essential because the students could learn nothing of "proper" home life in the homes then present at Tuskegee.

Stripped of phrases, the early program at Tuskegee Institute was derived from a glorified common sense amounting in this instance to genius. The elaborations of "industrial education" came later. The students were raw, uncultivated, undisciplined country youth; Washington started to induct them into the American culture through a discipline based on the fundamentals which they lacked. That was the process which had touched him when, as a ragged, hungry boy, he had applied for admission to Hampton Institute, and had been asked to sweep a room as his entrance examination. In all of his speeches and writings Washington exhibited a deep contempt for "Latin and Greek" as the subjects of instruction in Negro colleges. It was his misfortune to have attended, after leaving Hampton, one of the pretentious institutions for the higher education of the Negro, Wayland Seminary, in the District of Columbia. But if Washington had attended Talladega College, or Fisk University, or Atlanta University, he would have met there men and women from New England who possessed the same idea as to disciplinary regimentation of the plantation Negroes which he found at Hampton. He would have found, in all of these schools, men and women with New England ideas of cleanliness and order. He would have been in school with fellow students who were as poverty-stricken as he, and who worked their way through school with the same eagerness to learn he showed at Hampton. At Tuskegee the use of the toothbrush, the daily bath, the absence of grease spots from clothing, neatness and order—these evidences of what Washington called "civilization"—were as important, in the writing, and perhaps in the thinking, of its founder, as "industrial education." The brickyard which he established at Tuskegee was preceded by one set up at an American Missionary School in Athens, Alabama, for the same purpose—furnishing work for students, and necessary bricks which the school was too poor to purchase. In 1853 Frederick Douglass, the runaway slave who became a leading figure in the abolitionist agitation, had asked Harriet Beecher Stowe to go to England to raise funds with which to establish an industrial trade school for Negroes.

The principal difference does not wholly lie in the kind of subject matter which the leaders of these schools believed in as fundamental media for the required discipline. Armstrong, the Hawaiian-born, New England-educated, ex-soldier, believed in the general discipline of "military training," and in the dignity of labor for members of an "undeveloped" race. Cravath, at Fisk, and Ware and Bumstead at Atlanta, believed in the discipline of Latin and Greek. With all their belief, however, in the virtue of the "classic," they established these curricula as goals to be achieved rather than as immediate studies. Established in 1867, it was not until 1881 that Talladega College in Alabama gave its first college degree, and not until after 1920 did the "college" number more than 20 percent of the entire student body.

The difference between these two types of school—the "industrial" and the "college"—was indubitably affected by the fundamental attitude toward racial equalitarianism. The strict humanitarians were, to this extent, "misguided fanatics," as Curry called them. They were placed in an alien environment and they refused to compromise with it. There is a profound educational significance in the effect of these personalities, whether "fanatical" or "practical," upon the habits and attitudes of the young Negroes who came to them from slavery, and who received from both types an impress that was revolutionary.

It is important also to remember that both Curry and Washington saw "industrial education" as a technique to be used to obtain support from people who otherwise would have been opposed to any kind of education. Washington said industrial education "kills two birds with one stone"; it secured the cooperation of the whites, and "does the best possible thing for the blacks." Curry hoped that industrial education would reduce "idleness, pauperism, and crime," and thereby meet "prevalent and plausible objections to general education." The motives of Washington in appealing for money for the support of industrial education may not always have been the same as those of the men who gave him money.

Educational Influence of Washington and Tuskegee in Alabama

There are certain intangibles connected with the life of Booker T. Washington which cannot be statistically evaluated. The school was operated as a propaganda agency; the effects of this propaganda in influencing public opinion favorable to the education of Negroes cannot be measured.

One outcome of Washington's work is obvious. His assured position made him the arbiter of affairs bearing on the Negro. The philanthropic organizations consulted Washington, not only with regard to the education of Negroes, but also regarding certain schools for white persons in the state. . . . Since Tuskegee theory was that the school should begin first in its own community to transform the life of the people, various efforts were initiated in this direction by Washington. In 1896 he said that many Tuskegee graduates were "showing the people how to extend the school term to 4, 5, and even 7 months, when before they went there the school term was only three months." At this early date he had the conception of philanthropic aid to communities which twenty years later developed into the Julius Rosenwald Fund. He claimed Tuskegee graduates "are very seldom in a place long before they secure a good schoolhouse which is usually built by the contributions of the country people themselves in labor and money." H. H. Rogers gave his money to aid Negro communities in Macon County build rural schoolhouses; and, through aid given by Rosenwald, Washintgon said in 1912 that "forty-seven school buildings have been erected in Macon County by colored people themselves."

The stimulating force in this school-building program was furnished by the Extension Department of Tuskegee Institute. Washington was, indisputably, a man of the folk. The written speeches printed as having been delivered by him can give no hint as to the wealth of anecdote and ready sympathy, while talking to plantation Negroes, for which he is still remembered. He wished to make all of the country folk thoroughly at home at Tuskegee Institute. He organized a Farmers Conference to which Negroes from the surrounding countryside came, as they still do, "in ox-carts, mule-carts, buggies, on mule back and horseback, on foot." Free forage for animal and food for man was provided in limitless quantities for the visitors.

> *The matters considered at the Conference are those that the colored people have it in their own power to control—such as the evils of the mortgage system, the one-room cabin, buying on credit, the importance of owning a home and of putting money in the bank, how to build schoolhouses and prolong the school term, and to improve moral and religious conditions.*

The agricultural extension department sent speakers and teachers into the rural areas to teach Negroes better methods of agriculture. This work was inaugurated as early as 1897.

Washington was a ceaseless educational propagandist. On the platform, through periodicals and in the white and Negro press, he lost no opportunity to plead for education. In a series of annual letters published in white and Negro newspapers in the South, he gave advice to Negroes on the improvement of their schools. Where Negroes were being discriminated against in the distribution of the school fund, they were advised to "bear in mind that we are citizens," to make "a direct appeal to the public school authorities for a more just distribution of the public school fund." If the authorities did not immediately give the Negroes a fair share of the fund they should ask until they did receive it. . . .

Booker T. Washington and the "Great Man Theory" of Educational History

Appraisals of Booker T. Washington may easily fall into the common error of attributing momentous social and economic changes to the impress of a great personality whose life was contemporary with these changes. Such great men, because they are identified in time with social change, come to be regarded as essential causative factors when more correctly their lives merely illumine, through their numerous contacts, the slow and subsurface movements of human events.

There is another error as fundamental; and it is to decry the positive contribution of great personalities because we have no adequate statistical measure of their effect upon human history. Such statistical measures as we have might give the impression that

Booker T. Washington lived and died in Macon County without leaving behind him any permanent impress upon the educational institutions supported at public expense by the citizens (and, politically defined, this means "white" citizens) of that county. But this impression would be a gross underestimation. There is a dim and shadowy area of social forces which, from lack of perspective, we have no adequate means of presenting to the imagination. In this survey, in addition, little reference has been made to the immense influence which Booker T. Washington had upon private philanthropy, and so, through these agencies, upon public education for Negroes. The building of Tuskegee Institute, the service of its many graduates throughout the South, the profound effect upon public opinion of the man himself; these are among the positive, immeasurable influences generated by this great personality, which in themselves constitute unique social forces, transcending the spheres of his own and our generation, and giving promise of increasing power through successive generations in an undiminished flow into the future.

It would appear that the evidences of greatness are to be found, not in immediate institutional results, nor even in those claims upon which the personality itself rests its petition for present and future acknowledgment; but in the long-time contribution which that personality can make to the area of thought and feeling and opinion. It is so with Booker T. Washington. Another generation may evolve more delicate instruments for such appraisal; until that time, the historian of educational events may find in the life of the builder of Tuskegee Institute perhaps the most illuminating point of departure from which to evaluate the times and the social and economic forces in which he was involved. In his own time Booker T. Washington was a vivid, towering personality; even in our time he has become a legend.

And who shall deny the importance of legends, as social forces, in affecting the course of human history?

C. Vann Woodward

THE ATLANTA COMPROMISE

The next contribution treats Washington's program in the context of the disfranchisement movement in the South (1890–1910) and the general deterioration of black life. To picture Washington as the framer of "the modus vivendi of race relations" in such circumstances invites contrasting interpretations. He can be admired for realistic adjustment to threatening forces, or he can be criticized for willingness to give such a society a large degree of support through compromise. Although granting an element of tragic inevitability, C. Vann Woodward's dominant judgment of the man and his program is negative. Woodward teaches history at Yale University.

In place of the improvement in race relations promised by the disfranchisers as a result of their work there occurred a serious deterioration in almost all departments. In part this was a direct result of the methods used by the disfranchisers themselves. It became standard practice to support disfranchising campaigns with white-supremacy propaganda in which race hatred, suspicion, and jealousy were whipped up to a dangerous pitch. Politicians and newspapers cooperated in circulating Negro atrocity propaganda in the form of feature stories, cartoons, photographs, and posters.

[Charles B.] Aycock's campaign managers staged "White Supremacy Jubilees," in which hundreds of armed men paraded in red shirts. Ben Tillman came up from South Carolina to lend a hand, and sympathizers in Richmond told of 50,000 rounds of ammunition and a carload of firearms shipped to North Carolina a few days before the election of 1898. The Negroes remained quiet. Shortly after the whites of Wilmington won the election over a thoroughly cowed black majority, a mob of 400 men led by a former congressman demolished a Negro newspaper office, set it on fire, shot up the Negro district, killed 11 Negroes, wounded a large number, and chased hundreds into the woods. The leader of the mob was then elected mayor of the city. He proclaimed that "all further violence" should cease.

The sequel of the white-supremacy election in Georgia was sim-

From C. Vann Woodward, *Origins of the New South, 1877–1913*, pp. 350–360, 364–367.
 Footnotes omitted.

ilar, except that the Atlanta mobs looted, plundered, lynched, and murdered for four days. Race riots were not transient products of propaganda that passed with the campaigns. Three years after Tillman's disfranchising constitution went into effect some twelve Negroes were killed and several wounded during an election near his home. In 1900, two years after Louisiana adopted the grandfather clause, several mobs of white men roamed the city of New Orleans for three days, assaulting Negroes, looting, burning, and shooting. "The bloody horseplay of the mobs is full of instruction for the whole South," observed a New Orleans paper. "It is evident that the grand idea of white supremacy has become the stalking-horse of anarchy in this part of the Union."

But mob rule and race riots were not confined to one part of the Union. Within a month of the riot in New Orleans race riots occurred in New York City and Akron, Ohio. "Rioting in the North," according to a Negro historian, "was as vicious and almost as prevalent as in the South." With the cry, "Lincoln freed you, we'll show you where you belong," mobs took possession of Lincoln's home town of Springfield, Illinois, for two days in 1908 and waged brutal war on Negro life and property. Governor James K. Vardaman of Mississippi believed the experience would "cause people of the North to look with more toleration upon the methods employed by the Southern people."

Lynch law still took a savage toll of Negro life, though the number of lynchings in the country declined markedly from the peak reached in the nineties, a tendency happily not in conformity with the deterioration in race relations already noted. From 1889 to 1899 the average number of lynchings per year was 187.5, while in the following decade the number was 92.5, or less than half. Two other significant changes, however, occurred over the same period. The proportion of the lynchings taking place in the South increased from about 82 percent of the total in the earlier decade to about 92 percent in the period 1900–1909. At the same time, the proportion of lynching victims who were white decreased from 32.2 percent in the earlier decade to 11.4 percent in the latter. In other words, while lynching was decreasing in the South, it was decreasing more slowly than elsewhere. It was becoming an increasingly Southern and racial phenomenon.

In the first decade of the new century the extremists of Southern racism probably reached a wider audience, both within their own region and in the nation, than ever before. Thomas Dixon's popular "series of historical novels . . . on the race conflict," as the author described the trilogy, appeared between 1902 and 1907. One of them, *The Clansman,* a bitter indictment of the Negro, was dramatized on the stage and later on the screen for an even wider audience. Within the same five-year period were published such works as *"The Negro a Beast": or, "In the Image of God," The Caucasian and the Negro in the United States, The Color Line: A Brief in Behalf of the Unborn,* and *The Negro, A Menace to American Civilization,* books characterizing the race as degraded, bestial, and incapable of improvement. Between 1901 and 1909 Ben Tillman made "countless speeches" to Chautauqua audiences in all parts of the country, popularizing his racial views. The Negroes were "akin to the monkey," an "ignorant and debased and debauched race," declared the senator, and "To hell with the Constitution" if it interfered with lynching rapists. Ten years removed from the equalitarianism of his Populist days, Tom Watson was preaching "the superiority of the Aryan" and the "hideous, ominous, national menace" of Negro domination.

Southerners of the older generation were sometimes shocked at the fierce, ungovernable passions abroad in the South. Old Governor Oates thought "the change in public opinion in regard to the status of the Negro" was "most startling" in Alabama. "Why, sir," he exclaimed to the men of [J. Thomas] Heflin's generation, "the sentiment is altogether different now, when the Negro is doing no harm, why the people want to kill him and wipe him from the face of the earth." Edgar Gardner Murphy, one of the young humanitarians, deplored the same fateful trend. Extremists, he said, had proceeded "from an undiscriminating attack upon the Negro's ballot to a like attack upon his schools, his labor, his life—from the contention that no Negro shall vote to the contention that no Negro shall learn, that no Negro shall labor, and (by implication) that no Negro shall live." They ended by preaching an "all-absorbing autocracy of race," an "absolute identification of the stronger race with the very being of the state."

It was little wonder that in the speeches at a Southern conference on race problems held in Montgomery in 1900, "The overruling note sounded through all their words is pessimistic." According to a report of the conference, "Economically, morally, religiously, even physically, this sad key was struck time and again." The pessimism of the Montgomery conference persisted in the South for more than a decade. It pertained not only to the relations between races, but to the condition and progress of the Negro himself. William Garrott Brown reported evidence of the sentiment everywhere in his tour of the South in the spring of 1904. "The great majority of those with whom I have talked," he wrote, "declare that the Negro is not adapting himself to the new era, that he is not 'making good.' " Three Southern governors agreed that the Negro was deteriorating as a laborer. Two Northern investigators, Ray Stannard Baker and Albert Bushnell Hart, encountered sentiment of the same kind in the South. Three British travelers with experience in race problems of South Africa and the West Indies took an extremely discouraging view of relations in the South and saw in complete segregation or colonization of the Negro the only alternative to disaster. In the North it was "generally acknowledged" in 1903 "that the new Negro at the South is less industrious, less thrifty, less trustworthy, and less self-controlled than was his father or his grandfather."

Upon one opinion both whites and blacks, Northerners and Southerners appeared to be in agreement—that the transition from the slavery system to the caste system had been accomplished at the cost of grave deterioration in race relations. The intimacy of contact under slavery, especially that between the better type of both races, was succeeded by a harsh and rigid separation. Under slavery, as W. E. B. Du Bois, for example, pointed out, the two races sometimes "lived in the same home, shared in the family life, often attended the same church, and talked and conversed with each other," while under the caste system there was "little or no intellectual commerce" between races. "Ours is a world of inexorable divisions," wrote Murphy. Segregation had "made of our eating and drinking, our buying and selling, our labor and housing, our rents, our railroads, our orphanages and prisons, our recreations, our very institutions of religion, a problem of race as well as a problem of maintenance."

As the old type of Negro bred in slavery died off and the new type bred to caste increased, it seemed from within the white world that the Negro was losing his manners and his morals. Crowding into the slums of the cities in great numbers, the Negro population of Southern urban communities increased 32 percent between 1890 and 1900 and 35.8 percent in the following decade. As the urban Negro population increased, the proportion of crime committed by the race mounted—from 256 imprisoned per 100,000 Negro population in 1904 to 1,079 in 1910. Homicide rates in Atlanta, Birmingham, Memphis, and New Orleans reached appalling heights, and in the country at large the rate for colored persons became almost seven times the rate for whites.

The walls of segregation and caste were raised higher and higher by law and custom. Between 1900 and 1911 ten Southern states elaborated their laws requiring separation of races in transportation facilities, all of them including laws for street railways, and some for ferries and steamboats. Atlanta carried the tendency to the point of having separate elevators, though not by compulsion of law, by 1908. Between 1911 and 1914 the cities of Norfolk, Richmond, Ashland, Roanoke, Winston-Salem, Greensboro, Greenville, Augusta, and Atlanta passed ordinances segregating residential areas, and in 1913 an agitation was started by Clarence Poe of the *Progressive Farmer* for the segregation of farm lands in North Carolina.

On both sides of the wall of caste grew suspicion, uneasiness, and mistrust. Governor N. B. Broward told the Florida legislature in 1907 that "relations between the races are becoming more strained and acute." Writing in 1903, John Spencer Bassett concluded that "there is today more hatred of whites for blacks and blacks for whites than ever before." Speaking for the Negro, Charles W. Chesnutt said the same year that "the rights of the Negroes are at a lower ebb than at any time during the thirty-five years of their freedom, and the race prejudice more intense and uncompromising."

Over the years there evolved along with the caste system a generally accepted credo of race among white Southerners. In 1913 Thomas Pearce Bailey, a Southern educator, set down this "racial creed of the Southern people" with such candor and accuracy that it may serve as the best available summary:

1. *"Blood will tell."*
2. *The white race must dominate.*
3. *The Teutonic peoples stand for race purity.*
4. *The Negro is inferior and will remain so.*
5. *"This is a white man's country."*
6. *No social equality.*

7. *No political equality.*
8. *In matters of civil rights and legal adjustments give the white man, as opposed to the colored man, the benefit of the doubt; and under no circumstances interfere with the prestige of the white race.*
9. *In educational policy let the Negro have the crumbs that fall from the white man's table.*
10. *Let there be such industrial education of the Negro as will best fit him to serve the white man.*
11. *Only Southerners understand the Negro question.*
12. *Let the South settle the Negro question.*
13. *The status of peasantry is all the Negro may hope for, if the races are to live together in peace.*
14. *Let the lowest white man count for more than the highest Negro.*
15. *The above statements indicate the leadings of Providence.*

Not all Southern whites subscribed to the credo. Men of Murphy's school struggled in perplexity with the race question, always conscious that their motives and honesty might be impugned at home and abroad. Occasionally an outsider perceived and sympathized. "Deeply religious and intensely democratic as are the mass of whites," wrote Du Bois, "they feel acutely the false position in which the Negro problems place them." And Henry James breathed "a soft inward dirge over the eternal 'false position' of the afflicted South."

It was an ex-slave who eventually framed the modus vivendi of race relations in the New South. Booker T. Washington was more than the leader of his race. He was also a leader of white opinion with a national following, and he propounded not merely an educational theory but a social philosophy. The historical stage was set for the entrance of this remarkable man. It was a time when the hope born of Reconstruction had all but died for the Negro, when disfranchisement blocked his political advance and the caste system closed the door to integration in the white world, when the North had abandoned him to the South and the South was yielding to the clamor of her extremists. The defiant spirit of the old Negro leaders of emancipation and Reconstruction appeared increasingly quixotic under these circumstances.

The year 1895 marked both the death of Frederick Douglass and the acclaim of Booker Washington as the new leader of the race. The new doctrine came to be known as the "Atlanta Compromise," so called because in a famous speech before an audience of both races at the opening of the Atlanta Cotton States and International Exposition Washington gained instantaneous and nationwide recognition. "Nothing has happened since Henry Grady's immortal speech before the New England society in New York that indicates so profoundly the spirit of the New South," reported James Creelman in the New York *World.* The comparison was not without historical validity. Washington's life mission was to find a pragmatic compromise that would resolve the antagonisms, suspicions, and aspirations of "all three classes directly concerned—The Southern white man, the Northern white man, and the Negro." It proved, he admitted, "a difficult and at times a puzzling task." But he moved with consummate diplomacy, trading renunciation for concession and playing sentiment against interest.

To the white South (always "of the better class") he made a disarming concession. "I was born in the South," he said, "and I understand thoroughly the prejudices, the customs, the traditions of the South," and, he added, "I love the South." He had learned that "these prejudices are something that it does not pay to disturb," and "that the agitation of questions of social equality is the extremist folly." In the second place, he had early renounced Northern intervention and subscribed to Southern white views on that sore point. "My faith is that reforms in the South are to come from within," he said. He gave assurances that the Negro was more interested in industrial education and economic opportunity than in political rights and privileges, and he agreed that property and educational qualifications were desirable for the franchise. This did not mean that he gave up ultimate realization of any kind of rights, but he said nothing of ultimate aims. He appealed to sentiment, reminding the South of the "fidelity and love" of the Negro during the Civil War, and, identifying his race with the industrial hopes of the region, asked consideration for those who "without strikes and labor wars" had built up the South's industries.

To the Northern whites Washington, like the older type of Negro leader, came in search of friends for his race. He fully appreciated "those Christ-like philanthropists" who opened their pockets to his people. But instead of appealing to the agitators and doctrinaires he sought out the very type of men whom Southern whites were trying to interest in the development of Southern industry. He thus identified himself with the Eastern affiliations of the conservative

South. These Northern capitalists were actual or potential investors in the region and sometimes large-scale employers of black labor. Washington found his way with amazing ease among such men. He was more than once a guest aboard the yacht of H. H. Rogers of Standard Oil, a man he admired for his "practical grasp of public and social questions." William H. Baldwin, Jr., vice-president of the Southern Railway, employer of thousands of Negroes, spent hours with Washington over the latter's speeches, "going into minute details of verbal expression." He was an intimate of Collis P. Huntington, builder of Newport News and railway owner, and a guest of Andrew Carnegie at Skibo Castle. Again and again he pointed out the practical significance of his message for labor problems. Speaking to a convention of industrialists in Alabama, he said: "It is here alone, by reason of the presence of the Negro, that capital is freed from the tyranny and despotism that prevents you from employing whom you please." Elsewhere he expressed unfriendliness for labor unions, revolutionary tactics, and socialism, and professed devotion to the laissez-faire theory of government.

To his own race he preached a gospel of conservatism, patience, and material progress. "I fear that the Negro race lays too much stress on its grievances and not enough on its opportunities," he told a Fisk University audience. The prejudices and injustices of the caste system and the barbarities of the mob (subjects he rarely mentioned) should be met with "few words and conservative action"; it was wise "to suffer in silence" and exercise "patience, forbearance, and self-control in the midst of trying conditions." He was "not asking that the Negro act the coward," he added; "we are not cowards." The friendship of the conservative, upper-class Southern whites and wealthy Northern capitalists, however, offered more hope than agitation and protest. Security and recognition would follow material gain, and his people should begin not at the top, but at the bottom, in both education and industry, and work up in the American way. "This country demands that every race shall measure itself by the American standard," he said. All Negroes admitted that "the black man has far better opportunity to rise in his business in the South than in the North."

The power this man came to wield over the destinies of his race and over the New South stood in striking contrast to his incorrigible humility. The man who abjured "social equality" in the South moved in circles of the elite in the North and aristocracy abroad that were opened to extremely few Southern whites. The man who disparaged the importance of political power for his race came to exercise political power such as few if any Southern white men of his time enjoyed. A sampling of his vast correspondence indicates the extent of this power. As chief patronage referee in the South for federal appointments during the administrations of Roosevelt and Taft, he was consulted on virtually all Negro appointments and on the merits of many Southern whites. He corrected the messages of presidents and blighted careers by his silence. His influence was sought in all parts of the United States, and his power over the Negro press was known and feared. More directly he influenced the distribution of the vast patronage of Northern philanthropy.

During the two decades from 1895 to Washington's death in 1915, Negro thought and policy in matters of race relations, labor, education, and business enterprise conformed in large measure to the Tuskegee philosophy. This was not due so much to the genius and personal influence of Booker Washington as to the remarkable congeniality between his doctrines and the dominant forces of his age and society, forces that found an eloquent voice in the brown orator, but that would have made themselves felt in any case. . . .

Booker Washington was certainly not responsible for the Negro's diminishing position in the crafts, his exclusion from unions, and his employment as a strikebreaker. Finding Negro labor in this plight, he plotted what seemed to him the most practical course. "The Negro is not given to 'strikes,' " he said. "His policy is to leave each individual free to work when, where, and for whom he pleases." He pronounced trade unionism "that form of slavery which prevents a man from selling his labor to whom he pleases on account of his color." The Negro worker should rely not upon collective bargaining but upon the paternalism of well-disposed employers. "You should remember," he reminded Southern industrialists, "that you are in debt to the black man for furnishing you with labor that is almost a stranger to strikes."

After the strike of 1908 was crushed, the big Alabama operators, Tennessee Coal and Iron (United States Steel) and the De Bardeleben Coal Company, introduced an elaborate welfare and educational program for their labor. In order to convert illiterate common Negro workers into efficient skilled workers and assure a stable bulwark against unionism, the operators built schools, hospitals, welfare and recreational centers, and improved housing on a grand scale. This welfare capitalism, according to a journal of the Hampton Institute, was working toward "the same ends as those which Hampton and Tuskegee and the whole system of education they represent are striving for. Moreover, in many cases, these parallel efforts and aims are drawn closer together by the fact that Hampton and Tuskegee graduates are having a large part in such work." Alumni of these institutions did in large measure direct the program of welfare work and company unionism, and one of the companies established annual scholarships to Tuskegee for children of its employees.

Washington's "industrial" education philosophy was an integral part of his labor philosophy. By teaching the crafts he hoped to encourage the Negro to recoup to some extent his position of post-emancipation days. "A large element of people at the South favored manual training for the Negro," he said, "because they were wise enough to see that the South was largely free from the restrictive influences of the Northern trade unions, and that such organizations would secure little hold in the South so long as the Negro kept abreast in intelligence and skill with the same class of people elsewhere." Such a concept, he believed, would appeal to men of wealth and position who "see the close connection between labor, industry, education and political institutions." Brickmaking, blacksmithing, wheelwrighting, harness making, basketry, tinsmithing—the type of crafts taught at Tuskegee—had more relevance to the South of Booker Washington's boyhood than to the South of United States Steel, but his teachings of orderliness, cleanliness, discipline, and a "cooperative spirit" had relevance for the new era as well.

The enormous vogue that industrial education enjoyed among Negro educators in the South and the extent to which the older institutions, some of them without enthusiasm, fell in with the movement are to be explained to some degree by the influence that Washington exercised over the distribution of Northern philanthropic funds. There is considerable evidence to support the view of an unfriendly critic that Washington's influence became so powerful that "almost no Negro institution could collect funds without the recommendation or acquiescence of Mr. Washington."

One of the most important developments in Negro history, not to say the history of the South, was the rise of a whole separate system of society and economy on the other side of the color line. Excluded from equal participation in the white world, the Negro constructed a copy of it—of its churches, schools, banks, theaters, professions, services, and other institutions. Beginning as a largely undifferentiated class of former slaves, the race was soon sorted out into all the social and economic classes of the white capitalistic society upon which it was modeled. And as in the white society of the time, the businessman occupied a foremost rank of prestige. The Negro middle and upper class was caught in the curious dilemma of suffering from segregation and at the same time having a vested interest in it, since it provided what opportunity and protection from white competition the Negro did enjoy in the uphill struggle for the patronage and business of his own race. The Negro middle class, like the working class, therefore stood in need of a philosophy that could somehow reconcile the disadvantages and the advantages of segregation.

In 1900 Booker Washington took the leadership of the rising Negro business community of the country by organizing the Negro Business League and serving as president for several years. By 1907 there were 320 local Business Leagues with a wide influence in the Negro world. In speeches and books Washington held up the self-made black capitalist as a hero of his race. The businessman's gospel of free enterprise, competition, and laissez-faire never had a more loyal exponent than the master of Tuskegee. Washington went back to a bygone day for his economic philosophy. It consisted of the mousetrap-maker-and-beaten-path maxims of thrift, virtue, enterprise, and free competition. It was the faith by which the white middle-class preceptors of his youth had explained success, combined with a belief that, as he expressed it, "there is little race prejudice in the American dollar." Washington's individualistic doctrine never took into account the realities of mass production, industrial integration, financial combination, and monopoly. Since the Negro capitalist was nearly always a small capitalist, he was among the first to suffer and the last to rally under the new pressures. He was largely confined to petty trade and a declining proportion of that.

The shortcomings of the Atlanta Compromise, whether in education, labor, or business, were the shortcomings of a philosophy that dealt with the present in terms of the past. Not that a certain realism was lacking in the Washington approach. It is indeed hard to see how he could have preached or his people practiced a radically different philosophy in his time and place. The fact remains that Washington's training school, and the many schools he inspired, taught crafts and attitudes more congenial to the premachine age than to the twentieth century; that his labor doctrine was a compound of individualism, paternalism, and antiunionism in an age of collective labor action; and that his business philosophy was an anachronism. It is hardly necessary to add that white leaders of the South adhered pretty generally to the same doctrines and that the larger part of them subscribed to Washington's race policy.

Samuel R. Spencer, Jr.

THE ACHIEVEMENT OF BOOKER T. WASHINGTON

Like Woodward a white Southerner by birth, Samuel R. Spencer, Jr., reaches a far more favorable verdict in this passage from his 1955 biography of Washington. Spencer emphasizes Washington's sharpened public criticisms of racial injustice in the years between the formation of the NAACP and his death (1910–1915). The positive judgment, however, rests less on admiration for this tactical change than on the argument that Washington made an intelligently pragmatic adjustment of means to possibilities. Implicit here is the assumption that Washington stood fundamentally for the same goals as the integrationist movement that was gaining power in the 1950s. Spencer is president of Davidson College.

Washington himself, realizing that discrimination was mounting in many areas despite the Negro's economic and cultural advancement, moved toward a stronger position on civil rights during the last few years of his life. He had always defended the Negro's right

From Samuel R. Spencer, Jr., *Booker T. Washington and the Negro's Place in American Life,* pp. 190–193, 195–201.

to enter complaints "in a conservative and sensible manner," but later his own utterances became less and less conservative. "I am not deceived," he stated emphatically to the National Colored Teachers' Association in 1911. "I do not overlook the wrongs that often perplex and embarrass us in this country. I condemn with all the strength of my nature the barbarous habit of lynching a human being, whether black or white, without legal trial. I condemn any practice in any state that results in not enforcing the law with a certainty and justice, regardless of race or color." A year later, his article for the *Century* magazine entitled, "Is the Negro Having a Fair Chance?" left no doubt that the answer was, "No."

This shift was perceptible all along the line. Discrimination in public education particularly galled him. As early as 1905, his interest in this question had prompted him to ask Villard to publicize one situation in which the Negro's share of state funds for education amounted to a startlingly small fraction of the amount allotted to whites. "As no color line is drawn in the courts in the matter of punishing crime," he said, "neither should any color line be drawn in the opportunity to get education in the public schools." Over and over again he condemned the inequity in state appropriations for whites and Negroes, pointing out that in some instances more money was paid for the labor of Negro convicts under the convict lease system than for Negro teachers.

As he grew older, his willingness to abide by Southern custom became somewhat frayed. On one occasion he went onto the stage of a theater in Tampa to speak, only to find that Negroes and whites in the audience had been separated by a row of sheets hung down the aisle. Visibly annoyed, he said without a word of introduction or greeting, "I have traveled all over this country and in many foreign lands, but this is the first time that I have ever seen white people and colored people separated by sheets. Now, before I begin my remarks, I want that thing taken down from there." When the sheets came down, he went on with his speech.

He had just as little patience with the residential segregation laws which were going into effect all over the South. "You cannot help the Negro very much and you do not help the white man very much by yielding to the temptation of trying to shut the race off in certain segregated parts of American cities," he told a Battle Creek audience in 1914. Such legislation, he declared, was not only unnecessary, but unjust. "Every thoughtful Negro" resented a segregated system, because his people never got equal health facilities, lighting, cleanliness, police protection, or the use of public services like libraries and hospitals—though they were compelled to pay taxes on the same basis as the whites. The Negro knew, he said in a prophetic phrase, that segregation meant "an unfair deal."

He also inveighed against discrimination in travel accommodations and did his best to hold railroad companies to the spirit and letter of the "separate but equal" principle. His approach, as always, was reasonable. He urged Negroes, for example, to keep themselves clean and neat while traveling so as to remove any grounds for criticism. But on "Railroad Days," which he organized through the Negro Business League, he also urged Negro patrons to lay before railroad-company officials specific abuses and suggestions for improvement.

That Southern justice made the Negro consider the courts places of punishment rather than protection also disturbed him. He sent to the press articles asking jury representation for Negroes and spoke out against the practice of "arresting so many of our people for petty and trivial offenses." The convict lease system, under which prisoners were hired out to persons who cared little that they were human beings—a custom which opened the way to flagrant abuse of Negroes in particular—drew Washington's fire. He also protested against another form of slavery, the peonage permitted by Southern contract-labor laws. Since economic independence for the Negro farmer had always been one of his central objectives, he considered the Supreme Court decision of 1911, voiding the labor law of Alabama, "the most important national event that has occurred within recent years."

Above all he continued to hammer at lynching. Though he rarely failed to point out that progress was being made (the number of lynchings per year had been decreasing slowly since 1892), he did not fail to condemn where condemnation was due. By coincidence he happened to be speaking in Jacksonville, Florida, shortly after a murder had been committed by two Negroes. Washington refused to cancel the engagement; instead he delivered a strong denunciation of lynching to the accompaniment of shouts from a would-be lynch mob on its way to the prison nearby. . . .

To a generation of white Americans who had never known any

Negro leader other than Booker T. Washington, his death left a curious void in the accepted pattern of thinking about race problems. In the hearts and minds of the vast majority of his own race as well, there was no one to replace him. Still, the end of his personal leadership did pave the way for the kind of harmony for which Washington himself had so often spoken. "We must have a united race," he had said in one of his last words of advice to Negroes. "We must have men big enough and broad enough . . . to lay aside all personal differences, all petty jealousies," men "who are willing to lay their lives upon the altar of our race's welfare as a sacrifice." Less impatient at the end with what he termed "abstract" protest, he recognized that organizations of all kinds—"the religious, the educational, the political, the literary, the secret and fraternal bodies, as well as those that deal with the civil rights of our people"—had to work together to solve the Negro's complex problem.

General agreement on the principles to be emphasized in a cooperative program for race advancement came about through a conference of distinguished Negro leaders held near Amenia, New York, the year after Washington's death. One in their desire to forget old factional alignments and promote racial unity, the delegates agreed to encourage all forms of education for the Negro, work for his enfranchisement, and to recognize special circumstances affecting Negro work in the South. They openly accepted as their goal complete and unqualified integration of the Negro into American society.

This had been Washington's goal as well, but realizing that the Negro could do little at that time to block the current of discrimination, he had put his emphasis on the practical and the possible. Like a seasoned boxer, he never took the full force of his opponent's attack, but rolled with the punch, attempting to protect himself and his race for more effective battles later. His policy was distinctly realistic. He began by looking at his race with a critical and remarkably objective eye, admitting the prevalence of ignorance, immorality, and irresponsibility; thereby he disarmed his white listeners and gave logic and common sense to his proposed remedies.

His strategy was just as realistic as his estimate of the situation. "I do not deny," he wrote, "that I was frequently tempted during the early years of my work, to join in the denunciation of the evils and injustice that I saw about me. But when I thought the matter over, I saw that such a course would accomplish no good and that it would do a great deal of harm." Washington believed that his alternative approach was not only constructive but aggressive. "I felt that the millions of Negroes needed something more than to be reminded of their sufferings and of their political rights, that they needed to do more than defend themselves," he explained. For obvious reasons the average Southern Negro could take no part in agitation or protest; he could only vaguely hope that he or his children might eventually benefit from efforts carried on in his behalf by men far removed from his day-to-day existence. But Washington fired the imagination of even the poorest tenant farmer by offering him an active role in a creative, dynamic program which affected him personally and directly. By setting tangible goals and demonstrating how they could be reached, he pointed the way to a better life for the Negro in his own home and community. Furthermore, a wealth of evidence existed to show that the program got results which were understandable and real.

The really new element in Washington's program was his emphasis on economic independence and security. Here he was making a decided break with the past, and part of the opposition to him sprang from the unwillingness of many "radicals" to give up traditional political remedies as the exclusive means to race advancement. Many did not recognize, as Washington did, that the color line was being redrawn to exclude Negroes from occupations which had been theirs by custom. Washington correctly concluded that many Negroes considered economic opportunity more essential than the ballot, social equality, or other objectives of those who pinned their faith primarily on protest. In his struggle to keep the door of economic opportunity open, he was fighting for an objective closely related to that of "Fair Employment Practices" legislation more than a quarter of a century later.

By overemphasizing industrial education, he highlighted the fact that economic progress offered a means to full integration no less important than political means, and that the two complemented each other. Furthermore, by schooling his race in such traditional American virtues as hard work, thrift, integrity, responsibility, and initiative, he helped Negroes forge a common bond with their white neighbors. His predecessors had taken their lead from Thomas

Jefferson. Washington took his from Benjamin Franklin, and by doing so, introduced a strain into the Negro's Americanism which strengthened his claim to full citizenship.

Unfortunately, his economic emphasis had its weaknesses as well as its strength. His accurate judgment that the Negro's economic ills contributed to his vulnerability in other areas was partly offset by the fact that he conceived of economics in terms more valid for Franklin's day than for the twentieth century. Though he accurately forecast that for many years the vast majority of Negroes would have to train themselves for the basic occupations, he did not foresee developments which were to alter drastically the nature of these industries. In the first place, he had geared his program to the training of craftsmen and small entrepreneurs, whereas twentieth-century industry demanded labor for the mass-production jobs of the assembly line. In the second place, he failed to see that mechanical farming and consolidation were fast eliminating the necessity for the large agricultural labor force which he had considered a constant in the economic equation, and that the urban migration of Negroes which he so heartily disapproved was only part of a general population shift from farm to city. Still, the later adjustment of Tuskegee and other industrial schools to the needs of a new era showed that these weaknesses could be overcome.

Of more serious consequence were two assumptions on which he based his hope for the elimination of discrimination. He believed, first, that successful competition with whites in the economic realm would raise the Negro in the estimation of the white man and thereby break down prejudice. Experience was to prove just the opposite, especially among the large group of white people closest to the Negro in the social and economic scale.

He also assumed, optimistically, that the tendency of the "best" white people to treat Negroes differently depending on their education, character, and general merit would continue. This tendency, which had allowed a successful Negro like Lewis Adams to command the respect of the entire Tuskegee community, led Washington to believe that the problem of race would be solved as the number of Lewis Adamses could be multiplied. When the advent of discriminatory laws lumped all Negroes together regardless of individual merit, Washington's faith in "progress" made him continue to insist, even while he spoke out more sharply against discrimination, that race relations were steadily improving.

Perhaps the most justified criticism is that Washington's monopoly of leadership prevented those with a different point of view from working effectively in their own way while he continued to work in his. Since the nature of his program and his method of carrying it out kept him from emphasizing complete integration forcefully or in sufficiently specific terms, it was desirable that others do so in order to keep before coming generations of Negroes an ideal and a hope for the future. The rallying to this standard immediately after Washington's death showed that his strong influence had at least to some extent stood in the way of this self-assertion.

Still, most of Washington's weaknesses must be qualified. It is difficult, for example, to condemn him for faith in his fellow man; yet one of the flaws in his program was the fact that it relied too heavily on the cooperation and enlightenment of the Negro's white neighbor. Washington realized that he was taking a chance. "Much will depend," he wrote, "upon the sense of justice which can be kept alive in the breast of the American people." Had white Americans, and particularly white Southerners, been willing to carry out their part of the bargain which Washington offered at Atlanta in 1895, their continuing plea for gradualism would have carried more weight. Instead, only when faced with threatened elimination of the entire segregation system half a century later did most Southern states hasten to implement the "separate but equal" principle to which they had so long paid lip service.

If the years did not fully justify Washington's faith in the white man, what of his faith in his own race? He said many times that he was proud of being a Negro, and that he would not exchange the Negro's future for the future of any race on earth. By midcentury, thirty-five years after Washington's death, the Negro had by no means reached the promised land. Still denied opportunities in many areas of American life, he had earned a name for himself in the fields of entertainment, athletics, and the arts, but had produced only a few men and women of national stature in such areas as statecraft, industry, scholarship, and law. In Washington's phrase, the Negro was still passing through the "severe American crucible." But obvious cracks were appearing in the walls of prejudice and discrimination, and by 1950 the Negro could hope with more realism than at any time since emancipation for the day of liberty and justice for all.

That Booker T. Washington looked forward to this day cannot be doubted; he accepted half a loaf, not as a permanent settlement, but as a means toward obtaining the whole loaf later. To criticize his methods is to make the facile assumption that he had some choice in the matter. He did what was possible, given the time and place in which he lived, and did it to the utmost.

Furthermore, had he offered nothing in the way of precept, he would still have given a great deal by example. He practiced what he preached: courage, self-reliance, integrity, humility, dignity, and consideration for his fellow man. Completely free from race prejudice, he had the ability to lift himself above the level of petty hatreds and selfish ambition. "More and more," he said late in his life, "we must learn to think not in terms of race or color or language or religion or political boundaries, but in terms of humanity." Such vision belonged not to the past, but to the future. In an age which was just beginning to learn that the color of a man's skin has nothing to do with his potential contribution to society, the entire human family benefited from the life of such a man as Booker T. Washington.

Harold Cruse

BEHIND THE BLACK POWER SLOGAN

In spite of interpretations such as Spencer's, Booker T. Washington's reputation was in decline among black Americans during the civil rights movement of the 1950s and 1960s. Then came the dramatic emergence in 1966 of the slogan "Black Power." It began to seem possible that Washington deserved recognition as a forerunner of those blacks who rejected the integrationists' program and stressed black economic and cultural autonomy. Harold Cruse, professor of history at the University of Michigan, Ann Arbor, argues that Black Power does indeed represent a continuation of Washing-

ton's essential ideology. For the full exchange between Herbert Aptheker and Eugene Genovese to which Cruse refers, the student should consult the panel on "The Legacy of Slavery and the Roots of Black Nationalism," in Studies on the Left *6 (1966): 3–65.*

The recent Black Power Conference in Newark, New Jersey, produced so many resolutions of an economic, political and cultural nature that they cannot be quoted or analyzed here. But previous to this, the Harlem CORE organization published last winter an issue of their magazine *Rights and Reviews* called the "Black Power Issue" (Winter 1966/67). A number of spokesmen described Black Power as follows:

Julian Bond:

> *Black Power must be seen as a natural extension of the work of the civil rights movement over the past few years. From the courtroom to the streets in favor of integrated public facilities; from the streets onto backwoods roads in quest of the right to vote; from the ballot box to the meat of politics, the organization of voters into self-interest units.*

Floyd McKissick:

> *The doctrine of Black Power is this new thrust which seeks to achieve economic power and to develop political movements that would make changes that are vast and significant.*

Lorenzo Thomas:

> *Our attempts to think out loud have often been taken up by the news and represented to the nation as our plan of action. Black Power, for instance. Forget Black Power. There is more to it than that, and our life might perhaps become the truth of the moment we seek without the need of slogans. In times past people were content to* experience *their lives, but today one is not really living unless one has a program.*

Ralph Edwards:

> *Any true proponent of Black Power should be* committed *to a special kind of violence*—defensive violence. *Yes, defensive violence as opposed to the aggressive violence heaped upon us.*

(It is not clear whether Edwards considers defensive violence and the urban rebellions of Watts and Detroit, etc., as one and the same thing. If he does, then we have a new form of American revolutionary anarchism which demands a more critical examination.)

Yosef Ben-Jochannan:

> *What is Black Power? It is that power which black peoples had in Africa*

before the invasion and domination of Africa by the Europeans under the guise of "taking Christianity to the heathen Africans."

(This definition of Black Power comes from the old Garveyite back-to-Africa movement. At a Harlem Black Nationalist Youth Conference in May 1965, this tendency said that any Negro who opposed "back-to-Africa" with fighting for equality in the US is an Uncle Tom–House Nigger. It is not clear how the Garveyite tendency views Black Power in the USA.)

Roy Inniss:

There is a compelling need to emphasize the socio-psychological aspect of Black Power. We can cry "Black Power" until doomsday . . . [*but*] *until black people accept values meaningful to themselves, there can be no completely effective organizing for the development of black power.*

(Note that both Inniss and Ben-Jochannan consider Denmark Vesey, Harriet Tubman, Nat Turner, Marcus Garvey, Elijah Muhammad, and Malcolm X as representative leaders of black people in America, but *not* Booker T. Washington and W. E. B. Du Bois.)

So much for Harlem CORE's definition of Black Power—and there are other definitions to come. However, the *Amsterdam News* of July 29, 1967, asks the question, What was accomplished at the Black Power Conference? It then says, "Despite the encomiums of success from many at the conference, a definitive meaning for the phrase Black Power eluded circumscription and remained . . . dangerously ambiguous." So let us examine certain other attitudes on Black Power.

In the New York *Post* series on Black Power (week of June 19), Bayard Rustin says of the slogan:

Three times Negroes have engaged in these politics. First with Booker T. Washington at the turn of the century, after the failure of Reconstruction. His slogans were "Self-Help" and "Drop Down Your Buckets Where You Are." Then with Marcus Garvey in the 1920's, during the racist regression just after World War I. Garvey had two slogans: "Build the Negro Economy" and "Back to Africa." Now aren't they inconsistent? Slogan politics are always inconsistent.

Another critic, Tom Kahn, along with Rustin believes that "Black Power is conservative, is a retreat." An NAACP official, Henry Lee Moon, thinks Black Power is a "naive expression, at worst diabolical, in the sense that at worst it's designed to create chaos." He added, "Actually people with power never speak of power." Roy Wilkins agrees generally with Moon.

John R. Lewis, a former chairman of SNCC, does not see any hope in the future of Black Power. However, a present member of the leading echelons of SNCC, Ivanhoe Donaldson, when asked by Rustin what kind of *program* SNCC offers for Black Power, answered, "I'm not sure we have to justify ourselves with a program in this country. We have a program because we have a base." This reply brings us face to face with one of the most challenging problems of the Black Power slogan. We have a situation wherein Stokely Carmichael, who has been the most vocal exponent of Black Power within SNCC, is described as a spokesman whose strong points are not structure and plan (i.e. program); his gift is speech. The same was true of Malcolm X, who could inspire but who did not plan, structure, or plot an organized course. Martin Luther King believes that the slogan of Black Power is "really a cry of disappointment, it is a cry of hurt, it is a cry of despair."

What really lies behind all of the varied and conflicting reactions to the slogan of Black Power? Strange to conclude, there happens to be a certain validity in nearly all these reactions. For any slogan that has not been adequately defined, there will be reasons for doubt as well as for strong support. Bayard Rustin has put his finger on something very crucial about the Black Power slogan. *Black Power is nothing but the economic and political philosophy of Booker T. Washington given a 1960s militant shot in the arm and brought up to date.* The curious fact about it is that the very last people to admit that Black Power is militant Booker T-ism are the Black Power theorists themselves. A Roy Inniss and a Ben-Jochannan, for example, will characterize Booker T. Washington as a historical conservative (if not an Uncle Tom) and refuse to recognize him as a part of their black nationalist tradition. Both of them will, of course, uphold Marcus Garvey with much nationalist fervor—completely overlooking the fact that Garvey was a disciple of Booker T. Washington. When Garvey came to the United States in 1916, he came to see Booker T. Washington, who had died in 1915. Both

Garvey and his wife Amy-Jacques Garvey thought: "Since the death of Booker T. Washington, there was no one with a positive and practical uplift program for the masses—North or South."[1] But the NAACP "radicals" of the time, especially the Du Bois tendency, were staunchly opposed to Washington's program. Later on all the Marxist Communist and Socialist tendencies combined to relegate poor old conservative Booker T. Washington to historical purgatory for having failed to conduct himself like a respectable militant or radical in Negro affairs. Dr. Herbert Aptheker, the chief Communist party historian on the Negro, for example, also became the chief castigator of Washington. The prejudice of the political left against Washington accounts in part for Bayard Rustin's denigration of Black Power in 1967, the only difference being that Rustin is perceptive enough to see that Black Power is, clearly, Booker T-ism. Few Marxist Socialists and other radicals will see the truth of this when they honor Black Power with a political economy. Even Bayard Rustin did not point out that W. E. B. Du Bois put forth a program for economic and political Black Power in his autobiography, *Dusk of Dawn* (1940) when he clearly enunciated his abandonment of the NAACP philosophy. Du Bois did not call his plan "Black Power"; he called it a plan for the Negro "economic cooperative commonwealth." The radical left, especially Aptheker, will also overlook this fact in their estimate of Du Bois's career. A Bayard Rustin did not see that Du Bois, along with Washington and Garvey (with whom Du Bois fought bitterly) also had a "self-help" phase of "Drop Down Your Buckets Where You Are." This phase has (and will) always recur in Negro life from era to era. In fact, this nationalist (self-help, self-identification, black unity) phase appeared simultaneously with the civil rights–radical protest tradition of which Frederick Douglass was the first outstanding historical prophet. The spokesman for the black nationalist phase of Douglass's day was Martin R. Delany, who was, for a time, Douglass's co-editor of the abolitionist newspaper *The North Star.* Thus the civil rights protest phase of Negro leadership began simultaneously with its opposition, the black nationalist phase, within the abolitionist movement.

The ambiguity, the lingering vagueness over the exact definition of Black Power is rooted, first of all, in an exceedingly faulty and

[1] Amy-Jacques Garvey, *Garvey and Garveyism,* published by the author, 1963, p. 26.

unscientific interpretation of Negro historical trends in the United States. This faulty interpretation of black social trends in America negates any attempt to deal *theoretically* with the Black Power concept in any definitive way. In other words, the subjectively faulty way in which Negro history has been interpreted by all conservative, liberal, and left schools has cut the ground from under any possibility of setting up a theoretical structure around both the nationalist–separatist–black power trends and the civil rights protest–integrationist trends. The result is *the black American as part of an ethnic group has no definitive social theory relative to* his *status, presence, or impact on American society.* It is for this reason that when a Black Power phase repeats itself in the sixties, it comes at such a crucial moment in the history of American race relations that a Black Power movement cannot escape being taken over and commandeered by a *revolutionary anarchist tendency.* Coming at a moment of racial crisis in America, there has been no school of *social theory* prepared in advance for Black Power that could channel the concept along the lines of positive, radical, and constructive social change. In this regard, the most derelict and irresponsible school of thought has been the Marxist tendency in America. The abject forty-five-year-old failure of the American Marxist movement to comprehend the meaning of the Negro presence in America amounts to an historical disaster of the first magnitude.

Consider the case of the leading Marxist historian (on blacks and whites alike), the perennial Dr. Herbert Aptheker of the Communist party. This historian published his first pamphlet on Negroes about thirty years ago and still has not grasped the basic fundamentals of Negro social development to this day. I quote Aptheker's comments in *Studies on the Left* to illustrate this problem:

> *I do not find an "enormous influence" exerted by Booker T. Washington upon black nationalism. And Genovese's acceptance of Mr. Washington's own public rationalizations for his program of acquiescence is extraordinary. Thus, Washington justified his insistence that Negroes avoid political activity on the grounds that they were not experienced in such activity; but this was not why he put forth the program of acquiescence. He put forth that program because of the insistence of Baldwin of the Southern Railroad, and Carnegie and Rockefeller who subsidized the Tuskegee machine. And they insisted on that program for obvious reasons.*

The differences between Du Bois and Washington were basic and not simply tactical, and no single quotation from a 1903 essay will change that. Du Bois rejected subordination; Washington accepted it. Du Bois rejected colonialism; Washington assumed its continuance. Du Bois was intensely critical of capitalism, long before World War I; Washington worshipped it . . .

. . . Further, integration is necessary to this nation exactly because the Negro is integral to it. . . .

. . . The realities of black nationalism are exaggerated by Genovese; the power and force of Negro-white efforts are minimized by him.[2]

One could quote more, but this is enough to demonstrate that Herbert Aptheker is one of the most un-Marxist Marxists quotable these days when it comes to heaping radical mystification on the Negro movement. In native American terms, Aptheker's Marxism is European "book" Marxism; hence his approach to the Negro is totally lacking in imagination, depth, or perception. For one to see no "enormous influence" of Washington on black nationalists is like seeing no enormous influence of Hegel or the Greeks—Democritus or Heraclitus—on Karl Marx's dialectical materialism. For Aptheker to quibble in 1966 about Washington's avoidance of political activity throws absolutely no light at all on the nature of Washington's Tuskegee Machine in 1905. This machine got a Negro, Charles Anderson, appointed to the post of collector of Internal Revenue in 1905, which was no mean achievement in the New York City of those days. Aptheker does not distinguish between what Washington said (tactically) and what he *did* practically, both North and South. In 1900 he established the National Negro Business League, which still exists in Washington, D.C. Long before Du Bois's Niagara Movement (which sold itself out inside the NAACP) Washington was organizing Southern Negro farmers, sharecroppers, and small businessmen through yearly Tuskegee conferences. During the same period, it was Washington's protegés in the North, Philip A. Payton and others, who organized the Afro-American Realty Company, which waged a most militant economic struggle against entrenched white real estate interests in order to win living space in the previously all-white Harlem of 1900. The winning of Harlem

[2] *Studies on the Left*, Vol. 6, No. 6, 1966, pp. 33, 34.

and better housing for Negroes between 1903 and World War I was a direct outgrowth of Washington's National Negro Business League, of which both Payton and Anderson were members.

Booker T. Washington built a school in Alabama, a permanent, lasting, and functional institution in the Deep South. Aptheker is rather naive about Southern life-realities in 1900 if he thinks that one built institutions in Dixie without "acquiescing" to something sacred within the status quo. Apparently Aptheker does not have much respect for such all-black institutions where they are socially necessary and tactical compromises are required to create them. What Aptheker says reveals that not only does he not understand the social imperatives behind these institutions, he also does not understand the nature and imperatives of black nationalism as a trend (and this is not to imply that he *must* be sympathetic to black nationalism). The point is that as a *historian* he should understand certain facts that he doesn't. Marcus Garvey had so much admiration for what Washington had done with Tuskegee that he wanted to get his advice on how such a school could be developed in Jamaica, B.W.I. When Garvey established his U.N.I.A. headquarters in New York, Emmett J. Scott, who was Washington's personal secretary at Tuskegee, became a close working colleague of Garvey's. Now since black nationalists admire the memory of Garvey, it stands to reason historically and ideologically that Washington's influence on black nationalism was rather enormous. But Aptheker professes not to understand this phenomenon; and this is because Aptheker refuses to understand what black nationalism is all about. A historian *must* understand *all* social phenomena out of history or stop pretending to be a historian. Negro historians are not much better. Many of the young black nationalists of today are misinformed on the real meaning of Booker T. Washington's role because of the obfuscation that permeates Negro historiography and that has prevented the development of a black social theory on historical and class trends in Negro history. . . .

[The] Nation of Islam was nothing but a form of Booker T. Washington's economic self-help, black unity, bourgeois hard work, law-abiding, vocational training, stay-out-of-the-civil-rights-struggle agitation, separate-from-the-white-man, etc., etc., morality. The only difference was that Elijah Muhammad added the potent factor of the Muslim religion to a race, economic, and social philosophy of which the first prophet was none other than Booker T. Washington. Elijah also added an element of "hate Whitey" ideology which Washington, of course, would never have accepted. The reason that a Washington would have considered a Malcolm X a madman was that Washington practiced moderate accommodationist separatism while Malcolm and Elijah preached militant separatism. *But it is still the same separatism whose quality only changes from one era to another.* The Marxists and other radicals cannot see that when Booker T. Washington said to the Southern whites—"In all things purely social we can be as *separate* as the five fingers, yet one as the hand in all things essential to mutual progress"—that Washington was saying in 1895 what Elijah Muhammad was to say under changed conditions sixty-five years later. They were both prophets of a kind of nationalist-separatism, one moderate, one assertive. When Malcolm X was in the Nation of Islam he, too, believed in this separatism, but it was a militant separatism that Malcolm X preached at the behest of Elijah Muhammad. Washington preached a form of separatism which laid the ideological groundwork for both Garvey and Muhammad. But can anybody be serious if he thinks that Booker T. Washington could have preached Muhammad's kind of militant separatism *in 1895 in the deep Alabama South?* . . .

The Negro is politically compromised today because he owns nothing. He can exert little political power because he owns nothing. He has little voice in the affairs of state because he owns nothing. The fundamental reason why the Negro bourgeois-democratic revolution has been aborted is because American capitalism has prevented the development of a black class of capitalist owners of institutions and economic tools. To take one crucial example, Negro radicals today are severely hampered in their tasks of educating the black masses on political issues because Negroes do not own any of the necessary means of propaganda and communication. The Negro owns no printing presses, he has no stake in the networks of the means of communication. Inside his own communities he does not own the houses he lives in, the property he lives on, nor the wholesale and retail sources from which he buys his commodities. He does not own the edifices in which he enjoys culture and entertainment or in which he socializes. In capitalist society, an individual or group that does not own anything is powerless. In capitalist society, a group that has not experienced the many sides of capitalistic development, that has not learned the techniques of business ownership, or the intricacies of profit and loss, or the responsibilities of managing even small or medium enterprises, has not been prepared in the social disciplines required to transcend the functional limitations of the capitalistic order. Thus, to paraphrase Lenin, it is not that the Negro suffers so much from capitalism in America, but from a *lack of capitalistic development.* This is why the Black Power Conference heard so many procapitalistic resolutions, such as the old "buy black" slogan of Harlem's 1930s nationalist movements. Not a single one of the economic resolutions of this conference was new; they were all voiced ten, twenty, thirty, forty years ago. The followers of Washington raised them, the followers of Garvey raised them, even Du Bois raised them in his nationalistic moments.

Louis R. Harlan

THE SECRET LIFE OF BOOKER T. WASHINGTON

Author of the most recent and most thorough biography of Booker T. Washington and editor of Washington's papers, Louis R. Harlan of the University of Maryland distills his deep knowledge of the man in this essay. What Washington did in his "secret life" seems to call for a mixed verdict. He supported more daring challenges to discrimination than most historians have suspected, and yet he went further in sabotaging his critics than they ever imagined. These activities suggest a personality at sharp variance from Washington's public image of openness and trust. His secretiveness, which appears to have exceeded the "masking" often required of blacks in a white-dominated society, becomes in itself an important factor in any estimate of the man and his work.

From Louis R. Harlan, "The Secret Life of Booker T. Washington," *Journal of Southern History* 37 (August 1971): 393–416. Footnotes abridged.

The historian inquiring into the black people's experience in America must sooner or later confront the presence in the black past of men who do not fit the conventional mold of heroic history. Nevertheless, a study of their lives may be instructive. One such man was Booker T. Washington, the conservative black leader of the early twentieth century. What strikes a later generation about Washington is not so much his accommodation to segregation and other aspects of white supremacy, which has long been recognized, but his complexity, his richness of strategic resource, his wizardry. He used the white money and favor won by his bland accommodationism to build a personal political machine, sometimes by ruthless methods. While he smiled and nodded in his public life, like the man in the moon he had his dark side, a secret life in which he could cast off the restraints of conventional morality and conservatism and be himself. Surreptitiously, Washington supplied money and leadership for an assault on racially discriminatory laws in the courts. With more success, he employed spies, secret agents, and provocateurs to countermaneuver against his black-militant enemies.

Washington's public image, which in time became a deception, was fixed in the minds of his generation by two highly publicized events, a speech and a book. In 1895 he suddenly moved out of the ranks of obscure young black men through his Atlanta Compromise address, which eloquently presented the conventional formula for interracial cooperation to which most whites and many blacks of the day subscribed. Holding out his hand in a dramatic gesture, Washington promised that Negroes would accept segregation "as separate as the fingers," if whites would provide them with opportunity for economic progress and unite with them, "one as the hand in all things essential to mutual progress." Washington's speech was delivered when a tide of white aggression was engulfing the black communities and when white Americans were either joyfully or sadly proclaiming the final failure of the political approach of Reconstruction. Washington offered both races a negotiated peace. This peace was never actually consummated, but Washington's proposal of it enhanced his influence as a black spokesman who had the ear of whites. In 1901 he added his personal example to strengthen the formula. In his autobiography, *Up from Slavery,* Washington carefully edited his past to present himself as the black version of the American success-hero, the slave boy who "by luck and pluck" made good. Like the white heroes of the Horatio Alger novels, Washington lived a virtuous life, manfully overcame odds, and saved his pennies, and though he did not in the end marry the boss's daughter, he received other substantial blessings from white millionaires.

There were many signs of white approval, North and South, of Washington's racial leadership. Andrew Carnegie not only gave a large sum to Tuskegee Institute but also $150,000 to Washington himself and additional sums to aid several of Washington's black enterprises. John D. Rockefeller, Collis P. Huntington, Jacob Henry Schiff, and Julius Rosenwald, all "sainted philanthropists" in Washington's eyes, aided not only Tuskegee Institute but other schools and organizations Washington approved. Harvard University awarded him an honorary master's degree without noticing the irony of the title. Southern governors praised and consulted him. Queen Victoria served him tea. And he was the man who came to dinner with the Theodore Roosevelts in the White House. Washington hobnobbed with the wealthy and famous to a degree that no other black man of the segregation era achieved, and the reports of his life gave vicarious satisfaction to many humbler blacks. By a system of indirect rule, white Americans crowned Washington "king of a captive people." The price of his power, however, was acceptance of the overruling power of the whites. His public utterances were limited to what whites approved. He urged Negroes to have faith that their rewards would come through the white man's Puritan ethic of work and striving, the conventional moral philosophy and economic thought of the day. He endorsed not only the beatitudes but all the platitudes—the Sunday school lesson, Polonius, Poor Richard, and the Gospel of Wealth.

While Washington publicly seemed to accept a separate and unequal life for black people, behind the mask of acquiescence he was busy with many schemes for black strength, self-improvement, and mutual aid. At his all-black school, Tuskegee Institute, and dozens of other schools under his influence, he promoted industrial education as the way to meet the practical needs of a depressed rural people. Farmers' conferences, land-purchase revolving funds, all-black towns, and countless speeches were his instruments for building black rural economic strength and his own leadership. Meanwhile, he also built what came to be called the Tuskegee Machine by methods similar to those of urban political bosses.

Through the National Negro Business League he not only encouraged Negro businessmen but secured their organized support for his conservative faction in the Northern cities. He became Theodore Roosevelt's closest adviser on race matters and the Negro patronage broker for the Republican party. He dominated the Negro press by ownership of several leading newspapers and by advertising and subsidies to others. Partly through his power to dispense philanthropic funds but also through his close personal attention to every detail, Washington exerted a remarkable influence over black colleges and schools, church leaders, and even secret fraternal orders. Weaving many strands into an intricate web of influence and power, Washington became a minority-group boss whose power went beyond politics into almost every aspect of the life that black people were compelled to live in early twentieth-century America.

While Washington's staff of secretaries and ghost-writers operated his Tuskegee Machine, at a deeper level of secrecy his confidants and spies helped him carry on a shadow life in which he was neither a black Christ nor an Uncle Tom but a cunning Brer Rabbit, "born and bred in the brier patch" of tangled American race relations. Here both white and black enemies were made to feel the secret stiletto of a Machiavellian prince.

It was in many ways unfortunate for Washington's historical reputation that he personally prospered in a time of black racial disaster. He was the Herbert Hoover of a Negro "Great Depression." Perhaps he could not have reached the top in any other time, and perhaps as he claimed, it was a world he never made. His militant black critics, nevertheless, deeply believed that his efforts at appeasement had led the whites to the very aggressions he was trying to check. This conviction gave a certain ruthlessness to the black infighting on both sides.

As a rural Southern Negro whose career had been based on compromise, Washington was less sensitive to racial slights than some Northern blacks of the professional class, but he was appalled by the "final solution" approach of extreme white racists at the end of the nineteenth century. Yet an open and direct challenge to Jim Crow would wreck his precarious relationship with Southern whites. Even the Northern philanthropists who aided him would frown on tactics of social conflict. He had frequent reminders that the violent race relations of the era could touch him as well as others, and several times when racial tensions were high he employed private detectives as bodyguards. Washington in these circumstances decided to launch a secret but direct attack on racially restrictive laws. He secretly paid for and directed a succession of court suits against discrimination in voting, exclusion of Negroes from jury panels, Jim Crow railroad facilities, and various kinds of exploitation of the black poor.[1] In all of this secret activism, it is clear that Washington was not merely trying to make a favorable impression on his militant critics or to spike their guns, for he took every precaution to keep information of his secret actions from leaking out. Only a handful of confidants knew of his involvement.

The contrast between Washington's public stance and his private thought and behavior appeared first in connection with the issue of Southern disfranchisement of Negroes. As state after state placed property and educational restrictions on voting, he publicly pleaded with disfranchising conventions to apply the restrictions equally to both races. When the new constitutions protected the pedigreed white vote with grandfather clauses and other loopholes, however, Washington refused to fight openly against ratification of the new state constitutions. The registrars in his Alabama county gave him a special invitation to come in and awarded him a lifetime voting certificate, which he framed and proudly hung in his den at The Oaks. He voted like a solid citizen and urged his faculty members to do likewise, but both publicly and privately he favored restrictions that would prevent the ignorant and propertyless of both races from voting.

Secretly, meanwhile, Washington went to New Orleans to persuade Negro leaders there to launch a test case against the Louisiana grandfather clause. To raise the money for court costs, Washington goaded into action the legal committee of the Afro-American Council, the leading Negro rights organization of that time. To help the committee's fund raiser, he arranged for free railroad passes from philanthropist friends. He himself gave some money and was listed as "X.Y.Z." in the council records; he also

[1] This interpretation owes a debt to August Meier for his pioneer article, "Toward a Reinterpretation of Booker T. Washington," *Journal of Southern History* 23 (May 1957): 220–27, and for his critique of the present article, read before the Association for the Study of Negro Life and History. Washington's motivation is more fully discussed in the author's article, "Booker T. Washington in Biographical Perspective," *American Historical Review* 75 (October 1970): 1581-99.

raised other money from white liberals, noted in the records as "per X.Y.Z." Washington urged his coworkers never to use his name, and they reassured him that he could be of more service to them in a secret and advisory way than otherwise. The outcome of the Louisiana case was disappointing. There was such endless wrangling over strategy between the local sponsors, the Afro-American Council lawyers, and the three white lawyers that the case was dropped without appealing to the federal courts after a four-year effort. Washington swore he would never work with a committee of lawyers again.

Washington was more successful in two Alabama suffrage cases, *Giles* v. *Harris* (1903) and *Giles* v. *Teasley* (1904), both of which reached the United States Supreme Court. The plaintiff in both cases was Jackson Giles, a minor federal official in Montgomery. In this effort, Washington chose and paid the only lawyer involved, his friend and personal lawyer Wilford H. Smith of New York City. Washington doubly guarded his secrecy by having his private secretary Emmett J. Scott handle all the correspondence with Smith and by using code names to hide identities in case the letters were intercepted. Scott at first called Smith by the code name "Filipino," but Washington warned Scott: "It seems to me in case any of these communications were found, it would be less suspicious should some real name, such as 'John Smith' by found on the letters." Scott could do better than "John Smith." He began a lively correspondence with Wilford Smith using the names R. C. Black and J. C. May, respectively, though Smith sometimes took the name "McAdoo" in telegrams. As the secret partners in the civil rights actions passed on money, news, and advice, they invented other code words also. Booker Washington was referred to as "His Nibs"; "D" stood for dollars, and "M" for Montgomery.

The Giles cases in the end were as disappointing as the Louisiana case. Washington had hoped for a favorable decision from the local district judge, Thomas G. Jones, a Southern conservative whom Washington had persuaded President Theodore Roosevelt to appoint. But Judge Jones ruled against Giles, as did the United States Supreme Court. Either because of Smith's carelessness or because of bias in the high court, or both, the Giles cases were thrown out on technicalities, the first because Giles had attacked the validity of the state constitution under which he sought to register and the second because he had failed to claim in the state courts that his rights as a United States citizen were denied, although that was the basis of his appeal. Smith wrote to Washington: "To my mind the Supreme Court took advantage of the only loop-hole in sight to get around the decision of a question fraught with so many important political consequences. We will have to find a way to hem them in as they do in playing checkers. . . ." Washington urged Smith to press a new case, to, "at least, put the Supreme Court in an awkward position," but Smith and other lawyers convinced him it would be useless.

Washington and Smith also collaborated successfully in a test of the exclusion of Negroes from jury panels. With secret money from Washington, Smith carried the Dan Rogers case from Alabama to successful issue before the United States Supreme Court in 1904. They secured the freedom of a black man convicted in a criminal case because qualified blacks were excluded from the jury.

Washington fought the unfairness of the Jim Crow railroad cars both openly and secretly. Publicly, he protested only against unequal facilities rather than separation itself. For example, in a national magazine article in 1912, he quoted another Southern Negro approvingly: "I pay the same money, but I cannot have a chair or a lavatory and rarely a through car. I must crawl out at all times of night, and in all kinds of weather, in order to catch another dirty 'Jim Crow' coach to make my connections. I do not ask to ride with white people. I do ask for equal accommodations for the same money."

Behind the scenes, however, Washington was more militant. When the state of Georgia segregated sleeping cars in 1900, Washington urged Georgia black leaders to protest and also sought the help of William H. Baldwin, Jr., a railroad president who was chairman of the Tuskegee Board of Trustees. Through Baldwin, Washington secured a private conference with the president of the Pullman Company, none other than Abraham Lincoln's son Robert Lincoln. When Lincoln refused to join a Negro group in protesting the Georgia law, Baldwin advised Washington to look for "a light mulatto of good appearance, but unquestionably colored" for a test case. But going to court is not a philanthropist's way of accomplishing an object, and Baldwin soon began to urge that Washington "let the matter drift a little longer" on the dubious ground that "if a test case is not made it will soon become a dead letter."

Washington ignored Baldwin's advice. He and Wilford H. Smith secretly assisted W. E. Burghardt Du Bois of Atlanta in a case against the Georgia law in 1902, and though Du Bois rather clearly broke with Washington with the publication of his *Souls of Black Folk* in 1903, Du Bois and Washington were secretly cooperating as late as December 1904 in an effort to test the Tennessee Jim Crow law. Later, Emmett Scott criticized the militant Du Bois for not pushing these cases vigorously enough. Washington also persuaded Giles B. Jackson of Richmond to begin a similar suit in 1900 against the Virginia railroad segregation law. He talked another friend, James C. Napier, into a suit in Tennessee against a Pullman segregation law. When the man chosen for the Tennessee test case lost his nerve, Washington tried another round of conferences with the Pullman officials. This time the son of the Great Emancipator refused even to reply to the letters of the Great Accommodator.

Washington was caught on both horns of the "separate but equal" dilemma, as was shown in 1906 by his agents' secret lobbying during the congressional debate on the Hepburn railway rate bill. Senators William Warner of Missouri and Joseph B. Foraker of Ohio proposed amendments that would guarantee equal railroad passenger facilities for Negroes. Washington at first lobbied for the Warner-Foraker amendment, apparently being as insensitive as its sponsors to the implicit approval of separate facilities that such a guarantee carried. Through Negro friends in Washington, the Tuskegee educator paid $300 to Henry W. Blair, former senator from New Hampshire, to lobby for the amendment. Then he learned that militant blacks who were more sensitive to the implied racial exclusion were on their way from Boston to fight the amendment. Always alert to even the most subtle challenge to his power, Washington sent word to Blair to reverse himself and lobby against the amendment. When it was defeated, Washington urged his secret Negro collaborators to claim the credit, but he personally was still undecided about the merits of the case. As in the Atlanta Compromise speech, social-equality abstractions had for him a low priority. He wrote to one of his collaborators: "In fact the more I think of it the more I am convinced that the Warner Amendment would have been a good measure, and very helpful."

Washington also championed the rural black poor in their enjoyment of the most basic right of all, the right to live and to labor in their own behalf. He responded warmly and effectively, for example, to the predicament of Pink Franklin, an illiterate South Carolina farmer. Franklin shot and killed two white men in 1910 when they broke into his cabin before daylight without announcement of their purpose to arrest him for violating a state peonage statute already declared unconstitutional by the South Carolina Supreme Court. After the United States Supreme Court refused to reverse Franklin's conviction for murder, Oswald Garrison Villard, an officer of the newly formed National Association for the Advancement of Colored People, enlisted Washington's help in seeking a commutation of the sentence. Washington suggested two courses: (1) to employ a leading South Carolina white lawyer to go directly to the governor and (2) to ask Reverend Richard Carroll to intercede with a plea for clemency. An ultra-conservative and rather sycophantic Negro, Carroll had "many qualities that neither you nor I would admire," Washington wrote, but he had "tremendous influence with the white people of South Carolina." Villard replied that he had no money to pay a lawyer, but he urged Washington to do all he could through Carroll. Whether it was Carroll's influence, a persuasive letter from Washington's friend Robert C. Ogden, a Tuskegee trustee, or possibly a letter from President William Howard Taft that tipped the balance, the South Carolina governor did commute Pink Franklin's sentence to one of life imprisonment.

The most significant example of Washington's secret aid to Southern Negroes threatened with peonage, however, was the Alonzo Bailey case, which Washington secretly aided all the way to its success in the United States Supreme Court. A farmworker in Montgomery County, Alabama, Bailey had signed a year contract with a corporate farm to work for $12 a month. When he borrowed $20 against his future wages and then left the farm without repaying, he was tried and convicted under the Alabama peonage statute, not in a civil suit for debt but in a criminal suit for signing a contract with intent to defraud. Washington and some of his upper-class Southern white friends had long sought such a test case to prove the benevolence of their leadership, as had agents of the Justice Department under Roosevelt's attorney general Charles J. Bonaparte. Washington sent a discreet Tuskegeen instructor, Ernest T. Attwell, to contact his secret collaborators in the Bailey case, Judge W. H. Thomas of the Montgomery city court and United States District Judge Thomas G. Jones. The two judges secretly gave counsel in the case, but because of their judicial position they were barred from being the lawyers of record. With Washington's secret encouragement and financial assistance, therefore, they persuaded two local white lawyers to take the Bailey case without fee. Washington raised the other court costs from Northern liberal friends, and Attorney General Bonaparte submitted an amicus curiae brief. Washington may have viewed the Bailey case as evidence of the viability of the bargain he had made with the Southern white elite in his Atlanta Compromise speech, but his circumstances made it necessary to keep his part in the case hidden from public view. The Supreme Court in 1911 declared that peonage was involuntary servitude and that the Alabama law was therefore unconstitutional. Peonage continued illegally in Alabama, but, as Pete Daniel has shown, it was less common than in other Southern states where contract labor laws were enforced. Alonozo Bailey soon unheroically found employment in a local country club, and Washington could take no public credit for this rare legal victory in an era when the whites were winning most of the power and the glory.

In his personal conduct Booker T. Washington could never allow himself to forget that he represented his race and that any breach of decorum on his part would be blamed on his race. For this reason, and because he had been trained at Hampton Institute by strait-laced New Englanders, Washington lived a life of scrupulous puritanism. He avoided even such minor vices as tobacco and gave earnest public support to all the tenets of Sunday school morality. Despite all the honors heaped upon him, his demeanor was one of incorrigible humility. His life was the very model of the way white men wished to see black men behave. His secret actions against his Negro opponents, however, showed little forbearance and drew less from the teachings of Jesus than from those of Machiavelli.

When Washington said in his Atlanta Compromise address in 1895 that whites and blacks could be "as separate as the fingers," he set the teeth of some Negroes on edge. Because they challenged his conservative doctrines, his opponents came to be known as "radicals," though in a later day their tactics would seem moderate. These men fairly gnashed their teeth when Washington won white applause and laughter by stories in which black men, chickens, and mules figured prominently, when he flattered or amused whites by making blacks the scapegoats of their own misfortunes, when he pointed the finger of scorn at what he considered the pretensions of educated, middle-class, urban Negroes.

The first to challenge Washington's leadership and philosophy was a nervous young Harvard graduate, William Monroe Trotter, whose outspoken weekly newspaper, the Boston *Guardian,* trod the border line between personal journalism and libel. When Washington spoke in 1903 at a Negro church in Boston before a tightly packed audience of two thousand, Trotter dramatized his disagreement with Washington by disrupting the meeting. Standing on a chair, he read off nine accusatory questions in a high, shrill voice that pierced the hubbub. The police finally made their way to him and evicted him and nine others for disorderly conduct. The meeting continued, but Trotter had achieved his purpose, for the incident appeared on the front pages of the white press as "the Boston riot," penetrating Washington's news screen and letting the country know all Negroes were not behind him. Washington's lawyer promised to "put them in the jug"; and after a trial which Washington's Boston friends pushed vigorously, Trotter and one cohort served thirty days in jail. The incident drove a wedge between the two factions. A final effort to settle their differences, the Carnegie Hall Conference in 1904, was unsuccessful, largely because Washington insisted on a more conservative line than the militants could accept. The militant minority survived in the Niagara Movement after 1905 and grew more rapidly with the aid of white liberals in the NAACP after 1909.

Washington viewed this Negro criticism through a distorted personal lens. In his own eyes he was a heroic, constructive racial statesman beset by yapping dogs. He believed he had won leadership by open means and that his enemies were trying to wrest it from him by underhanded methods of distortion and innuendo. Washington egocentrically exaggerated the personal element in the opposition. It seemed to him mere jealousy of his standing and achievements. He felt justified in using ruthless means to retain his power; and those means were at hand. About the time of the Boston riot, Washington employed a spy to help him outwit his enemies.

About a week before the Boston affair, a plump, possum-shaped young Texan, Melvin J. Chisum, offered Washington his services. An old friend of Emmett Scott, Chisum was then editing a shaky little Negro magazine, the *Impending Conflict,* in partnership with John E. Bruce. "I don't think Chisum is a very brainy man," Scott commented, "but I do know he is resourceful and I think at the same time honorable. . . . Our New York friend can use Chisum in any way that we desire." Washington's faction soon found work for Chisum when they learned Trotter and his followers were planning to disrupt another Washington speech, this time in a Negro church in Cambridge. At a final meeting in Trotter's home Chisum was present. His report later mysteriously disappeared from Washington's files, but it was the basis of Emmett Scott's account two years later:

> *. . . it was finally decided in Trotter's home that when the meeting should be in full sway one of their number would light a bonfire in a near-by vacant lot, that another in the church should yell "fire" and that a third should cut the electric wire, thereby throwing the church into darkness and confusion. This program of wrath, disorder and possibly murder, which Trotter and his gang had planned came near succeeding. At their final meeting to perfect their arrangements a colored attorney of Boston, who had learned of their scheme, threw open the door, walked into the midst of the band and gave them to understand in no Sunday-School language that he had the names of every man and knew all the details of their plans. He further told them that if a single one of them attempted to carry out the plan, he would have them all in jail in a few hours. At this revelation the little gang was thunderstruck and scattered in every direction; not one of them dared to show his face at the meeting.*

Washington wanted to publicize what he called a "dastardly attempt on the part of that Boston crowd to disgrace the race," but William H. Lewis, the Boston lawyer who had burst into the meeting, said: "I rather prefer to hold it as a club over their heads." He warned that Chisum's unsupported affidavit would be insufficient safeguard against a libel suit. "Besides I am not inclined to believe absolutely the story of our confidential friend. I think he has overdrawn it somewhat, and I am not sure that he did not himself make some of the propositions purporting to have been made by others."

Washington publicly ignored Trotter but secretly seized the first opportunity to counterattack. For months he and Scott combed the *Guardian* for evidence of libel, not against Washington but against someone else. Using their findings, they persuaded William Pickens, a black student at Yale whom Washington had befriended, to sue Trotter and his coeditor George R. Forbes for libel. Washington and Wilford Smith gave Pickens financial and legal aid, and when the case was settled out of court, Washington gleefully reported to friends "the apology made by Trotter and Forbes so as to prevent wearing stripes." The pro-Washington faction in Boston meanwhile sought to have Forbes removed from his job at the Boston Public Library.

The next time Washington's New England black friends honored him, in Cambridge in 1904, they chose a banquet for which tickets would have to be purchased rather than risk an open meeting. Not to be outdone so easily, Trotter and his group schemed to hold an anti-Washington indignation meeting on the same night. They hired a hall and secretly printed advertising circulars for their rally. Once again, however, they had in their midst an unsuspected spy, Clifford H. Plummer, who had begun negotiating with Washington a year earlier while he was serving as lawyer for one of the Boston rioters. Forewarned by Plummer, Washington's friends went to the owner of the hall and got the reservation for their enemies' meeting place canceled, while Plummer quietly gathered up and destroyed the circulars. Plummer succeeded in concealing his clandestine partnership with Washington. "I informed 'the gang' that I do not expect to attend the dinner," he wrote Washington, "which declaration by me made me eligible to any office within their gift, from the presidency of the United States, to a member of the common council from any ward in Boston or Cambridge."

Hearing rumors in the summer of 1905 of a new national black protest organization, Washington through his secretary Emmett Scott sent Plummer fifty dollars and orders by telegram to "go to Buffalo . . . ostensibly to attend Elks convention but to report fully what goes on at meeting to be held there Wednesday and Thursday. Get into meeting if possible but be sure name of all who attend and what they do." This was the first meeting of the Niagara Movement, so named because the group crossed to Niagara Falls, Canada, after discrimination at a Buffalo hotel. Plummer went to the Associated Press to prevent publicity about the meeting. "Few of them here," he wired Washington from Buffalo, "nothing serious so far[,] will try to stop their declaration of principles from appearing." Washington and Scott meanwhile wired all the Negro and white newspapermen they could absolutely trust, urging them to ignore the Niagara meeting. In this and subsequent years the silence of the press was effective in limiting the influence of the Niagara Movement.

When the Niagarites met the following year at Harpers Ferry, Washington had a new agent to report on their affairs, Richard T. Greener, first Negro graduate of Harvard and onetime professor of law at the University of South Carolina. Greener in 1906 was an old, broken, out-of-office politician. After a distinguished career as dean of the Howard University Law School, he sought a consular post. The State Department assigned him to Bombay, and when he complained of the climate there, they reassigned him to Vladivostok. Removed from office under circumstances which involved racial bias, he wrote Washington from Harpers Ferry, asking his help in regaining his office. "Here is a good chance to get a good friend into the inner portals of the Niagara meeting," suggested Emmett Scott. "I hope you will spare no pains to get on the inside of everything," Washington wrote Greener. He attributed motives to his opponents which help explain why he had few qualms about spying on them: "You will find, in the last analysis, that the whole object of the Niag[a]ra Movement is to defeat and oppose every thing I do. I have done all I could to work in harmony with DuBois, but he has permitted Trotter and others to fool him into the idea that he was some sort of a leader, consequently he has fritt[er]ed away his time in agitation when he could succeed as a scientist or Socologist [*sic*]."

Other sleuths, paid and unpaid, also did Washington's bidding. Pinkerton detectives on a half-dozen occasions protected him or his distinguished guests from threatened attacks and eavesdropped on white conversations about him in hotel lobbies and trains. He hired a white detective in Boston to find out whether Trotter's wife was employed as a domestic and, if so, for whom. Washington was probably disappointed to learn that Mrs. Trotter worked every day in her husband's office. Soon afterward the same detective was clumsy enough to be discovered as a Washington agent by the man he was shadowing.

Washington had more success with the less professional Negro spies. His correspondence was filled with confidential information. Chicagoans and New Yorkers, for example, sent him lists of Niagara delegates from those cities. Another agent searched the Atlanta tax records for evidence that Du Bois had failed to pay his poll tax. Friends in New York, Washington, Boston, and Chicago transmitted Washington's bribes to Negro newspapers for favorable editorial treatment. When a Tuskegee faculty member broke his contract, an agent of Washington stole the teacher's letters from his pastor's desk so as to embarrass the man with his new employer and force an apology. Such tactics, however, hardly disproved the teacher's assertion in the offending letters that Washington had "absolute control over his teachers" and kept them in "a modified form of slavery." To promote Tuskegee, Washington paid a lecturer with stereopticon slides to tour the Northern Negro churches, ostensibly presenting impartially the story of Negro education. "Of course the minute people get the idea that you are an agent of Tuskegee," Washington warned him, "that minute in a very large degree your influence would be modified."

Washington's most active spy, however, was Melvin J. Chisum, whose Boston success naturally brought him to mind when the Niagara Movement posed a threat. Washington sought out Chisum again through Charles W. Anderson, collector of internal revenue in New York City, local black political boss, and Washington's intimate friend. Chisum proved worthy of his hire. Securing a position as a reporter on the anti-Booker newspaper, the Washington *Bee,* he convinced its editor, W. Calvin Chase, that even though they both hated Washington as much as any other upstanding, race-loving black man, they should not let that stand in the way of profitable business dealings with him. Chisum persuaded Chase to accept a bribe offered at the strategic moment by two friends of Washington to pay for several pro-Washington editorials. "I have him, Doctor, I have him," Chisum almost crowed to Washington when Chase took the bait. "But, rest perfectly sure, that my plan is so carefully lain that he will not see." After the editorials were written, the cream of the jest came when Chase's militant friends began criticizing him, and Chisum counted on Chase's hot temper to further his plan. Chisum wrote to Washington:

> *Now! The Bee will be a surprise to everybody that knows it the forthcoming week and the war is on between his highness bub Trotter and bub Chase. Are you willing that I remain here for a couple of weeks and make shure* [sic] *of Chase's broadsides being properly directed so as to put them beyond the point of repair, or reconnection? I know Trotter will fire on the Bee, and I think I ought to be in the con[n]ing tower with Chase when he does.*

Chisum privately considered Chase "at heart, a vile, malicious, jealous—heartless 'cuss,'" but in talking with Chase he was careful to knock Washington and then add, confidentially, "Mr. Chase, I would let no one but you hear me say this." Chisum's scheme to trap Chase into dependency on Washington was successful, but in the years that followed Washington could not depend with certainty on Chase. Like many another impecunious Negro editor whose bondage was economic and whose real sympathy was with the other side, Chase was loyal to Washington only when paid. Washington, however, expressed himself as "most grateful" to Chisum, and Charles Anderson, who thought Chisum too expensive a luxury, grudgingly admitted that the spy had "his valuable points."

Chisum obviously delighted in his work and in his closeness to the throne. "I am, Your obedient humble servant, Chisum," he ended one letter in picaresque style, "your own property, to use as your Eminence desires, absolutely." He offered to go to Chicago and seek employment as a waiter in a Negro restaurant, but Washington decided he would be more useful spying on the Brooklyn branch of the Niagara Movement. "I am almost sure I will be able to attend the secret conference at the Convention," Chisum reported. He shuttled between his Harlem residence and the Niagara meetings in Brooklyn Heights, often getting home long after midnight. His reports to Washington were usually oral, and their letters recorded only the times and places of meeting, usually on park benches in Manhattan. "I sat in the park today from 12:45 to now," he wrote Washington one day at 3:30, "and will be there near where we sat again tomorrow Friday at 1 sharp." A few weeks later Washington wrote to Chisum: "I plan to be in New York about the 13th and shall hope to see you at the usual place at that time." After 1906 Chisum engaged in a succession of small business enterprises, and his spying tapered off. "Questions are to be asked you tonight," he informed Washington on one occasion. "I will, I think, succeed in stopping them." Chisum remained, as he said, Washington's "obedient, humble servant," but the master no longer rubbed the lamp.

While Washington both openly and secretly attacked the Negro radicals, some of his influential white supporters began to have doubts about his own effectiveness as a black leader. As segregation and race riots spread rather than diminished, it was increasingly clear that Washington's concessions and bland optimism were insufficient to bring racial harmony and justice. A race riot in Springfield, Illinois, in 1908 startled two of Washington's white liberal supporters into taking a leading role in founding the National Association for the Advancement of Colored People. These were Oswald Garrison Villard and Mary White Ovington. Grandson of the abolitionist William Lloyd Garrison and son of a railroad baron, Villard edited the influential *Nation* and the New York *Evening Post.* In the years of the Niagara Movement he raised $157,000 as chairman of the Tuskegee endowment committee, and for a decade he allowed Washington and Scott to help write his editorials on race matters. Villard became chairman of the board of the NAACP, and he continued to try to bring the organization and Washington together, but Washington refused to attend its meetings. Miss Ovington, a wealthy white settlement-house worker in the Negro slums of New York, had visited Tuskegee and had written articles favoring the school and its head. Persistent white racism turned her toward protest, however, and she became an NAACP staff member. One of Washington's principal critics, Du Bois, became the editor of the NAACP magazine, the *Crisis.*

Washington's response to the NAACP was more ambiguous than it had been in the cases of Trotter and the Niagara Movement. For a time he encouraged his friend Robert R. Moton to seek an accord with the NAACP group, but a sharply critical circular by Du Bois and others on stationery of "the National Negro Committee" angered him so that he broke off negotiations. Washington encouraged William H. Baldwin's widow to help found the National Urban League, an organization whose approach indirectly challenged that of the NAACP.

Toward the end of his life Washington seemed to move ideologically toward the NAACP position. He joined with it in protesting federal segregation in the Wilson administration, and he cooperated with it in efforts to ban the racist film *The Birth of a Nation.* Washington's posthumous article in the *New Republic,* entitled "My View of Segregation Laws," opposed residential segregation laws so forthrightly that the NAACP Board of Directors voted to reprint it as a pamphlet. On the other hand, writing in 1914 to a Birmingham city official to argue against a proposed segregation ordinance, Washington warned that such legislation would "stir up racial strife and bring about bitterness to an extent that will result in discouraging a number of the best colored people in the state." He foxily suggested an alternative approach:

> *Of course I do not know just in detail what the local conditions in Birmingham are, but I do know that taking the two races generally in the South that one seldom buys property in a section of a community or city where he is not wanted. The general custom has settled the matter it seems to me, and custom in this case I sometimes think is stronger than a law. I believe if it were made known to a half dozen of the leading colored men in Birmingham that certain things were desired in reference to the purchase of property in the future that the same results could be obtained as by passing a law which I very much fear will be misunderstood throughout the country and, I repeat, stir up racial strife.*

During the formative years of the NAACP Washington launched a devastating secret attack on the white liberals who were working with his black enemies. This is illustrated by the Cosmopolitan Club dinner incidents in 1908 and 1911. A social club of liberal whites and members of the darker races, the Cosmopolitan Club was founded in Mary White Ovington's home in Brooklyn Heights and continued to meet quietly in private homes. In the spring of 1908, however, at Miss Ovington's suggestion they invited guests to meet with them at a midtown New York restaurant. About a hundred attended. Villard was one of the speakers, as was Hamilton Holt, editor of the *Independent,* a progressive weekly. About halfway through the dinner reporters entered the room, and a photographer stood on a chair to take flash pictures of the entire assemblage. The photographing was prevented after messages of protest were sent to the head table, but the New York *American,* a Hearst paper, reported next day: "Social equality and intermarriage between the races were advocated last night at a banquet... where twenty white girls and women dined side by side at table with negro men and women." The New York *Times* denounced the affair as a "banquet, of which brotherhood was the 'note' and the promotion of Socialism the moving spirit and intent...." The publicity brought Miss Ovington such obscene mail that she was forced to have her letters opened by male relatives.

Booker T. Washington was in New York at the time of the dinner, staying at the Manhattan Hotel. According to a newspaper report, "He sent word to the desk of the hotel that he was 'not to be disturbed,' and notified his two secretaries that he was 'not at home' to reporters." As the news spread southward, suggestion became assertion, and the news became even more titillating as the sober diners were depicted as drinking and making love at a "Bacchanal feast." The incident reminded some Southern newspapers of Booker Washington's dinner years earlier at the White House. One woman wrote him from Washington: "I think you better not try to see me as I asked you to, owing to the very strong race feeling here just now —some reporter might get hold of the fact that you called to see me, and misrepresent you...." She felt that Washington's Atlanta address had done much to promote racial amity, "but temporarily this N.Y. episode has set things back greatly. I hope you will make another speech soon and reassure the public."

Washington's secret cooperation with the racially biased white press in reporting another Cosmopolitan Club dinner in 1911 strongly suggests that he may have inspired the 1908 publicity also. In January 1911 Washington received from Charles W. Anderson a copy of an invitation to a Cosmopolitan Club dinner. "One needs only to glance over this invitation," Anderson commented, "printed as it is on yellow paper, and note the names of the speakers and the long-winded topics they are to discuss, to be convinced that they are a bunch of freaks." Washington wired in reply: "Regarding black and white dinner be sure get hold of same reporter who reported for American year or two ago. Would see that copies of printed announcement reach all city editors in advance. Think New York Times will work in harmony with you."

Anderson contacted not only the leading New York dailies but the City News Association and the Associated Press as well. He was disappointed that the story was crowded out of some local papers by other news. "The man who handled it last year could not be found," he wrote Washington, "but a 'good friend' on the Press took care of that end of it . . . and I hope the Associated Press did likewise." The next day one edition of the New York *Press* carried the headline: "THREE RACES SIT AT BANQUET FOR MIXED MARRIAGE." Another edition carried the headline: "THREE RACES MIX AT BANQUET FOR MAN'S BROTHERHOOD/Fashionable White Women Sit at Board with Negroes, Japs and Chinamen to Promote 'Cause' of Miscegenation." In the text of the news story it was clear that miscegenation had not been advocated, but the *Press* reported: "White women, evidently of the cultured and wealthier classes, fashionably attired in low-cut gowns, leaned over the tables to chat confidentially to negro men of the true African type." Even Washington's sharpest critics did not dream of his cooperation with the white reporters. Miss Ovington, a very proper old maid, was still upset by the incidents when she wrote her memoirs in 1947. Still wondering who had tipped off the reporters, she spoke of "the connivance of a few club members" and recalled suspiciously a Gallic twinkle in the eye of the club's treasurer, the Frenchman André Tridon. She had no idea of Washington's secret role.

Washington's secret life is probably more significant as a revelation of his character than because of its effects. It did not change materially the shape of the Color Line, and he had other, more effective means to use against his Negro opponents. Washington's private papers afford a glimpse, however, behind his conventional mask of accommodation and morality, showing a man who, under trying circumstances, sought in his own peculiar way to play a more aggressive and manly role. In both his secret struggle against Jim Crow laws and his espionage among his Negro and white liberal critics he exhibited more of what the Mexicans call *machismo* than his public role allowed. It is also clear that he sometimes confused his own interests with those of the race, assuming that what was good for Booker Washington was good for "the brother." He illustrated the uneasiness of every head that wears a crown. He was sure that history would vindicate his actions when the whole tale was told. That verdict is uncertain, but there is no doubt that he was far more than a foot-dragging "Uncle Tom." He was a man, with all that the name implies of strength and weakness. Some will see him sympathetically as a Brer Rabbit moving adroitly through the brier patch.

Others will view him unfavorably as a classical deep-dyed villain. Whatever the judgment that black history pronounces on Booker T. Washington, it is clear that black history, if it is to be more than a procession of cardboard figures, must like other history have its shades of gray, its villains as well as heroes, its imperfect human characters as well as saints.

Suggestions for Additional Reading

The Booker T. Washington Papers, edited by Louis R. Harlan (Urbana, 1971–) begin with a volume of Washington's autobiographical writings, which were not limited to the widely known *Up from Slavery.* As volumes containing his correspondence appear, there will be readily accessible evidence of his methods of putting his ideas into practice. Although Washington tended to repeat himself, there is enough variation according to intended audience, time of composition, and topic to make wide reading in his works worthwhile. The student can learn of his winning way with an audience from E. Davidson Washington, ed., *Selected Speeches of Booker T. Washington* (Garden City, 1932), and of the historical interpretation which underlay his racial strategy in *The Future of the American Negro,* partly reprinted here, and *The Story of the Negro,* 2 vols. (New York, 1909).

Writings of Washington's black contemporaries show the range of reaction to his policies and provide standards of comparison. Although several valuable anthologies of W. E. Burghardt Du Bois's writings have recently appeared, the student is still advised to turn first to the classic *Souls of Black Folk. The Negro in the South: His Economic Progress in Relation to His Moral and Religious Development* (Philadelphia, 1907) dramatically juxtaposes two lectures by Washington with two by Du Bois. Seven black Americans air their often diverse views in Booker T. Washington et al., *The Negro Problem: A Series of Articles by Representative American Negroes of To-Day* (New York, 1903). The writings of Kelly Miller, notably *Race Adjustment: Essays on the Negro in America* (New York, 1908), point to virtues in both Washington and Du Bois. The leading black journalist of Washington's day, T. Thomas Fortune, spoke his mind in *Black and White: Land, Labor, and Politics in the South* (New York, 1884). *The Autobiography of an Ex-Colored Man* (Boston, 1912), a novel by James Weldon Johnson, offers insights into the subjective reactions of blacks to American discrimination.

In black biography, Louis R. Harlan, *Booker T. Washington: The Making of a Black Leader, 1856–1901* (New York, 1972) takes front rank; a second volume is projected. For certain details and as evidence of changing attitudes toward Washington, however, the biographies by Scott and Stowe, Matthews, and Spencer will continue to be of value. Of two biographies of Du Bois, Broderick's, represented here, is richer in interpretation, but Elliott M. Rudwick, *W. E. B. Du Bois: A Study in Minority Group Leadership* (Philadelphia, 1960), is often more detailed. Du Bois himself traced his life story in two books: *Dusk of Dawn* and *The Autobiography of W. E. B. Du Bois: A Soliloquy on Viewing My Life from the Last Decade of Its First Century* (New York, 1968). The projected volumes of Du Bois's correspondence, edited by Herbert Aptheker, will be a major addition to scholarship. A protest leader more "radical" than Du Bois is the subject of Stephen R. Fox, *The Guardian of Boston: William Monroe Trotter* (New York, 1970), while an editor who shared some of Washington's "secret life" is described in Emma Lou Thornbrough, *T. Thomas Fortune: Militant Journalist* (Chicago, 1972).

To learn more about black nationalism and the relationship of Afro-Americans to Africa, the student should consult Henry M. Turner, *Respect Black: Writings and Speeches,* ed. Edwin S. Redkey, as well as the Redkey volume *Black Exodus,* represented in these readings. An excellent anthology that traces these themes through two centuries is John H. Bracey, Jr., August Meier, and Elliott Rudwick, eds., *Black Nationalism in America* (Indianapolis, 1970). Washington's own dealings with Africa and Africans are detailed in Louis R. Harlan, "Booker T. Washington and the White Man's Burden," *American Historical Review* 71 (Jan. 1966): 441–67. Studies of three very different men who worked for emigrationist goals are Edmund David Cronon, *Black Moses: The Story of Marcus Garvey and the Universal Negro Improvement Association* (Madison, 1955); Hollis R. Lynch, *Edward Wilmot Blyden: Pan-Negro Patriot, 1832–1912* (London, 1967); and William Bittle and Gilbert Geis, *The Longest Way Home: Chief Alfred C. Sam's Back to Africa Movement* (Detroit, 1964). For migrationism, of not only the back-to-Africa variety, see Carter G. Woodson, *A Century of Negro Migration* (Washington, 1918).

The rise of the most important organizational challenge to Washington's leadership is chronicled in Charles Flint Kellogg, *NAACP: A History of the National Association for the Advancement of Colored People,* vol. 1, *1909–1920* (Baltimore, 1967). Autobiographies of two NAACP activists, one black, one white, are Alfreda M. Duster, ed., *Crusade for Justice: The Autobiography of Ida B. Wells* (Chicago, 1970), and Mary White Ovington, *The Walls Came Tumbling Down* (New York, 1947). For information on the Urban League, which began almost simultaneously with the NAACP, but was oriented toward employment opportunities and social welfare, a good starting place is Arvarh E. Strickland, *History of the Chicago Urban League* (Urbana, 1966).

Where should the student turn if he wants a general history of black Americans during the era of Booker T. Washington? Meier's *Negro Thought in America,* excerpted here, is without equal. Organized around black social strategies, it concerns itself with all the issues raised in this collection and many more. Surveys of the entire sweep of black history in America include John Hope Franklin, *From Slavery to Freedom: A History of Negro Americans* (rev. ed., New York, 1969); August Meier and Elliott Rudwick, *From Plantation to Ghetto* (rev. ed., New York, 1970); and Benjamin Quarles, *The Negro in the Making of America* (New York, 1964). Three studies made interesting by their authors' efforts to drive home their central theses are Robert L. Factor, *The Black Response to America: Men, Ideals, and Organizations from Frederick Douglass to the NAACP* (Reading, Mass., 1970); S. P. Fullinwider, *The Mind and Mood of Black America: 20th Century Thought* (Homewood, Ill., 1969); and Earl E. Thorpe, *The Mind of the Negro: An Intellectual History of Afro-Americans* (Baton Rouge, 1961). Gunnar Myrdal's massive synthesis, *An American Dilemma: The Negro Problem and Modern Democracy,* 2 vols. (New York, 1944), valuable throughout, includes insightful treatments of Washington, Du Bois, and emigrationism.

To explore more fully the social context which has been used sometimes to condemn, sometimes to exculpate, Washington, see besides the volume by C. Vann Woodward represented in these readings, his *The Strange Career of Jim Crow* (rev. ed., New York, 1966) and his *American Counterpoint* (Boston, 1971). Especially useful for its survey of the national press is Rayford W. Logan, *The Negro in American Life and Thought: The Nadir, 1877–1901* (New York, 1954), retitled in paperback *The Betrayal of the Negro.* The ideas that whites carried in their heads about blacks are analyzed in George M. Fredrickson, *The Black Image in the White Mind: The Debate on Afro-American Character and Destiny, 1817–1914* (New York, 1971); Claude F. Nolen, *The Negro's Image in the South: The*

Anatomy of White Supremacy (Lexington, Ky., 1967); and Idus A. Newby, *Jim Crow's Defense: Anti-Negro Thought in America, 1900–1930* (Baton Rouge, 1965). For the record of the Supreme Court in race relations, see Loren Miller, *The Petitioners: The Story of the Supreme Court of the United States and the Negro* (New York, 1966), and for a particularly fateful case, Otto H. Olsen, ed., *The Thin Disguise: The Turning Point in Negro History,* Plessy *v.* Ferguson (New York, 1968).

For the political background of Washington's policies consult Paul Lewinson, *Race, Class, & Party: A History of Negro Suffrage and White Politics in the South* (London, 1932). Political developments in Washington's home state are skillfully interpreted in Sheldon Hackney, *Populism to Progressivism in Alabama* (Princeton, 1969). A good idea of what blacks encountered in the White House can be gained from George Sinkler, *The Racial Attitudes of American Presidents: From Abraham Lincoln to Theodore Roosevelt* (Garden City, 1971).

A Northern newspaperman's laudatory account of Washington's educational enterprise is Max Bennett Thrasher, *Tuskegee: Its Story and Its Work* (Boston, 1901). To see Washington's program in educational context, the student should consult Henry A. Bullock, *A History of Negro Education in the South* (Cambridge, Mass., 1967) and Horace Mann Bond, *The Education of the Negro in the American Social Order* (New York, 1934), as well as the Bond volume represented in the readings. Other important studies of black education are Louis R. Harlan, *Separate and Unequal: Public School Campaigns and Racism in the Southern Seaboard States, 1901–1915* (Chapel Hill, 1958) and Thomas Jesse Jones, ed., *Negro Education: A Study of the Private and Higher Schools for Colored People in the United States,* 2 vols. (Washington, 1917, Bureau of Education Bul. 38, 1916).

Volumes providing useful economic background for Washington's policies are Pete Daniel, *The Shadow of Slavery: Peonage in the South, 1901–1969* (Urbana, 1972); Carl Kelsey, *The Negro Farmer* (Chicago, 1903); Sterling D. Spero and Abram L. Harris, *The Black Worker: The Negro and the Labor Movement* (New York, 1931); Charles H. Wesley, *Negro Labor in the United States, 1850–1925* (New York, 1927); and Abram L. Harris, *The Negro as Capitalist: A*

Study of Banking and Business among American Negroes (Philadelphia, 1936). Washington's own business philosophy sets the tone of his *The Negro in Business* (New York, 1907).

Most phases of black life at the turn of the century were dealt with in various volumes of the *Atlanta University Publications,* ed. Du Bois (Atlanta, 1897–1911). As is the case with many older studies of black affairs, these have been recently reprinted.

In conclusion, the student is urged to become acquainted with James M. McPherson et al., *Blacks in America: Bibliographical Essays* (Garden City, 1971), a splendid interpretive guide. Through it can be located items generally excluded from the paragraphs above—articles, studies of single cities and states, and anthologies.

1785 1

1 2 3 4 5 6 7 8 9 0